*The stained glass window at the former*
*King's Daughters Home was a glowing beacon*
*welcoming many visitors. It was donated to the home*
*from Christ Church in Springfield, Illinois in honor of one of*
*the first local circles – "In His Name Circle." It was relocated*
*to the front entrance in 1988 which is when they added*
*the back lighting to enhance its beautiful colors.*

# Dining
## WITH THE
# Daughters

Recipes Galore from
King's Daughters and More

**King's Daughters Organization**
Springfield, Illinois

## Dining with the Daughters
*Recipes Galore from King's Daughters and More*

First Printing 2012

---

Book design and layout by Erin Weller, Erin Weller Graphic Design, and Polly Danforth, Morning Star Design, both of Springfield, Illinois.

Printed in the United States of America

ISBN: 978-0-615-67350-9

10 9 8 7 6 5 4 3 2 1

---

The mission of the King's Daughters Organization is to charitably aid the elderly in our community through our volunteer efforts. The profit realized from the sale of *Dining with the Daughters – Recipes Galore from King's Daughters and More* will be used for community projects sponsored by King's Daughters Organization.

For information on ordering copies of the cookbook published by King's Daughters Organization, contact:

**Cookbook Committee**
**King's Daughters Organization**
205 S Fifth Street, Suite #930
Springfield, IL 62701

www.kdospringfield.org

# *Dining* WITH THE *Daughters*

Family traditions pass from generation to generation and some of our most treasured memories bring a smile to our face, or a tear to our eye. They weave our past with our present and anchor future generations. Many of these memories are created in the one special room in the home where everyone seems to gather: the kitchen.

The King's Daughters Organization is a group of multi-generational women dedicated to serving the elderly in our community. Enjoying and appreciating the wide range of ages gives our organization the feeling of community and family. Our members gather monthly to share a meal and a meeting, and our annual fundraiser is a style show and luncheon which has become a popular Springfield tradition.

So it is not surprising that this cookbook, *Dining with the Daughters*, is a tribute to mother and daughter relationships and the many traditions that are present in our organization as well as in our community. There is a special bond between a mother and her daughter; it begins the first day a mother sees her daughter and lasts a lifetime and beyond.

*Dining with the Daughters* has been a labor of love for our cookbook committee and members. Countless volunteer hours have been spent collecting, creating, cooking, taste testing, designing and editing this cookbook. Our goal was to share a special collection of our favorite family recipes along with a sampling of recipes from some of Springfield's most celebrated chefs and eateries. We hope that you will enjoy these recipes and create new memories and traditions in your own family.

We encourage you to spend time looking through the rich history and photos from our historic city. It is our hope that when you prepare these recipes, you will feel a touch of the passion we put into capturing the traditions as mothers and daughters, and experience love for our elders that we hold dear.

This book is dedicated to all those members, friends and celebrities who have contributed time and talent to this enterprise. Thank you, and Bon Appétit!

*Posy    Barbara    Cathy    Donna*

*Katie    Suzie    Brenda    Diana*

# King's Daughters Organization

King's Daughters Organization (KDO) is a group of vibrant Circles of Friendship — talented, compassionate women whose mission is **to charitably aid the elderly in our community.** The corporation is managed by a Board of Directors comprised of members who represent each of the Circles, and a volunteer Advisory Board of professionals. Our members bring the mission to life through personal volunteerism with a wide variety of organizations serving the elderly, and by actively supporting the expansion of our endowment fund, ensuring our mission's life for years to come.

## Our Past

*Above: The original Ladies who resided at the King's Daughters home.*

*Below: Painted portrait of Marjorie Merriweather Post.*

King's Daughters has a long and rich history. The International Order of King's Daughters' began as a Christian organization in 1886 which influenced the origin of our local organization for a few years. Our first Springfield Circle was established in 1888, with other circles forming rapidly. Each circle had its own mission. Twenty-six circles incorporated in 1893 as King's Daughters' Home for Women and purchased the stately Italianate mansion at 541 Black Avenue. The house had originally been the home of the cereal giant C.W. Post and his family. Marjorie Merriweather Post, leading American socialite and the founder of General Foods, was born in the family home. After the family relocated, the new owner was unable to keep the house in good repair. Financial support from the Springfield community provided improvements necessary before the opening of the home.

On June 6, 1895, the home opened debt free with nine Ladies and a waiting list. Eventually, we had as many as 38 residents. In 1902, a fire almost destroyed our precious home. The Post family became aware of this devastating event and provided the funds to rebuild the home. They were very pleased with what King's Daughters had done with their former family home. In the early years, each circle sponsored a resident and maintained a designated room at the home. Later,

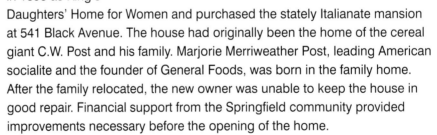

*Members of the Post family and former Home residents are laid to rest at Oak Ridge Cemetery in Springfield.*

*Above: After a devastating fire damaged the original home, the Post family provided resources to rebuild.*

Circles relinquished responsibility of their rooms and focused on maintaining personal relationships with our Ladies. We provided entertainment, lunched with them monthly and celebrated birthdays and holidays. In many cases, Circles became extensions of their families.

It should be noted that the Post family provided financial aid for many years; and in recognition of their support, the name was changed to Carrie Post King's Daughters Home in 1950. In 1988, a decision had to be made to allow the home to continue its mission. Generous community support made it possible for us to remodel the home providing individual bathrooms and more comfortable facilities for 26 residents.

Initially, we offered a Lifetime Care Program, which was discontinued in 1993 due to its rising cost. The program provided for skilled nursing home care for each lady when it became necessary.

In 2006, with increased costs of maintenance, funding of the Lifetime Care Program and resident care, King's Daughters membership made a painful decision to close the home while there were sufficient funds to provide for a smooth transition and a future for King's Daughters. Our members assisted the remaining nineteen Ladies in finding new homes and making their moves as smooth as possible. We continue our same traditions of personal relationships with them. The landmark decision to close the home ended an era but opened the door to a new, vibrant and impactful future. The home and its Ladies had been in our care for 111 years!

## ᏦᎠ *Our Future*

The home was sold to nearby Benedictine University, fittingly for a women's residence hall. With the proceeds from the home and our existing Endowment Fund, we turned to the Community Foundation of the Land of Lincoln (formerly Sangamon County Community Foundation) for guidance. We became

**COMMUNITY**
**F O U N D A T I O N**
for the *Land of Lincoln*

*— continued on next page*

King's Daughters Organization in 2007. We established The KDO Fund to support grants for not-for-profit organizations providing services to senior citizens. A member from each Circle serves on the annual Grants Committee. Today our grant program is a very vital part of our mission, along with significant personal volunteerism projects by each Circle. KDO is the only local grant giving body dedicated to solely supporting seniors in its mission.

Throughout our history, the Springfield community has supported KDO through major fundraising events. Progress Circle, with assistance from all circles,

*Above: Members enjoy fellowship at the annual meeting.*

presents an annual luncheon and style show. This Springfield tradition began over 65 years ago. Developing the cookbook, *Dining with the Daughters,* was another collaborative fundraising effort. Fundraising proceeds expand our KDO Fund; interest on the investment supports grants to accommodate the expanding senior population. At the time of this first edition, we have provided $470,000 in grants to 22 local nonprofit organizations. These grants strongly support our mission.

*Above: Diana Dedrick, Maryann Walker, Sharon Zook and Polly Roesch reflect the generations of KDO members.*

Our KDO history spans from the end of the nineteenth century, through the twentieth, and now well into the twenty-first century. Today, we are eight circles strong and a vital part of our local community. As an organization, we have sustained many changes but have continuously continued to grow and change to meet the needs of our ever-changing society. We will continue to honor our past and to maintain our niche in the history of Springfield, as we promote the well-being of the elderly in our community. ♔

# *Contents*

# Menu Creations

Cocktails and Tidbits

Dinner with Friends

Grillin' and Chillin'

Fall Dinner

Elegant Dinner

Seafood Soirée

Brunch for Your Bunch

Luncheon Temptations

Warm Weather Ladies Luncheon

Cold Weather Ladies Luncheon

# Cocktails and Tidbits

# *Dinner with Friends*

Loaded Potato and Sweet Corn Chowder  (page 93)

Braised Pork Shoulder Roast  (page 129)  or
Herb Roasted Rack of Lamb  (page 137)

Ratatouille Niçoise  (page 174)

Potato Dumplings  (page 165)  or
Parmesan Grits (page 173)

Sour Cream Orange Cake with Burnt Sugar Frosting  (page 195)

*Thanks to American Harvest, Sangamo Club and Illini Country Club.*


# *Grillin' and Chillin'*

Gazpacho  (page 92)  or
Scallop Rockefeller Soup  (page 100)  or
Walnut and Stilton Salad with Pomegranate Vinaigrette  (page 72)

Barbeque Flank Steak with Mango and Sweet Chili Glaze  (page 124)

Couscous  (page 172 )  or
Potato Cups with Onions and Westphalian Ham  (page 29)

Red Cabbage  (page 159)

Chocolate Raspberry Cakes  (page 200)

*Thanks to Augie's Front Burner, Carol Jean Fraase and 5flavors.*

# Fall Dinner

Butternut Squash and Apple Bisque  (page 95)  or
Lettuce Salad with Apples and Pecans  (page 73)

Sage Marinated Roast Pork with
Braised Apples and Onions  (page 132)

Nana's German Spinach  (page 164)

Miniature Cheddar Apple Butter Tarts  (page 43)

*Cheers to Julianne Glatz. Thanks*


# Elegant Dinner

Lemon Martini  (page 22)

Portobello Mushrooms and Asparagus  (page 157)

Osso Buco  (page 139)

Creamy Garlic Mashed Potatoes  (page 165)

Tres Leches Cake  (page 203)

*Maldaner's, you've been so helpful.*

# Seafood Soiré

Crab Cakes  (page 141)

Shrimp Madagascar  (page 146)

Spinach Flambé  (page 82)

Wheat Bran Yeast Rolls  (page 55)

Sin Chocolate Cake  (page 195)

*By popular demand from Island Bay Yacht Club and Sebastian's Hideout.*


# Brunch for Your Bunch

Avocado Grapefruit Salad  (page 73)

Florentine Sausage  (page 64)

Raspberry Almond Coffee Cake  (page 68)

Baked Raspberry French Toast with Almond Syrup  (page 58)  or
Blueberry French Toast Casserole  (page 59)

Sausage Spinach Swiss Strata  (page 61)  or
Scrambled Egg and Ham Bake  (page 62)

Fruit Salad with Limoncello  (page 75)


# Luncheon Temptations

Chilled Strawberry Soup  (page 92)  or
Mushroom Bisque  (page 97)

Chicken Salad  (page 79)  or
Ham Paté  (page 28)

Parmesan Bread  (page 49)

Cookies: see Tempting Treats chapter.
*We appreciate the Feed Store's contribution.*

# Warm Weather Ladies Luncheon

Sweet Tea  (page 20)  or
Apricot Punch  (page 18)

Vidalia Custard Bread  (page 50)  or
Addy Bread  (page 46)

Grilled Chicken Pita Salad  (page 80)  or
Raspberry Chicken Salad  (page 80)  or
Chilled Chicken Curried Salad  (page 81)

French Raspberry Custard  (page 211)  or
Français Fudge Cookies  (page 182)


# Cold Weather Ladies Luncheon

Hot Buttered Cranberry Peach Punch  (page 19)  or
Coffee Grog  (page 18)

Cheddar Bacon Biscuits  (page 52)  or
Cornfetti Muffins  (page 52)

Spinach and Vidalia Salad  (page 84)

Chicken Artichoke Casserole  (page 112) or
Poppy Seed Chicken Casserole  (page 118)

Apple Cake with Amaretto Caramel Sauce  (page 194)  or
Chocolate Nut Surprise Cookies  (page 182)

# *Thirst Quenchers*

 *The crown indicates a celebrity's recipe.*

## Apricot Punch

*Note: Different gelatin flavors may be substituted.*

3 **(3 ounce) packages apricot gelatin**
2 1/2 **cups sugar**
3 1/2 **cups boiling water**
5 1/4 **cups (40 ounces) unsweetened pineapple juice**
1 **cup plus 2 tablespoons (9 ounces) unsweetened grapefruit juice**

1 **cup bottled lemon juice**
7 **cups water**
2 **(1 gallon) empty containers**
2 **(2 liter) bottles ginger ale**

Mix gelatin, sugar and boiling water until dissolved. Cool. Add pineapple juice, grapefruit juice, lemon juice and water to gelatin sugar mixture. Pour mixture evenly into the 1 gallon containers and freeze. Thaw 4 hours before using. Add 1 bottle ginger ale to each gallon of punch mixture when ready to serve.

2 gallons

## Coffee Grog

*Note: Grog base can be refrigerated until ready to use.*

**Grog Base:**
2 **tablespoons butter**
1 **cup firmly packed brown sugar**
 **Dash of salt**
1/8 **teaspoon ground cinnamon**
1/8 **teaspoon ground nutmeg**
1/8 **teaspoon ground allspice**
1/8 **teaspoon ground cloves**

**Grog Beverage:**
16 **tablespoons grog base, divided**
3 **cups light rum, divided**
4 **cups heavy cream, divided**
16 **strips lemon peel, divided**
16 **strips orange peel, divided**
12 **cups hot, brewed coffee, divided**

Cream butter and brown sugar together until thoroughly mixed. Stir in salt, cinnamon, nutmeg, allspice and cloves until thoroughly blended.

16 servings

To prepare a cup of grog, combine 1 tablespoon grog base, 3 tablespoons rum, 2 tablespoons cream, I strip lemon peel and 1 strip orange peel in a heated mug. Stir in 2/3 cup coffee.

## Hot Buttered Cranberry Peach Punch

1   (16 ounce) can jellied cranberry sauce

1/3  cup light brown sugar, firmly packed

1/4  teaspoon cinnamon

1/4  teaspoon allspice

1/8  teaspoon cloves

1/8  teaspoon nutmeg or mace

1/8  teaspoon salt

2   cups water

2   cups unsweetened pineapple juice

2   cups peaches, blended to slush

3   tablespoons butter, each cut into quarters

With a fork, crush the cranberry sauce. Put sauce into the mixer bowl; add the sugar, cinnamon, allspice, cloves, nutmeg and salt. Gradually add the water, blending with the whisk attachment. Add pineapple juice and peach slush. Heat to boiling point and simmer about 5 minutes. When serving, pour punch into a heavy mug and drop a quarter pat of butter on top

10 – 12 servings

## King's Daughters Home Punch

1   (2 liter) bottle 7-Up, chilled

36  ounces pineapple juice, chilled

1 1/2  gallons raspberry sherbet

*Note: This recipe was used for many years for the annual Christmas Tea and other events at the King's Daughters Home.*

Pour 7-Up and pineapple juice into a punch bowl. Place sherbet into the punch by large spoonfuls, to prevent a big lump.

1 1/2 gallons

*Three state war memorials are located on the west side of Oak Ridge Cemetery. They commemorate and honor the lives of Illinois military veterans lost in World War II, the Korean War and the Vietnam War.*

## Sweet Tea

3 quarts cold water
4 pitcher-size cold brew tea bags
Glucose Mixture, recipe follows
Lemon slices, for garnish
Mint sprigs, for garnish

Glucose Mixture:
1 cup water
3/4 cup sugar

For the tea mixture, put the water in a large pan and bring it to a boil. Remove from heat; steep tea bags in the water for about 5 minutes. Remove the tea bags. When cool enough, pour into a pitcher. Add glucose to the tea. Mix well. Pour tea over ice cubes in a glass. Garnish with a slice of lemon and/or a sprig of mint.

To prepare the glucose, combine the water and sugar in a pan and bring to a boil. Remove from heat. Stir to be sure the sugar is melted.

14 (8 ounce) servings

## Frozen Whiskey Sours

1 (6 ounce) can frozen lemonade, thawed
1 (6 ounce) can frozen orange juice, thawed
6 ounces water

10 ounces whiskey
1 quart (4 cups) 7-Up

Combine the lemonade, orange juice, water, whiskey and 7-up and pour into a freezer container with a lid; freeze 24 hours or until slushy. This will keep 3 – 4 months in the freezer. When filling freezer container, allow adequate head room at the top of container for expansion. Thaw to serving consistency.

10 (6 ounce) servings

## Slushy Bourbon

*Note: This has been a long time Christmas Eve favorite.*

1 cup sugar
1 (12 ounce) can frozen lemonade, defrosted
1 (6 ounce) can frozen orange juice concentrate, defrosted

2 cups strong tea
6 cups water
1 3/4 cups bourbon whiskey

Mix sugar, lemonade, orange juice concentrate, tea, water and whiskey together in a bowl. Cover and freeze for at least 12 hours. Defrost to serving consistency and serve the slush in small glasses with spoons.

15 servings

## Fruity White Sangria

1   (750 milliliter) bottle of your favorite white wine

1   lemon, cut into wedges, seeds removed

1   lime, cut into wedges, seeds removed

1   orange, cut into wedges, seeds removed

1   fresh peach, cut into wedges

1/2   cup prepared limeade

2   (1 1/2 ounce) shots peach or apricot brandy

1/2   cup sugar

1   cup fresh sliced strawberries (optional)

2   cups ginger ale, chilled

Pour wine into pitcher and squeeze the juice wedges from the lemon, lime and orange into the wine. Toss the fruit wedges into wine pitcher. Add sliced peaches, limeade, brandy, sugar and strawberries. Chill overnight. Add ginger ale and ice just before serving.

8 – 12 servings

## Greek Sangria

1   (750 milliliter) bottle of dry red wine (Cabernet Sauvignon, Tempranillo, Rioja, Zinfandel, Shiraz)

1   (750 milliliter) bottle of sweet red wine (Lambrusco)

1   lemon, cut into wedges, seeds removed

1   lime, cut into wedges, seeds removed

1   orange, cut into wedges, seeds removed

1/4   cup orange juice or lemonade

2   (1 1/2 ounce) shots of Brandy

4 – 6   cups of Sprite or 7-Up

Ice, as needed

*Note: The Lambrusco and Sprite or 7-Up replaces the sugar that is normally added.*

Pour red and dry wines into a large pitcher and squeeze the juice wedges from the lemon, lime and orange into the wine. Toss in the fruit wedges; add orange juice or lemonade and brandy. Chill a few hours or overnight. Add Sprite or 7-Up and ice just before serving. To serve right away, use chilled red wine and serve over lots of ice. Sangrias are best when chilled about 24 hours in the refrigerator to allow the flavors to meld.

24 – 26 servings

## Hot Buttered Rum Mix

*Variation: Use 3
teaspoons of
ground nutmeg
and 1 teaspoon of
ground mace.*

| | |
|---|---|
| 2 **teaspoons ground cloves** | 2 **pounds brown sugar** |
| 2 **teaspoons ground allspice** | 3 **eggs** |
| 1 **tablespoon ground cinnamon** | 1 **cup (8 ounces) hot water** |
| 1 **tablespoon ground nutmeg** | 1 **(1 1/2 ounce) shot Rum** |
| 1 **pound (4 sticks) butter, softened** | |

Combine cloves, allspice, cinnamon, and nutmeg. Add to butter and cream until mixed well. Add brown sugar and mix again. Add three eggs and mix thoroughly.

To serve, mix 1 teaspoon of mix with hot water and rum, to suit.

Makes at least a quart of buttered rum mixture.

## Kir

*Variation: For
Kir Royale, use
champagne instead
of wine.*

| | |
|---|---|
| 1 **part Crème de cassis** | 4 – 5 **parts white wine** |

Pour the crème de cassis into a white wine glass or a champagne flute. Pour in chilled white wine.

1 serving

## Maldaner's Restaurant
## Lemon Martini

*Note: Maldaner's
Lemon Martini is a
great preview for a fun
night of cooking. This
refreshing cocktail is a
favorite at both of our
bars.*

| | |
|---|---|
| 2 **ounces premium vodka** | 1 **martini shaker** |
| 1 **ounce limoncello** | 1 **martini glass** |
| **Lemon twist** | |

Fill your shaker with ice; pour in vodka and limoncello and shake until chilled. Pour into martini glass and garnish with lemon twist.

*"If people are injured
from the use of liquor,
the injury arises not
from the use of a
bad thing but from
the abuse of a good
thing." – Abraham
Lincoln*

## Limoncello

| | | | |
|---|---|---|---|
| 4 | cups vodka | 3 | cups water |
| 1/2 | cup lemon rind strips (about 7 lemons) | 1 1/2 | cups sugar |

Combine vodka and rind in a container. Cover and let it stand at room temperature for 2 weeks. Strain through a sieve, discarding the solids. Combine water and sugar in a large saucepan. Cook over medium heat until the sugar dissolves. Cool to room temperature and add to the vodka mixture.

This will keep for one month refrigerated. It lasts for 1 year refrigerated when divided among 3 sterilized 750 milliliter bottles, capped and sealed.

7 cups

*Tip: This is good over ice, in a lemon drop martini, mixed with sparkling wine or with club soda and mint.*

## Peach Melba

| | | | |
|---|---|---|---|
| 1/2 | cup sugar, plus more for glass rims | 1 | cup fresh lime juice, plus more for glass rims |
| 1/2 | cup boiling water | 2 | large or 3 small fresh peaches sliced (with skins) |
| 1 1/2 | cups (6 ounces) fresh or frozen raspberries | 1 | cup ice cubes |
| 3/4 | cup rum (to taste) | | |

Mix sugar in boiling water until completely dissolved to make simple syrup. Puree the raspberries with 2 tablespoons of the simple syrup; pour into a measuring cup and rinse blender. (Pour through a sieve to remove seeds if you wish.) Blend rum, lime juice, remaining simple syrup, peaches and ice until smooth. To serve, dip the rims of martini glasses (or small highball glasses) in fresh lime juice and then sugar. Put 2 tablespoons of the raspberry puree into the bottom of each glass; top with the peach mixture.

8 servings

*Variation: Substitute 16 ounces of frozen peaches for fresh peaches.*

*Notes: Do not use canned peaches. You can make the simple syrup ahead and store in refrigerator.*

*Your dining experience at the Fraase Farm in New Berlin is enhanced by the ambiance of eclectically decorated gardens.*

# For Starters

*The crown indicates a celebrity's recipe.*

# Tomato, Basil and Cheese Torta

*Tip: May be made a day in advance. This can be sliced into slices, wrapped tightly and frozen for up to 2 months. Well worth the effort.*

| | |
|---|---|
| 1 **cup pine nuts** | 1 **cup finely shredded Parmesan cheese** |
| 1 **(7 ounce) jar dried tomatoes in oil** | 1/3 **cup olive oil** |
| 4 **cloves of garlic** | 2 **(8 ounce) packages cream cheese** |
| 2 1/2 **cups fresh basil leaves** | 2 **cups (4 sticks) butter, softened** |
| 1/8 **teaspoon salt** | |
| 1/8 **teaspoon pepper** | |

Preheat oven 350°. Grease bottom and sides of a 3 x 5 x 9 – inch loaf pan. Line the pan with plastic wrap extending it over the sides of the pan. Set aside. Put the pine nuts in a pan in a single layer and roast for about 4 minutes. Remove pan from oven and shake to scatter the nuts. Return pan to the oven and roast 2 more minutes. Drain tomatoes and reserve 2 tablespoons of the oil. Process the tomatoes with the oil in a food processor. Empty tomatoes into a bowl and wipe out the processor container. Process garlic in the same container for 5 seconds; add basil, salt, pepper, cheese and pine nuts and process until finely chopped. Pour in olive oil and process until smooth. Empty processor container into another bowl and wipe out container. Put cream cheese and butter into the food processor and process slowly until smooth. Spread one cup of butter cheese mixture into loaf pan. Spread half of the basil mixture over cream cheese mixture. Layer one cup of butter mixture over basil layer. Spread tomato mixture over last butter/cream layer. Add remaining basil mixture and top it with cream cheese mixture and chill for 8 hours. Unmold and serve the whole loaf or for a smaller group slice in approximately 1 1/2 – inch slices from end to end so that you can see the layers.

Serve with assorted crackers.

Serves a large group.

# Gorgonzola Truffles

*Note: Truffles may be chilled up to three days. Let warm slightly before serving.*

| | |
|---|---|
| 4 **ounces cream cheese, softened** | 1/4 **teaspoon freshly ground black pepper** |
| 1 **(5 ounce) container crumbled Gorgonzola cheese** | 1/2 **cup cooked and crumbled bacon** |
| 2 **teaspoons finely chopped onion** | **Apple slices** |
| 1/2 **teaspoon Worcestershire sauce** | **Pear slices** |
| | **Grapes** |

Combine cream cheese, Gorgonzola cheese, onion, Worcestershire sauce and pepper in electric mixer bowl until mixed well. Cover mixture with a lid and refrigerate 1 hour. Form mixture into 3/4 – inch balls and roll in bacon. Serve with fruits.

6 servings

# Pot Stickers

**Dipping Sauce:**

- 1/3   **cup soy sauce**
- 1/4   **cup wine vinegar**
- 1   **teaspoon sesame oil**
- 3   **tablespoons sliced or grated fresh ginger**

**Pot stickers:**

- 1/2   **cup minced green onion**
- 1   **cup finely chopped water chestnuts**
- 1   **clove garlic, minced**
- 1   **teaspoon fresh minced ginger root**
- 1/2   **pound ground meat (turkey, pork or chicken)**
- 2   **tablespoons soy sauce**
- 2   **teaspoons sesame oil**
- 1   **tablespoon cornstarch**
-   **Dash of white pepper**
- 1   **packet pot sticker or wonton wrappers**
- 1/2   **cup water**

*Note: You can freeze pot stickers on a baking sheet before cooking. When frozen, put them into airtight bags and use them as needed. Cook in the same manner, allowing longer cooking time. Pot sticker and wonton wrappers are available at most stores in the produce section.*

Combine soy sauce, vinegar, sesame oil and ginger and set aside for dipping.

Combine the green onion, water chestnuts, garlic and ginger root in a food processor, mixing with a pulsing action until finely chopped. Add meat and pulse until mixed. Add soy sauce, sesame oil, cornstarch and pepper and pulse a few times to mix all together. Place one heaping teaspoon of filling into center of each wrapper. Moisten edges with water and fold wrapper in half to enclose the filling. Firmly press the edges together to seal.

Heat a frying pan which has a tight fitting lid. Spray with cooking spray or coat with oil. When pan is quite hot add the pot stickers and brown the bottoms for about 2 minutes. Then add water, cover pan and cook for approximately 5 minutes or until the pan is dry and the bottoms crisp. Serve immediately with dipping sauce or keep warm until ready to serve.

30 pot stickers

# Pancetta Goat Cheese Crisps

- 12   **thin slices (1/3 pound) pancetta**
- 1   **Bartlett pear**
- 4   **ounces goat cheese, crumbled**
-   **Freshly cracked pepper**

**Honey for garnish**

**Fresh thyme sprigs for garnish (optional)**

Preheat oven to 450°. Arrange pancetta slices in a single layer on an aluminum foil lined baking sheet. Bake 8 – 10 minutes or until golden. Remove from oven and transfer to a paper towel-lined wire rack. Let stand 10 minutes or until crisp.

Core pear with an apple corer. Cut crosswise into 12 thin rings and arrange on a serving platter. Top evenly with pancetta and goat cheese. Sprinkle with pepper. Drizzle with honey just before serving. Garnish with thyme sprigs, if desired.

12 appetizers

## Brie Cheese with Cranberry Glaze

3 cups cranberries

3/4 cup firmly packed light brown sugar

2/3 cup dried currants

1/3 cup water

1/8 teaspoon dry mustard

1/8 teaspoon allspice

1/8 teaspoon cardamom

1/8 teaspoon ground cloves

1/8 teaspoon powdered ginger

1 Brie cheese wheel, approximately 2 pounds or 8 – inches in diameter

Crackers, apple slices or pear wedges

Combine cranberries, sugar, currants, water, mustard, allspice, cardamom, cloves and ginger in a heavy saucepan. Cook over medium high heat, stirring frequently until most of the berries pop, approximately 5 – 8 minutes. Cool to room temperature and chill for at least 2 hours. This may be prepared up to 3 days in advance.

Preheat oven to 300°. Using a sharp knife, cut out a circle of rind about 3/4 the size of the wheel from the top of the Brie. Place cheese in a ceramic baking dish at least 8 – inches in diameter. Pour cranberry mixture over the top. Bake 15 – 20 minutes or until soft. Serve with crackers, apple slices and/or pear wedges.

16 - 24 servings

##  The Feed Store
## Ham Paté

1 1/2 cups chopped ham

1/4 cup mayonnaise

1 tablespoon Dijon mustard

1 teaspoon prepared horseradish

2 teaspoons dry sherry

1/4 teaspoon ground black pepper

Freshly chopped parsley (optional)

Place ham in food processor or blender container and cover. Use a pulsing action to process until finely chopped. Mix mayonnaise, mustard, horseradish, sherry and pepper in medium bowl until well blended. Stir in ham. Place in crock or bowl. Garnish with parsley, if desired.

Serve with crackers or cocktail rye bread slices.

Yield – 1 1/2 cups

# Jalapeño Crisps

1   (8 ounce) package cream
    cheese, softened (regular or
    reduced fat)
8   ounces grated Parmesan
    cheese

2   egg yolks
4   tablespoons finely chopped
    jalapeño peppers
    Bread crumbs

*Variation: Add sesame seeds to the bread crumbs before dusting the crisps.*

Preheat oven to 350°. Combine cream cheese, Parmesan cheese and egg yolks. Add jalapeño peppers. Form into a log and wrap in plastic wrap. Place in freezer for 20 – 30 minutes. Lightly grease a cookie sheet or a silicone sheet. Slice into 1/4 – inch rounds and dust both sides lightly with bread crumbs. Bake 17 minutes or until golden brown.

12 – 16 crisps

*Tip: Instead of freezing, refrigerate for an hour and drop by scant teaspoonfuls on to pan.*

# Augie's Front Burner
# Potato Cups with Onions and Westphalian Ham

2   pounds frozen hash brown
    potatoes, defrosted
    Salt
    Pepper
5   cups (about 8 medium) onions,
    thinly sliced
6   ounces heavy cream

1   teaspoon (2 ounces) cracked
    black pepper
1   cup Westphalian ham, diced
8   ounces raclette cheese, sliced
    Fresh thyme as needed for
    garnish

*Note: Raclette cheese is a semi-firm cow's milk cheese from the Swiss or French Alpine country. It has a nutty flavor and silky, smooth texture.*

Preheat oven to 425°. Brush four 12-section mini-muffin tins with oil. Toss hash browns with salt and pepper to taste and press into muffin cups. Bake 20 – 25 minutes until crisp and brown.

Grease or spray a Dutch oven. Reduce oven temperature to 350° and roast onion slices in the Dutch oven for 30 minutes or until slightly caramelized. Remove from oven and add heavy cream. Cook until thick. Season with black pepper.

Sauté ham until crisp. Place 1 tablespoon onion mixture in each cup. Sprinkle with ham and cheese. Heat in oven to melt cheese and garnish with thyme leaves.

48 potato cups

*Chef and owner Augie Mrzowski of Augie's Front Burner began his culinary career at the St. Nicholas Hotel right around the corner in the late 1960's and has been part of the Downtown "experience" for the last 15 years. Augie added that this sandblasted glass signifies the ocean and sunrise meeting, the place where all growth starts. Augie's Front Burner offers a unique dining experience for the adventurous in palate and spirit.*

## Sweet and Savory Wings

*Variation: Use a combination of chicken wings and thighs. Leftover meat makes great chicken salad.*

*Tip: For herb mixture, use 1/2 teaspoon each of rosemary, thyme, marjoram, savory and oregano and 1/4 teaspoon of tarragon and basil. Vary amounts to suit your taste.*

| | | | |
|---|---|---|---|
| 8 | chicken wings, with skin | 1/2 | cup white wine |
| | Juice of 1 lemon | 2 | garlic cloves, smashed |
| 1/4 | cup olive oil | 3 | tablespoons mixed dried herbs |
| 1/4 | cup honey | 1/2 | cup water |

Put chicken in a large sealable bag. Squeeze lemon juice into a small bowl and add olive oil, honey and wine. Stir until honey is dissolved. Pour into the bag with chicken. Add garlic and herbs. Seal bag and squeeze to mix contents well. Refrigerate overnight.

Preheat oven to 325°. Spray a flame-proof roasting pan with cooking spray. Place the chicken in the roasting pan skin side up. Pour marinade over chicken. Cover the pan with foil and bake for 2 hours. Remove the foil and turn oven to 425°. Bake an additional 15 – 25 minutes, or until chicken skin is browned. Check frequently as the honey in the marinade makes it burn quickly. Remove the chicken to a warmed platter. Spoon off the excess fat from the cooking liquid left in the pan. Place pan on a burner over medium heat. Make a sauce by scraping any browned bits sticking to the pan's surface and adding 1/2 cup of water to dilute. Stir until golden brown. Pour over chicken before serving.

4 servings

## Bacon Cheese Broils

| | | | |
|---|---|---|---|
| 1 | pound bacon | 1 | cup mayonnaise |
| 2 1/2 | cups finely shredded cheddar cheese | 1 | pound sliced pumpernickel party bread |
| 2 | tablespoons prepared mustard | | |

Preheat oven to broil setting. Fry bacon until crisp. Drain and crumble. In a medium bowl, combine bacon, cheese, mustard and mayonnaise. Spread mixture about 1/4 – inch thick onto each slice of party bread. Broil about 3 minutes or until bubbly.

24 appetizers

## Ham and Swiss Puffs

1    *package (2 sheets) frozen puff pastry, defrosted*
3    *tablespoons Dijon mustard*
1/4  *pound ham, thinly sliced*

1/2  *pound Swiss Gruyère cheese, sliced*
1    *egg, beaten with 1 tablespoon water, for egg wash*

Preheat oven to 450°. Place a piece of parchment paper or silicone mat on a sheet pan. Lay one sheet of puff pastry on a floured board and carefully roll it out to 10 x 12 – inches. Place it on the sheet pan and spread with the mustard, leaving a 1 – inch border around the edge. Layer the ham over the mustard and then layer cheese over the ham, leaving the 1 – inch border. Brush the border with the egg wash. Place the second sheet of puff pastry on the floured board and roll it out to 10 x 12 – inches. Place the second sheet on top of the filled pastry, lining up the edges and pressing together lightly. Brush the top with egg wash and cut a few slits to allow steam to escape. Bake for 20 – 25 minutes or until puffed and golden brown. Allow to cool for a few minutes before cutting. Serve hot, warm or at room temperature.

30 servings

## Crostini with Prosciutto Artichoke Dip

1 1/2  *cups sour cream*
1/2   *cup mayonnaise*
6     *artichoke hearts, cut into 1/2 – inch slices (1 14 ounce can)*
8     *ounces prosciutto, thinly sliced and diced*
      *Juice of 1 lemon*

2  *dashes Tabasco sauce*
   *Salt to taste*
   *Pepper to taste*
   *1 loaf Italian bread, thinly sliced*
   *Garlic oil*
   *Fresh oregano, minced*
1  *round loaf of Italian bread, not sliced*

Preheat oven to 350°. Mix sour cream, mayonnaise, artichoke hearts and prosciutto. Fold in lemon juice, Tabasco, salt and pepper, mixing well. Cut out 2 to 3 – inch rounds from the sliced bread to form the crostini. Place in a single layer on a baking sheet. Brush with garlic oil and sprinkle with fresh oregano, salt and pepper. Bake for 5 minutes or until golden. Meanwhile, cut out the center of a round loaf of Italian bread. Set center aside for another use. Toast hollowed bread in oven for 15 minutes. Cool. To serve, place toasted bread bowl on a large plate and fill with the prosciutto artichoke dip. Garnish the plate with crostini and serve immediately.

16 – 24 servings

## D'Arcy's Pint
# Spinach Artichoke Dip

*Note: See Roux on page 100.*

1/2   cup (1 stick) margarine
1/2   cup flour
  1   cup diced red onion
  1   pint heavy cream
  2   cups (8 ounces) shredded mozzarella cheese, plus more for sprinkling
  1   cup Parmesan cheese, plus more for sprinkling

  1   cup melted Velveeta or canned cheese sauce
1/4   cup fresh garlic, finely chopped
  1   (10 ounce) package frozen chopped spinach, drained
  2   (12 ounce) cans artichoke hearts, drained and chopped

Preheat oven to 350°. Melt margarine. Add flour and stir constantly for 1 – 2 minutes until it forms a roux. Add onion and cook until clear. Add cream, mozzarella, Parmesan and Velveeta. Simmer on low until it warms. Add garlic, spinach and artichokes. Mix thoroughly and simmer over low heat until heated through. Pour mixture into oven safe dish; sprinkle with more mozzarella and Parmesan. Bake until cheese is golden brown. Serve with warm pita bread or nacho chips.

Serves a large group

# Artichoke Dip

*Note: For a smaller group, make half a recipe.*

  1   medium red onion
  2   jars marinated artichoke hearts (7 1/2 ounce jars)
  1   cup real mayonnaise
  1   cup mozzarella cheese

  1   cup Parmesan cheese
  2   cups 4 cheese Italian blend
  1   tablespoon dill weed
  1   tablespoon plus 1 teaspoon dried parsley

Preheat oven to 350°. Spray a 9 x 13 – inch baking dish. Place red onion in a food blender and coarsely chop. Add artichoke hearts and marinade. Blend until almost smooth. Pour mixture into a bowl. Add mayonnaise, mozzarella cheese, Parmesan cheese and Italian cheese blend and mix well. Incorporate dill weed and parsley until well blended. Pour into a baking dish and bake until cheese is bubbly and slightly brown around the edges, about 35 – 40 minutes. Serve with crackers.

Serves a large group

## Oysters en Brochette

| | | | | |
|---|---|---|---|---|
| 1 | pint large oysters | 1/4 | teaspoon ground thyme | |
| 1 | cup dry vermouth | 4 | drops hot pepper sauce | |
| 3/4 | cup cooking oil | 1/8 | teaspoon ground sage | |
| 1/3 | cup freshly squeezed lemon juice | 1/4 | pound fresh button mushrooms | |
| 2 | tablespoons chopped chives | 1 | medium green pepper, cut into 3/4 – inch pieces | |
| 2 | teaspoons salt | 1 | medium red or white onion, cut into eighths | |
| 1 | clove garlic, minced | | | |
| 1/4 | teaspoon pepper | 4 | strips bacon cut into sixths | |

*Note: Use longer skewers and serve these as an entree.*

Preheat the broiler oven. Spray a large broiler pan with cooking spray. Remove any remaining shells from the oysters. Combine vermouth, oil, lemon juice, chives, salt, garlic, pepper, thyme, pepper sauce and sage for marinade. Add oysters, mushrooms, green pepper and onion to marinade. Cover and refrigerate for 1 hour. Thread oysters, bacon, mushrooms, peppers and onions evenly on 4 (3 to 4 – inch) skewers, placing a piece of bacon on each oyster. Broil 3 to 4 – inches from heat source for 4 – 6 minutes or until the oyster edges curl and the bacon is crisp. Watch carefully to prevent over-cooking.

4 servings

## LLCC Culinary Arts Center
## Pastrami Cured Salmon

| | | | | |
|---|---|---|---|---|
| 1 | cup coarse or kosher salt | 1/2 | cup molasses | |
| 1/2 | cup sugar | 1 | tablespoon cayenne pepper | |
| 1 | side salmon, about 2 to 2 1/2 pounds, skin-on and scored, bones removed | 6 | bay leaves | |
| | | 3 | tablespoons paprika | |
| | | 3 | tablespoons ground coriander seeds | |
| 2 | bunches fresh cilantro | | | |
| 1 | bunch fresh Italian parsley | 2 | tablespoons fresh ground black pepper | |
| 1/2 | pound shallots, peeled | | | |

Begin the curing process 3 – 4 days before planning to serve. Combine salt and sugar. Coat both sides of the salmon with the salt/sugar mixture and place salmon skin side down in an 8 x 12 – inch pan. Puree cilantro, parsley and shallots in a food processor until smooth. Coat both sides of the salmon with this mixture. Cover and allow salmon to cure in refrigerator for 2 – 3 days. Check daily and pour off any liquid that may be in pan.

The day before serving, scrape marinade from salmon and rinse. Dry with paper towels. Combine molasses, cayenne pepper, bay leaves, paprika, coriander seeds and ground black pepper in a saucepan. Bring to a boil, lower heat and simmer 5 minutes. Let cool and spread over both sides of the salmon. Refrigerate overnight.

To serve, slice thinly, and serve with bagels, crostini, cream cheese, chopped egg, capers and red onions.

## Seafood Crisps

8   ounces grated sharp cheddar cheese

1   tablespoon butter, softened or melted

1   tablespoons mayonnaise

2   small cloves garlic, chopped or 1/2 teaspoon garlic powder

1/3   teaspoon salt or seasoned salt or to your taste

1/8   teaspoon cayenne pepper (optional)

2   tablespoons chopped fresh parsley or 2 teaspoons dried parsley (optional)

1   (6 ounce) can tuna or crab or 1 (4 ounce) can tiny shrimp, drained

4   English muffins, sliced

Preheat oven to 400°. Mix cheese, butter and mayonnaise. Add garlic, salt or seasoned salt, cayenne (if using), parsley and seafood of your choice. Mix well. Spread mixture evenly on English muffin halves. Cut each muffin half into quarters. Place crisps on a baking sheet and bake 15 minutes. Remove from oven. Just before serving, heat broiler and broil briefly, until bubbly and lightly browned.

32 appetizers

## Golden Hour Onion Dip

1   package (8 ounce) cream cheese (regular or low fat), softened

1   tablespoons milk, as needed

6   strips bacon, crisply fried and crumbled

2   green onions, white and green parts chopped or 2 tablespoons chopped chives

Potato chips, crackers or cocktail rye bread for serving

Place cream cheese in food processor and pulse until smooth, adding enough milk to make dipping or spreading consistency. Scrape cheese into a bowl. Stir in bacon and onions. Refrigerate for 2 hours or more to meld flavors. Serve with potato chips, crackers or on cocktail rye bread for finger sandwiches.

Yield: 1 1/4 cups

## Bradfordton Cheese Ball

1 **(8 ounce) package cream cheese, softened**

4 **ounces Swiss cheese, finely shredded**

4 **ounces blue cheese, finely crumbled**

2 **tablespoons milk, more if needed**

2 **ounces walnuts, chopped**

*Variation: If your family is not overly fond of blue cheese, use 2 ounces.*

Combine the cream cheese, Swiss cheese and blue cheese in mixer bowl or food processor. Blend together. Add milk to create the desired consistency. Form into a ball or log and roll in walnuts. Cover in plastic wrap and refrigerate for at least 4 hours before serving. Serve with Fritos or Triscuits.

36 servings

## Shrimp Dip

2 **(4 ounce) cans shrimp or 10 – 12 fresh peeled and cooked shrimp, chopped into small pieces**

1 **(8 ounce) package cream cheese**

1 **(10 3/4 ounce) can cream of potato soup**

1/2 **cup shredded cheddar cheese**

1/2 **teaspoon pepper**

1/2 **teaspoon salt**

1/2 **teaspoon horseradish**

1 **cup sliced almonds, toasted**

*Variation: Substitute crab for shrimp.*

Preheat oven to 425°. Butter or spray a glass loaf pan or 1 1/2 quart casserole dish. Blend shrimp, cream cheese, potato soup and cheddar cheese and mix thoroughly. Add pepper, salt and horseradish. Dip into prepared pan and top with almonds. Bake for 30 minutes.

Yield: 3 – 4 cups

*This neoclassic gazebo or bandstand in historic Washington Park was built in 1926 to honor the memory of Professor Louis Lehman, director of the Illinois Watch Factory Band. It was dedicated to Springfield's beloved Music Master and is the site for many weddings and photo opportunities. It is a popular hangout at the upper pond.*

## HG's Steakhouse
# Cajun Crab Dip

| | |
|---|---|
| 1 cup diced red bell peppers | 2 teaspoons blackened seasoning spice |
| 1 cup diced green bell peppers | 2 teaspoons Cajun seasoning |
| 1 Roma tomato, diced | pinch of salt |
| 3 stalks celery, chopped | pinch of pepper |
| 1 red onion, diced | 2 (8 ounce) packages cream cheese, softened |
| 2 pounds lump crab | |
| 2 tablespoons sour cream | |

Combine red and green peppers, tomato, celery, onion, crab, sour cream, blackened seasoning, Cajun seasoning, salt and pepper and blend into cream cheese. Serve with crackers, vegetables or chips.

36 – 42 servings

# Spicy Southwest Dip

*Tip: This dish becomes more heat intense after the first day.*

*Variation: You may use a (1.1 ounce) package of Hidden Valley Dips Fiesta Ranch Mix adding 1/2 teaspoon of granulated garlic or garlic powder to the dip mixture.*

**Southwest Seasoning:**

2 teaspoons chili powder
2 teaspoons ground cumin
2 tablespoon paprika
1 teaspoon black pepper
1 tablespoon ground coriander
1 teaspoon cayenne pepper
1 tablespoon plus 1/2 teaspoon granulated garlic or garlic powder, divided
1 teaspoon crushed red pepper

1 tablespoon salt
1 tablespoon dried oregano

**Dip:**

2 cups sour cream
1/2 cup cheddar cheese, shredded
1/2 cup green onion, chopped
1 (4 ounce) can green chiles, chopped and drained
1 – 2 tablespoons diced black olives

Combine chili powder, cumin, paprika, black pepper, coriander, cayenne, 1 tablespoon granulated garlic (or garlic powder), crushed red pepper, salt and oregano; let meld.

Combine southwest seasoning with sour cream. Add the cheese, onions, chiles, black olives and 1/2 teaspoon granulated garlic and mix well. Refrigerate at least 4 hours before serving.

Serve with Frito Scoops or corn chips.

36 appetizer servings

## Pineapple Pecan Cheese Ball

2 **(8 ounce) packages cream cheese, softened**

1 **(8 ounce) can crushed pineapple, drained**

1/4 **cup chopped green pepper**

2 **tablespoons finely chopped onion**

1 **tablespoon seasoned salt**

2 **cups chopped pecans, toasted and divided**

Combine cream cheese, pineapple, green pepper, onion and seasoned salt. Stir in 1 cup pecans. Cover and chill until firm. Shape mixture into a ball and roll in remaining pecans. Serve with crackers and green and red bell pepper squares.

5 – inch cheese ball

## Swiss Cheese Spread

16 **ounces finely shredded Swiss cheese**

1 **bunch of green onion, finely chopped and trimmed, tops only**

1 1/3 **cups mayonnaise (regular or light)**

2 1/2 **teaspoons Lawry's pepper**

1 **teaspoon Accent or 1/2 teaspoon sugar and 1/2 teaspoon salt**

Stir together cheese, onions, mayonnaise, pepper and Accent. Let sit for at least 2 hours in refrigerator for flavors to meld. Serve with crackers.

*Maldaner's Restaurant and Catering in Springfield offers the best of contemporary American fine dining in the heart of downtown's historic district.*

## Mary A. Lawrence Cheese Ball

Tip: It is easier to make a professional looking log than a professional looking ball.

3 (8 ounce) packages cream cheese, softened

2 teaspoons Worcestershire sauce

2 teaspoons grated onion

2 teaspoons lemon juice

1 teaspoon dry mustard

1/2 teaspoon paprika

1/2 teaspoon garlic salt or 1/4 teaspoon garlic powder

1/2 teaspoon salt

8 ounces cheddar cheese, finely grated or finely shredded

2 tablespoons chopped parsley

2 tablespoons chopped pimientos

1 cup chopped pecans, other nuts or parsley for coating

Place cream cheese in food processor and process for 15 seconds. Add Worcestershire sauce, onion, lemon juice, mustard, paprika, garlic, salt and process until blended. Add cheddar cheese, parsley and pimiento processing until just blended. Remove from processor and divide the mixture in half. Place each half on a piece of plastic wrap and mold into a log. Refrigerate for 2 hours or overnight. Place chopped nuts or parsley on wax paper. Unwrap the cheese logs and roll in nuts or parsley. Place in fresh plastic wrap. Refrigerate until ready to use or freeze, well wrapped up to 2 months. Serve with assorted crackers.

32 – 40 servings

## Black Avenue Spread

1 (8 ounce) package cream cheese, softened

1/2 cup dried cranberries

6 ounces blue cheese, crumbled

2 green onions, white and part of green chopped

1 clove garlic, minced

1/2 cup chopped pecans

Combine cream cheese, cranberries, blue cheese, onions, garlic, and pecans. Form into a ball or roll. Serve with crackers.

12 – 16 servings

## LLCC Culinary Arts Center
# Chicken Liver Paté with Calvados

3/4 cup (1 1/2 sticks) unsalted butter, cut into cubes

1 cup small onion, diced

2 cloves garlic, minced

2 teaspoons fresh thyme, minced

1 pound chicken livers, rinsed and trimmed of all fat/sinew

1 1/2 ounces Calvados (French Apple Brandy)

1/2 cup heavy whipping cream

Salt

Pepper

Melt butter in a sauté pan and sauté onion, garlic and thyme until onion is translucent. Add chicken livers and brown about 7 minutes, leaving the centers pink. Remove from heat and add Calvados. Transfer to a bowl, cover and let cool in refrigerator overnight.

Blend chilled livers in food processor and slowly add heavy cream. Season mixture with salt and pepper to taste. Serve with baguettes, sliced apples and French cheeses.

This will serve a large group.

# Stuffed Peppadews

3 1/2 – 4 ounces feta cheese or herbed feta cheese, at room temperature

3 1/2 – 4 ounces cream cheese (light or regular), softened

Touch of milk or cream if necessary

20 peppadews

Combine feta and cream cheese in a food processor or blender. Whip until the mixture is soft and well blended. Add a touch of cream, if needed, to reach the desired consistency. Fill peppadews with cheese mixture and serve.

20 servings

*Variation: Use 4 ounces goat cheese in place of feta cheese and 1 – 2 tablespoons cream or half and half to reach the desired consistency, for a milder flavor. Combine and follow directions above. Garnish with a mint leaf.*

*Note: Peppadews are available at olive bars and in the deli section of larger grocery stores.*

# Caprese Skewers

3   ounces fresh mozzarella cheese, cut into 24 pieces, 1/4 to 1/2 – inch cubes

1 1/2   teaspoons extra-virgin olive oil

4   fresh basil leaves, chopped

2   pinches crushed red pepper flakes

Freshly ground black pepper, to taste

24   grape tomatoes cut in half crosswise

Basil leaves for garnish, chopped when ready to use

In a large bowl, stir mozzarella with oil, basil and crushed red pepper flakes. Season with black pepper. Add tomatoes and gently stir. The mixture can be refrigerated at this point for up to 24 hours. To assemble, place one tomato half on a toothpick, then one mozzarella cube and then one more tomato half. Arrange on a platter with fresh basil leaves for decoration.

24 skewers

# Ann Clark Corn Dip

*Tip: The canned chipotle peppers can be added to anything needing a smoky hot heat and kept in the refrigerator for a very long time.*

*Note: This can be heated in the microwave, although baking yields the best results.*

3   cups shredded cheddar/ Monterey Jack cheese

1/2   cup mayonnaise (regular or light)

1   (10 ounce) package frozen corn kernels

1   (4 ounce) can chopped green chili peppers, drained

2   teaspoons chopped canned chipotle peppers in adobo sauce

1/2   teaspoon garlic powder

Tortilla chips for dipping

Lightly coat a 9 – inch quiche dish or shallow 1 quart casserole with cooking spray. Stir together cheese, mayonnaise, corn, chili peppers, chipotle peppers and garlic powder in a large mixing bowl. Spread mixture into prepared dish. This may be done up to 24 hours ahead.

To serve, preheat oven to 350° and bake cheese mixture for 25 minutes or until heated through.

15 servings

## Island Guacamole

1 pomegranate

4 very ripe avocados, halved, seeded and peeled

1 cup finely chopped red onion (about 1 large)

2 fresh Serrano chili peppers, seeded and finely chopped

1/2 cup lime juice

3/4 cup peeled, seeded, and diced papaya

1/2 cup snipped cilantro
Coarse sea salt

*Tip: Look for arils in plastic containers at upscale and specialty markets.*

Remove arils (tiny fruit) from pomegranate and set aside. In a large bowl, use a fork or potato masher to coarsely mash avocados. Add red onion, chili peppers and lime juice; mix well. Fold in pomegranate seeds, papaya and cilantro. Season to taste with coarse sea salt. Serve immediately or cover surface tightly with plastic wrap and chill for up to 4 hours.

Yield: 4 cups

## Roasted Corn and Avocado Dip

1 cup frozen corn kernels, thawed

2 teaspoons olive oil

1 ripe avocado, peeled, half mashed and half chopped

3/4 cup seeded, diced tomato

3 tablespoons lime juice

3 tablespoon chopped fresh cilantro

2 tablespoons minced onion

2 jalapeño peppers, seeded and diced (use some of the seeds if you like heat)

2 garlic cloves, minced

1/2 teaspoon salt

1/4 teaspoon ground cumin

Preheat oven to 400°. Combine corn and oil in a shallow baking pan. Bake for 15 minutes or until corn is lightly browned, stirring occasionally. Cool. Combine corn, mashed avocado, chopped avocado, tomato, lime juice, cilantro, onion, jalapeño peppers, garlic, salt and cumin. Cover and chill at least 8 hours before serving. Serve with tortilla chips.

Yield: 2 1/4 cups

*The charm of yesteryear can still be appreciated at HG's Steakhouse, locally owned in the historic downtown building where Baur's Steakhouse operated for many decades.*

## Vegetable Ceviche

1 (14 ounce) can artichoke
  hearts, drained and chopped
1 large tomato, chopped
1/4 pound fresh button
  mushrooms, chopped
1/3 cup chopped green onion
1 large clove garlic, minced

1/4 cup fresh lime juice
1/4 cup vegetable oil
2 ripe avocados, chopped
  Garlic salt to taste
  Pepper to taste

Combine artichoke hearts, tomato, mushrooms, green onion, garlic, lime juice and oil. Cover and chill for 30 minutes. Stir in avocado and garlic salt and pepper to taste. Serve with pita bread or nacho chips.

Yield: 4 cups

## Zesty Tomato Relish (Bruschetta)

*Variation: Substitute an 8-ounce can of diced tomatoes, drained.*

1 cup diced fresh plum tomatoes,
  drained of excess juice
2 – 3 green onions chopped
4 ounces feta cheese
1/4 cup chopped black olives

1/8 cup finely chopped fresh basil
1 teaspoon olive oil
1 teaspoon Tabasco sauce
1/8 teaspoon salt

Gently combine diced tomatoes, onions, feta, olives, basil, olive oil, Tabasco and salt with fork until well blended. Prepare overnight or at least several hours before serving to allow flavors to meld. Serve on crackers, sliced bread or panetini.

20 – 24 servings

The Douglas Park covered band shell was constructed in the 1960's and has been the home of the Springfield Municipal Band ever since. The popular band continues to perform and entertain audiences at free performances throughout Springfield.

## Strawberry and Brie Bruschetta

1/3 cup butter, softened

1/3 cup packed brown sugar

2 teaspoons ground cinnamon

16 slices French bread (1/2 – inch)

12 slices Brie cheese, rind removed (about 12 ounces)

4 – 5 cups sliced stemmed strawberries (1 pound)

2 tablespoons balsamic vinegar

1/2 cup sugar

1/4 teaspoon black pepper or to taste

1 cup sliced almonds, toasted (optional)

*Tip: The Brie is easier to slice if partially frozen.*

Preheat oven to 375°. Combine butter, sugar and cinnamon in a small bowl and spread 2 teaspoons on each slice of bread. Place on a baking sheet and toast in oven for 5 minutes. Remove from oven and top each toast slice with 1 slice of cheese; return to oven. Bake an additional 4 – 6 minutes or until cheese is melted.

In large bowl, combine strawberries, balsamic vinegar, sugar and black pepper, mixing gently. Place two bruschetta on each serving plate. Spoon strawberry mixture over bruschetta, dividing equally; sprinkle with almonds if you wish. Serve immediately.

16 pieces or 8 servings

## Julianne Glatz
## Miniature Cheddar Apple Butter Tarts

1/2 pound sharp cheddar cheese, finely grated

1/4 cup (1/2 stick) unsalted butter, at room temperature

1 cup unbleached flour

1 tablespoon Worcestershire sauce

1/2 teaspoon dry mustard

1/2 teaspoon kosher or sea salt

Apple butter

*Note: These can be used immediately or refrigerated or frozen until needed, either as dough or as ready-to-bake tarts.*

*Note: These can also be served as a dessert.*

Preheat the oven to 400°. In a mixer or food processor combine cheese, butter, flour, Worcestershire sauce, mustard and salt. Mix until a smooth dough is formed.

Press tablespoons of the soft dough into miniature cups of a 1 1/4 – inch tart pan and press evenly around the bottom and sides with your fingers. Bake 8 – 10 minutes or until lightly browned. Tarts can be made ahead to this point. Fill the tartlets with apple butter just before serving.

24 – 30 tarts

# *Rise and Shine*

⬚ *The crown indicates a celebrity's recipe.*

## Addy Bread

Note: If fresh chives are not available, use minced scallion tops and chop into small pieces.

1 3/4 cups flour

1 tablespoon baking powder

1/2 – 1 teaspoon salt (depending on the cheese and other add-ins)

1/4 teaspoon freshly ground white pepper, or more to taste
Pinch of cayenne (optional)

3 large eggs, at room temperature

1/3 cup whole milk, at room temperature

1/3 cup extra-virgin olive oil

4 ounces Gruyère, Comte, Emmenthal or cheddar cheese, grated

2 ounces Gruyère, Comte, Emmenthal, or cheddar cheese, cut into small cubes

1/3 cup fresh chives minced (or other herb of choice)

1/3 cup toasted walnuts, chopped (optional)

Preheat oven to 350°. Generously butter a 5 x 9 – inch loaf pan. Whisk the flour, baking powder, salt, white pepper and cayenne, if using, together in a large bowl, set aside. Whisk the eggs until foamy; be sure that all egg whites are completely incorporated. Whisk in milk and olive oil. Pour the egg mixture into the flour mixture and mix with a heavy spoon until the dry ingredients are moistened. Stir in the grated and cubed cheese, chives and walnuts. Be sure the entire batter is moistened. The dough will be thick and heavy. Put into the prepared loaf pan. Pat the top level. Bake 35 – 45 minutes until bread is golden or a slim knife inserted in the center comes out clean. Cool about 3 minutes; run a thin knife around the edges and invert the pan to slip the bread onto a serving dish.

1 small loaf

## Blackstock Banana Bread

*Tip: Do not double!*

*Note: This truly is the best ever.*

3 ripe medium bananas, mashed

2 eggs

1 1/2 cups sugar

1/2 cup vegetable oil

1/4 cup plus 1 tablespoon buttermilk

1 teaspoon vanilla extract

1 3/4 cups unsifted flour

1 teaspoon baking soda

1/2 teaspoon salt

1 cup chopped walnuts

Preheat oven 325°. Grease and flour a 5 x 9 – inch loaf pan. Combine the bananas, eggs, sugar, oil, buttermilk and vanilla. Combine flour, baking soda and salt and add to banana mixture. Mix until blended, then fold in nuts. Pour into loaf pan and bake 1 hour and 20 minutes or until top is golden brown and splits slightly. Cool and remove from pan.

1 loaf

## Gloria Schwartz
## Challah Bread (Egg Bread)

| | |
|---|---|
| 1 (1/4 ounce) package active dry yeast | 1 egg, beaten |
| 1/2 cup sugar, divided | 2 egg yolks, divided |
| 1 cup warm water, 105° – 115° | 3 1/4 cups flour, divided |
| 1 teaspoon salt | Poppy seeds or sesame seeds for garnish |
| 1 tablespoon margarine, softened | |

Dissolve the yeast and 1 tablespoon sugar in warm water in a food processor mixing bowl fitted with steel or plastic blade. Let it stand until it gets foamy. Stir in the remaining sugar, salt, margarine, egg, 1 egg yolk and 2 cups flour. Mix for about 30 seconds. Add the remaining flour a little bit at a time until the dough leaves the sides of the bowl. It may be a bit sticky. Add flour if needed but not too much.

Place dough in a large greased bowl. Turn the dough over so that the top is greased to prevent it from drying out. Cover bowl tightly with plastic wrap and refrigerate overnight or up to 5 days. (You may need to place a plate on top with a heavy can on top of the plate to prevent the dough from rising out of the bowl.)

When ready to complete the bread, punch down the dough and divide it in half. Divide each half into 3 pieces. On a floured board, roll each piece of dough into a strand, tapering the ends. Braid the three strands together, pinching the ends to hold them together. Lay the braided challah on a greased baking pan. Repeat the same procedure with the other half of the dough. Cover with plastic wrap and let rise in a warm place until double in volume, about 1 – 2 hours.

When ready to bake, preheat oven to 375°. Beat the remaining egg yolk with 1 teaspoon of water. Brush the loaves with the mixture and sprinkle with the seeds. Bake for 25 – 30 minutes until the Challah sounds hollow when tapped. Remove from oven and cool on racks.

2 loaves.

## Blueberry Quick Bread

| | |
|---|---|
| 3 cups flour | 3 eggs, well beaten |
| 1 teaspoon salt | 1 1/4 cups salad oil |
| 1 teaspoon baking soda | 2 pints blueberries |
| 1 tablespoon ground cinnamon | 1 cup pecans, chopped |
| 2 cups sugar | |

Preheat oven to 350°. Lightly grease two 4 x 8 – inch loaf pans. Combine flour, salt, baking soda, cinnamon and sugar. Make a well in the center. Add eggs and oil to flour mixture and stir in only until dry ingredients are slightly wet. Fold in blueberries and then the pecans. Divide batter between prepared loaf pans. Bake for 1 hour or until a toothpick inserted in center comes out clean. Let cool in pans for 15 minutes before turning out onto a rack to cool. For best results let bread stand overnight before serving.

16 – 20 servings

## Illini Country Club
# Garlic Naan Bread

1 (1/4 ounce) package active dry yeast
1 cup warm water
1/4 cup white sugar
3 tablespoons milk
1 egg, beaten

2 teaspoons salt
2 teaspoons minced garlic
4 1/2 cups bread flour
1 tablespoon garlic powder
1/4 cup (1 stick) butter, melted

In a large bowl, dissolve yeast in warm water; let stand 10 minutes until frothy. Stir in sugar, milk, egg, salt, garlic, garlic powder; add flour last. Knead for 6 – 8 minutes on a lightly floured surface. Place dough in a lightly oiled bowl; cover with a damp towel. Let rise for 1 hour at room temperature. Place on a tray and let rise covered for 30 more minutes.

Preheat grill during the second rising. Roll dough out into a circle shape about 1/2 inch thick. Lightly oil grill, place naan on the grill and cook until lightly brown. Brush uncooked side with butter and turn over; brush cooked side with butter and finish grilling.

1 large flat loaf

# Grateful For This Bread

1 1/2 cups flour
2 teaspoons baking powder
1/4 teaspoon salt
1/4 cup brown sugar, packed
1/2 cup granulated sugar
1 cup pecans, chopped
2 eggs, lightly beaten

1/4 cup orange juice concentrate
1/3 cup canola oil
1 teaspoon vanilla extract
1/4 cup milk
1 cup cooked and mashed sweet potatoes

Preheat oven to 325°. Grease and lightly flour bottom of a 9 – inch loaf pan. Stir or whisk flour, baking powder and salt together in mixing bowl. Stir in the brown sugar, granulated sugar and pecans. In a separate bowl, combine eggs, orange juice concentrate, oil, vanilla, milk and mashed sweet potatoes. Stir until well blended. Add wet mixture to the dry ingredients and mix with a spoon just until the mixture is moistened. Pour batter into prepared pan. Bake for 60 minutes or until a toothpick inserted in center comes out clean. Cool in pan on a rack for 15 minutes. Remove from pan and continue cooling on wire rack. The orange flavor becomes more pronounced after the bread is completely cooled.

1 loaf

## The Feed Store
## Parmesan Bread

4 (1/4 ounce) packages yeast

4 teaspoons sugar

2 cups freshly grated Parmesan cheese

3 cups flour

2 teaspoons salt

4 large eggs plus 4 egg whites, beaten together lightly

3/4 cup (1 1/2 sticks) unsalted margarine, melted and cooled

3 1/4 cups bread flour

*Note: This can be used as an appetizer as well as with salad, soup or meals.*

In a small bowl, proof the yeast in 1/3 cup lukewarm water (100 degrees) with the sugar for 5 minutes or until the mixture is foamy. In the bowl of an electric mixer fitted with the dough hook, mix together the Parmesan and flour. Add the salt. Beat in the yeast mixture and the eggs at medium-low speed for 3 minutes. With the motor running, add the margarine and beat the mixture for 5 minutes or until a soft, smooth, and silky dough is formed, incorporating enough of the bread flour to keep the dough from sticking.

Preheat the oven to 200° for 2 minutes. Turn the oven off. Transfer the dough to an oiled bowl. Turn dough to coat it with the oil. Cover the bowl with plastic wrap. Using baking mitts put the bowl in the still-warm oven and let rise for 2 hours or until it has tripled in bulk. Punch down the dough again and let it rise, covered with plastic wrap, until it has doubled in size, around 1 hour. Butter three 4 x 8 x 3 – inch loaf pans. Punch down the dough and divide it into 3 pieces. Form each piece into a loaf shape and put each into a prepared pan. Let the dough rise for 1 1/2 – 2 hours, or until it is double in bulk.

Preheat oven to 425°. Place rack in the middle position of oven and bake loaves for 8 minutes. Reduce the heat to 350° and continue baking until the loaves are pale gold and sound hollow when tapped, about 10 minutes. Turn the loaves out onto a rack and let them cool completely.

3 loaves

## Dilled Garlic Bread

1 loaf French bread, about 14 – inches long

1/2 cup (1 stick) butter (no substitutes)

2 cloves of garlic, mashed to a puree

1/4 cup finely chopped fresh dill weed

1/4 cup freshly grated Parmesan cheese

Preheat oven to 375°. Slice bread in half lengthwise and place on a baking sheet, cut sides up. Melt butter in a small skillet over low heat. Add the garlic and heat gently for 2 – 3 minutes. Do not brown garlic. Brush the garlic butter generously on the cut sides of the bread halves. Sprinkle the dill and cheese evenly over the bread. Bake 5 – 8 minutes until golden brown. Cut each half crosswise into 1 – inch slices and serve immediately.

6 – 8 servings

## The Apple Barn
## Pullman Bread

| | |
|---|---|
| 3 **packages active dry yeast** | 10 **cups flour** |
| 1/2 **cup warm water** | 12 **tablespoons unsalted butter, room temperature** |
| 5 **teaspoons salt** | |
| 4 **cups warm milk** | |

*Note: The Pullman loaf is also called a sandwich loaf. It is made with white flour and baked in a long, narrow, lidded pan. The name Pullman was derived from its use in the compact kitchens of the Pullman railway cars. The Pullman Company is credited with inventing the pans used to create square loaves. It measures 4-1/2 x 5 x 13–inches.*

*Editor's Note: This recipe is published in honor and loving memory of Pearl Rank, who began the Apple Barn's Bakery. This was Pearl's favorite bread and they so graciously shared it for our KDO cookbook.*

Preheat oven to 425°. Butter 3 Pullman bread pans. Dissolve yeast in warm water. Dissolve the salt in the warm milk, not to exceed 100 degrees, or yeast may not proof. Put the liquids in a mixer with a dough hook. Add the flour 2 cups at a time, kneading until all the flour is incorporated after each addition. The dough should be somewhat smooth. Add the butter, 2 tablespoons at a time, until incorporated. Dough will be sticky. Put dough in large greased bowl, cover loosely and let rise until tripled in bulk. Punch down and knead for several minutes. Let rise second time. Turn dough out on floured board. Flatten into rectangular shapes the length of the pans. Put each rectangle into a prepared pan. Press dough into corners so air bubbles are broken. Cover with pan lid. Let rise again, until 2/3 of pan is full. Bake 30 – 40 minutes. Reduce heat to 350° and bake another 15 – 20 minutes. The crust should be golden brown and sides should have shrunk away from pan. Loaf should sound hollow when tapped. It is best if not cut until the second day. Great for French toast!

3 loaves

## Vidalia Custard Bread

| | |
|---|---|
| 3 **tablespoons butter, divided** | 3/4 **cup shredded cheddar cheese, divided** |
| 1 **large Vidalia onion, halved and sliced** | 1 1/2 **cups milk** |
| 1 3/4 **cups flour** | 1 **egg, lightly beaten** |
| 4 **teaspoons baking powder** | 1 **tablespoon poppy seeds** |
| 1/2 **teaspoon salt** | |

Preheat oven to 400°. In a large skillet, melt 2 tablespoons butter over medium heat. Sauté the onions until light golden brown, about 10 – 15 minutes. In a large bowl combine flour, baking powder and salt. Stir in 1/2 cup cheese. Gradually stir in milk and egg. Add onions, reserving 2 tablespoons for the topping. Pour mixture into a greased 9 – inch deep-dish pie plate. Sprinkle batter with the reserved onion, remaining cheese and poppy seeds. Drizzle 1 tablespoon of melted butter over top. Bake for 25 – 35 minutes or until set. Cool slightly. Cut into 8 wedges and serve warm.

8 servings

## Bread Pudding Casserole

4 **large eggs or 1 cup Egg Beaters**

3/4 **cup skim milk**

1 **teaspoon maple flavoring**

8 **slices whole wheat raisin or cinnamon raisin bread, cubed**

1 **cup peeled, thinly sliced apples**

1/4 **cup reduced fat cream cheese**

**Pancake syrup (optional)**

*Tip: This can be prepared ahead of time and refrigerated overnight. Remove from the refrigerator 30 minutes before baking and add 5 minutes to baking time.*

Preheat oven to 350°. Spray or grease an 8 x 8 – inch pan. Mix Egg Beaters, milk and maple flavoring together in a bowl. Toss bread and apple slices together and spread evenly in pan. Pour egg mixture over bread mix and lightly push down with fork. Drop small dollops of cream cheese evenly over the top. Bake 30 minutes or until browned and set. Remove from oven and let sit 15 minutes before serving. Serve with pancake syrup, if desired.

9 servings

## Banana Chocolate Chip Muffins

1 1/2 **cups flour**

2/3 **cup sugar**

1 1/2 **teaspoons baking powder**

1/4 **teaspoon salt**

2 **large (1 cup) mashed ripe bananas**

1 **large egg**

1/4 **cup (1/2 stick) butter, melted**

1/4 **cup milk**

3/4 **cup semisweet chocolate chips**

Preheat oven to 350°. Grease or spray six large size muffin cups with non-stick coating. Mix flour, sugar, baking powder and salt in large bowl. In another bowl, combine the bananas, egg, melted butter and milk. Fold banana mixture into flour mixture just until blended (do not over mix). Stir in chocolate chips. Divide batter among prepared muffin cups, filling each about 3/4 full. Bake 30 – 35 minutes, until tops are golden.

6 servings

*Springfield owes many thanks to those who spend time, effort and resources to restore so many of the beautiful older homes in our community. In so doing, they preserve beauty as well as usefulness.*

## Cornfetti Muffins

*Note: The vegetables prevent these muffins from rising as high as plain muffins. Wrap in a napkin or towel to keep warm while serving.*

| | |
|---|---|
| 3 scallions | 1 (8 1/2 ounce) can whole kernel corn, drained |
| 1 (8 1/2 ounce) package Jiffy corn muffin mix | 1/2 cup diced green bell pepper |
| 1 egg | 1/2 cup diced red bell pepper |
| 1 cup milk | |

Preheat oven to 400°. Grease or spray a standard size muffin tin or use baking cups. Trim scallions and thinly slice the white and crisp parts of the green tops. Set aside. Blend muffin mix, egg and milk. Add corn, green pepper, red pepper and scallions and mix just until well distributed. For the best crown, let dough rest 3 – 4 minutes and then stir lightly. Fill cups about 2/3 full. Bake 20 minutes or until light brown and firm on top.

11 – 12 muffins

## Cheddar Bacon Biscuits

*Tip: Hardwood smoked bacon is very good in this recipe.*

| | |
|---|---|
| 2 cups flour | 2 slices bacon, crisply cooked and crumbled |
| 1/2 teaspoons baking soda | |
| 1/4 teaspoon kosher salt | 1/3 cup finely grated sharp cheddar cheese |
| 4 tablespoons (1/2 stick) butter, cold and cut into small pieces | 1 cup buttermilk |

Preheat oven to 400°. Grease or spray a cookie sheet. Whisk flour, baking soda and salt in a bowl until well mixed. Cut the butter into the flour mixture, using two knives or a pastry blender, until mixture resembles coarse meal. Add the crumbled bacon and cheese. Stir the buttermilk in just until moist. Drop by the spoonful (approximately 2 tablespoons) onto the cookie sheet. Bake on middle rack for approximately 11 minutes, or until lightly browned. Best served hot or warm.

15 biscuits

*Established in 1884, Maldaner's Restaurant is the oldest restaurant in the city of Springfield and one of the oldest restaurants on Historic Route 66 in the State of Illinois.*

## Healthy Bran Muffins

| | | | | |
|---|---|---|---|---|
| 1 1/2 | cups wheat bran | | 1 | cup flour |
| 1 | cup buttermilk | | 1 | teaspoon baking soda |
| 1/3 | cup vegetable oil | | 1 | teaspoon baking powder |
| 1 | egg | | 1/2 | teaspoon salt |
| 2/3 | cup brown sugar, packed | | 1/2 | cup raisins, blueberries or |
| 1/2 | teaspoon vanilla extract | | | dried cranberries |

Preheat oven to 375°. Grease a 12 cup muffin tin or line with cupcake liners. Mix wheat bran and buttermilk and let stand for 10 minutes. Beat the oil, egg, brown sugar and vanilla together and add to the bran/buttermilk mixture. Sift flour, baking soda, baking powder and salt into a bowl. Stir the flour mixture into the buttermilk mixture until just blended. Do not over mix. Fold in the raisins, blueberries or cranberries and spoon into the prepared muffin tins. Bake 15 – 20 minutes or until a toothpick inserted into the center comes out clean. Remove from oven and cool 5 minutes. Remove from the muffin tin to a rack for cooling or serve immediately.

12 muffins

## Morning Glory Muffins

| | | | | |
|---|---|---|---|---|
| 2 1/4 | cups flour | | 2 | cups grated carrots |
| 1 1/4 | cups sugar | | 1 | apple peeled, cored and grated |
| 1 | tablespoon cinnamon | | 1/2 | cup shredded coconut |
| 2 | teaspoons baking soda | | 1/2 | cup raisins |
| 1/2 | teaspoon salt | | 1/2 | cup chopped pecans or |
| 3 | eggs | | | walnuts |
| 1 | cup vegetable oil | | 1 | (8 ounce) can crushed |
| 1 | teaspoon vanilla extract | | | pineapple, drained |

Preheat oven to 350°. Grease 16 muffin tins. Mix flour, sugar, cinnamon, baking soda and salt in a medium bowl. Whisk eggs, oil and vanilla together in a small bowl. Add carrot, apple, coconut, raisins, nuts and pineapple to the dry mixture. Stir in the egg mixture just until blended. Fill muffin tins to the top. Bake 35 minutes or until a toothpick inserted in the center comes out clean. Cool on a rack for 10 minutes before removing muffins from the tins.

16 muffins

# Dinner Potato Rolls

Note: Instant yeast may be called rapid-rise or bread machine yeast.

Baked rolls may be frozen, thawed at room temperature and reheated in a foil-covered pan for 15 minutes at 300 degrees.

|  |  |
|---|---|
| 1 **cup milk (whole or 2%)** | 1/3 **cup instant potato flakes** |
| 2 **tablespoons butter, cut in small pieces** | 1 **egg** |
| 2 **tablespoons oil** | 1 **teaspoon water** |
| 3 **cups flour** | **Sesame seeds, poppy seeds or coarse salt, if desired** |
| 2 **teaspoons instant yeast** | 1 **tablespoon butter, melted (if making Fan Tans)** |
| 1 1/4 **teaspoons salt** | |
| 3 **tablespoons light brown sugar, packed** | |

Lightly oil 16 muffin tins if making Cloverleaf Rolls or Fan Tans. If making Crescents, Knots or Snails, cover a baking sheet with parchment paper or spray lightly with cooking spray.

Heat the milk in a small saucepan over low heat until you can just comfortably swirl your fingertip in the milk. Remove from heat and add butter and oil. Set aside.

In a mixing bowl, combine flour (fluff it up before spooning into a measuring cup, then level with a knife), yeast, salt, brown sugar and potato flakes. Using a mixer or by hand, stir in the milk mixture, beating until the dough comes together and "cleans" the sides of the bowl.

Scrape dough onto a very lightly floured countertop and knead by stretching half the ball of dough away from you and folding it back upon itself. Give the dough a quarter-turn and repeat, stretching, folding and turning until the dough becomes smooth and springy, about 4 – 5 minutes. Try not to add any additional flour; it can make your rolls tough. If necessary, dust only your hands with flour. Spray a bowl with cooking spray. Place dough in the bowl and cover it with plastic wrap. Let it rise in a warm place for an hour. The dough will look puffy. Shape rolls as described in "Variations" below. Cover rolls with a light cloth and let rise about 45 minutes until puffy.

*(directions continued on top of next page)*

*Variations: To make Cloverleaf rolls, divide the dough into 16 pieces. Divide each piece into thirds. Roll each piece into a small ball and place 3 balls in each cup of prepared muffin tins.*

*To make Fan Tans, divide dough in half. On a lightly floured surface, roll one half into a 10-inch square. With a sharp knife or pizza cutter, cut dough into 4 equal strips. Brush each strip with butter and then stack them. With a sharp knife, cut stack into 8 equal pieces and place each piece on edge in prepared muffin cups. Repeat with remaining dough.*

*(Pour some water into any empty cups of the pan before baking.)*

*To make Crescents, divide dough in half. On a lightly floured surface, roll one half into a 10-inch circle. Cut into 8 wedges. Starting at the widest end, roll up each piece, taking care to tuck the "tail" under when placing it on prepared baking sheet.*

*To make Knots, divide dough into 16 pieces. Roll each piece into a 10-inch strand. Make a loop halfway up the strand, bringing the "tail" up through the hole. Bring the other end over the loop and tuck it inside the knot. Place on prepared baking sheet.*

*To make Snails, divide dough into 16 pieces. Roll each piece into a 10-inch strand. Wind up the strand to form a spiral, tucking under the outside end. Place on prepared baking sheet.*

Preheat oven to 350°. Pour some water into an empty cup of the muffin tin. Position the rack in middle of the oven. For a glossy crust, brush rolls with 1 egg beaten with a teaspoon of water. Sprinkle with sesame or poppy seeds, or a few grains of coarse salt, if desired. Bake for 18 – 20 minutes, or until golden. Cool on wire rack.

16 rolls

---

### Sebastian's Hideout
### Wheat Bran Yeast Rolls

| | |
|---|---|
| 2 **cups warm water (approximately 110°), divided** | 1 **cup vegetable oil** |
| 1 **tablespoon active dry yeast** | 3 1/2 **cups flour** |
| 6 **ounces honey** | 3 1/2 **cups whole wheat flour, divided plus extra flour for rolling** |
| 3 **eggs, lightly beaten** | 3 **teaspoons kosher salt** |
| 2 **cups bran flake cereal** | |

In an electric stand mixer with wire whisk attached, add 1 cup warm water, yeast and honey. Mix until frothy, 60 – 90 seconds. Allow to stand 5 minutes for yeast to activate creating foamy and frothy bubbles.

Attach the mixing paddle. With the mixer on medium slow speed, add the eggs and the remaining warm water and mix thoroughly.

Turn mixer off and add the bran flakes, vegetable oil, flour, 2 cups whole wheat flour and kosher salt. Turn mixer to medium-low speed and beat until all dry ingredients are incorporated. Scrape the bowl sides thoroughly. While continuing to mix, add and incorporate the remaining whole wheat flour.

When the dough has come together, scrape dough from sides of bowl and paddle. Attach dough hook and turn mixer on medium-low speed and mix until dough attaches to dough hook and separates from the sides of mixing bowl. Let rest 20 – 30 minutes in a covered mixing bowl. Dough should be soft, stretchy and not too damp at this point.

Preheat oven to 350°. Working in batches, liberally flour work surface and roll dough out with rolling pin to 3/4 – inch thickness. Cut circular rolls with floured biscuit cutter or water glass. Fold dough rings in half and press down. Arrange on a non-greased cookie sheet 1 – inch apart. Bake for 8 – 10 minutes.

5 dozen rolls

*An innovative fusion of classic French, Californian and Asian cuisine can be enjoyed from this downtown favorite eatery. The casual, yet elegant décor adds to this fine dining experience.*

## Popovers

*Note: Delicious as is or used as a cup to hold a favorite chicken a la king or similar recipe.*

| | | | |
|---|---|---|---|
| 1 | tablespoon shortening | 1 | tablespoon cooking oil |
| 2 | jumbo-sized eggs, beaten | 1 | cup flour |
| 3/4 | cup milk | 1/4 | teaspoon salt |
| 1/4 | cup heavy cream | | |

Preheat oven to 400°. Use about 1/2 teaspoon shortening to grease the bottoms and sides of each of 6 (6 ounce) custard cups. (Cups can be sprayed with nonstick coating.) Place the custard cups in a 10 x 15 x 1 – inch baking pan and set aside. Use a medium mixing bowl and a wire whisk to mix the eggs, milk, cream and oil until combined. Add flour and salt; beat until smooth. Fill the prepared cups half full with batter. Bake for about 40 minutes or until very firm. Immediately after removing from oven, use a fork to prick each popover to let steam escape. Turn off the oven. For crisper popovers, return popovers to the oven for 5 – 10 minutes or until desired crispness is reached. Remove popovers from cups. Serve immediately.

6 servings

## Augie's Front Burner
## Pizza Crust

*Note: This dough does not rise very much.*

| | | | |
|---|---|---|---|
| 1 | teaspoon yeast | 1 1/2 | teaspoons kosher salt |
| 1/4 | cup warm water | 1 | tablespoon olive oil |
| 3 | cups unbleached flour | | Stone-ground cornmeal |

Sprinkle the yeast over the surface of warm water to dissolve. Let it sit for 5 minutes or until the yeast is activated.

Sift flour and salt together. Stir the yeast mixture into the flour. Add the olive oil and continue to stir until it forms a fairly loose mass, adding more water if necessary. Turn onto a well-floured board. Flour your hands and knead the dough about 10 – 15 times. Form the dough into a ball and cover it with a towel. Let sit for 1 – 1 1/2 hours until it doubles in width.

Liberally sprinkle a pizza paddle or pizza pan with coarsely-ground cornmeal to prevent dough from sticking. Take 1/4 of the dough in your floured hands and pull, stretch and pinch it. Close your eyes and think of the pizza men that you have seen so often. Form a thin 10-inch circle of dough with slightly thicker edges. The thinness is very important. Place the dough on the paddle and cover.

Preheat oven to 425°. Add toppings of your choice and bake until crust edge is browned and cheese is melted.

4 (10 – inch) pizza crusts

## Sticky Buns

6 tablespoons (3/4 stick) butter, softened and divided
1/3 cup maple syrup
1 cup brown sugar, packed
3/4 cup chopped nuts
1 (8 ounce) package cream cheese, softened

1/2 cup confectioners' sugar
12 Pillsbury Grands Jr. refrigerator biscuits (not flaky ones), or mini frozen biscuits.

*Note: Recipe of Norie Russel, former member of Marjorie Post/Nightingale Circle and a past President of King's Daughters Organization.*

Preheat oven to 350°. Melt 4 tablespoons butter, maple syrup and brown sugar in a 9 x 13 – inch baking pan. Stir in nuts. Mix cream cheese, confectioners' sugar and 2 tablespoons butter together. Flatten the 12 biscuits or roll out with a rolling pin; about 1/4 – inch thick. Spread 1 tablespoon of the cream cheese mixture on each biscuit. Roll the biscuits and seal the ends; place seam side down in the pan. Bake 20 – 30 minutes or until golden brown. Remove from oven and turn out immediately onto a foil-lined tray.

12 servings

## Julianne Glatz
## Baked German Apple Pancake

1/2 cup unbleached flour
1 tablespoon sugar, preferably Baker's extra-fine sugar
1/2 teaspoon kosher or sea salt
2 eggs, beaten
2/3 cup half and half
1 teaspoon vanilla extract
3 – 4 large apples, about 1 1/4 pounds (see Note)

2 teaspoons cider vinegar
2 tablespoons unsalted butter
1/4 cup dark brown sugar, packed
1/2 teaspoon cinnamon
Confectioners' sugar for dusting
Powdered sugar for dusting

*Note: Use Granny Smith, Golden Blushing, Braeburn, seasonal Golden Delicious or other sweet/tart varieties that hold their shape well when cooked. If you prefer mixing the dry and liquid ingredients in a blender or food processor, put the liquid ingredients in first.*

*Tip: The batter may also be made the day before and refrigerated. Bring to room temperature before baking.*

Have all ingredients for the batter at room temperature. Combine the flour, sugar and salt in a bowl. Make a well in the center. Add the eggs, half and half and vanilla. Whisk together until no lumps remain. Set the batter aside to rest for at least 30 minutes.

Preheat the oven to 500°. Place rack in the middle position. Peel and core the apples and cut them into 1/2 – inch slices. Toss the slices with the vinegar. Heat butter in a 10-inch ovenproof skillet, preferably nonstick, over medium high heat. Add the apples, brown sugar and cinnamon and cook until the apples are golden brown, about 10 minutes. Stir frequently while cooking, but gently so as not to break up the apples. Remove the pan from the heat. Immediately pour a ring of batter around the edge of the pan and then pour the rest of the batter evenly over the apples. Place the skillet in the oven and immediately reduce the heat to 425°. Bake the pancake until the edges are brown and the pancake has puffed up, about 18 minutes. Loosen the edges with a heat-proof spatula. Invert the pancake onto a large plate, cut into wedges, and serve, dusted with confectioners' sugar.

6 servings

## Belgian Waffles

*Note: These make
very light waffles.*

| | |
|---|---|
| 1 3/4 cups flour | 2 cups buttermilk |
| 2 teaspoons baking powder | 2 egg yolks, beaten |
| 1/2 teaspoon baking soda | 1/2 cup unsalted butter, melted |
| 1/2 teaspoon salt | 2 egg whites |

Preheat the waffle iron to the temperature recommended by the waffle iron manufacturer and spray or grease the iron as recommended. Sift flour, baking powder, baking soda and salt together. Combine buttermilk, egg yolks and melted butter. Stir milk mixture into the dry ingredients. Beat the egg white to a hard peak. Fold batter gently into the egg whites. Pour 1/2 cup of the batter (or the amount recommended by the waffle iron maker) onto the waffle iron. Cook until golden. Remove from waffle iron and serve with butter or syrup.

3 – 4 full sized waffles

## Baked Raspberry French Toast with Almond Syrup

*Note: Challah Bread
recipe, see page 47.*

**French toast:**

| | |
|---|---|
| 1 1/4 | cups raspberry preserves |
| 1 | loaf of egg bread such as Challah bread, cut into 1 – inch slices |
| 1 1/4 | cups whole milk |
| 3/4 | cup whipping cream |
| 1/2 | cup sugar |
| 3 | egg yolks |
| 3 | eggs |

**Almond syrup:**

| | |
|---|---|
| 1 1/4 | cups light corn syrup |
| 3/4 | teaspoon almond extract |
| 4 | teaspoons sugar |
| 1/2 | cup sliced almonds, toasted Confectioners' sugar |

Butter a 9 x 13 – inch baking dish. Spread preserves evenly on 1 side of each bread slice. Cut slices diagonally in half and arrange in dish, preserves side up, and overlapping slightly. Whisk milk, whipping cream, sugar, egg yolks and eggs in a large bowl. Pour over bread. Let stand for one hour, basting occasionally, or cover and refrigerate overnight.

Warm corn syrup, almond extract and sugar over low heat, stirring until sugar dissolves. Let it stand at least 1 hour so flavors meld.

Preheat oven to 350°. Bake French toast uncovered, until puffed and golden brown, about 50 minutes. Sprinkle with toasted almonds and confectioners' sugar. Serve with almond syrup.

12 servings

## Blueberry French Toast Casserole

12  slices (8 cups) dry white bread, cut into 1/2 – inch cubes, divided

2  (8 ounce) packages cream cheese, cut into 3/4 – inch cubes

2  cups fresh or frozen blueberries

12  eggs

2  cups milk

1/2  cup maple syrup

*Tip: Low-fat (Neufchatel) cream cheese and skim milk can be used to reduce calories.*

**Blueberry or maple syrup**

Spray or butter a 9 x 13 – inch baking pan. Spread 1/2 of the bread cubes over bottom of baking pan. Sprinkle cream cheese and blueberries evenly over the bread cubes. Arrange remaining bread cubes over the cream cheese and blueberries. In a large mixing bowl, beat eggs, milk and the maple syrup. Carefully pour egg mixture over the bread mixture. Cover and chill in the refrigerator for 2 – 24 hours.

When ready to bake, preheat oven to 375°. Bake covered for 25 minutes. Uncover and bake 25 minutes more or until a knife inserted near the center comes out clean and the top is puffed and golden brown. Let stand 10 minutes before serving. Serve with warm blueberry or maple syrup.

8 – 12 servings

## Asparagus Quiche

2  cups grated Swiss cheese

1  tablespoon flour

1  unbaked (9 – inch) pie shell

1  large onion, thinly sliced

1  cup milk or 1/2 cup milk and 1/2 cup light cream

3  eggs, slightly beaten

3/4  teaspoon salt

1/2  teaspoon pepper

Nutmeg

1  (10 ounce) package frozen asparagus spears, thawed and drained

Shredded Parmesan cheese for sprinkling

*Note: If you are not concerned about appearance, cut the asparagus into 1 1/2 – inch pieces to make it more suitable to eating.*

Preheat oven to 425°. Mix cheese and flour and spread evenly into the unbaked pie shell. Cover the cheese with sliced onion. Heat milk to barely bubbling. Remove from heat. Beat eggs. Stir a small amount of hot milk into the eggs and mix well. Gradually add the egg mix into the milk. Add salt, pepper and nutmeg to taste. Stir and pour over the cheese and onions. Arrange the asparagus spears over the mix with tips towards center. Put into the oven and reduce oven temperature to 350°. Bake 30 minutes until nearly set. Sprinkle with Parmesan cheese and bake 10 more minutes or until set.

8 servings

## Ham and Swiss Quiche

| | | | |
|---|---|---|---|
| 1 | refrigerated pie crust | 4 | eggs, beaten well |
| 1 | tablespoon flour | 2 | cups half and half |
| 1 1/2 | cups shredded Swiss cheese | 1/4 | teaspoon salt |
| 1/2 | cup cooked diced ham | 1/2 | teaspoon dry mustard |

Preheat oven to 400°. Line a 9 – inch pie pan with pie crust. Trim and flute the edges. Prick tiny holes in the bottom and sides of the crust with a fork. Bake for 3 minutes. Remove from oven and prick again with fork. Bake another 5 minutes. Remove from oven.

Adjust the oven temperature to 325°. Combine flour and cheese; sprinkle into pie crust. Sprinkle ham on top of the cheese. Combine the eggs, half and half, salt and mustard and mix thoroughly. Pour egg mixture into the pastry shell. Bake for 55 – 60 minutes or until set. Let stand 10 minutes before serving.

10 servings

## Spinach and Bacon Quiche

*Note: This was a big hit when served at Circle meetings.*

| | | | |
|---|---|---|---|
| 1 | (10 ounce) package frozen chopped spinach, thawed | 10 | bacon slices, crisply cooked and crumbled |
| 4 | large eggs, beaten lightly | 1/2 | cup shredded sharp cheddar cheese |
| 1 1/2 | cups half and half | | |
| 1 | (1.8 ounce) package Knorr Leek Dry Soup Mix | 1/2 | cup shredded mozzarella cheese |
| 1/4 | teaspoon pepper | 1 | unbaked deep dish pastry crust |

Preheat oven to 375°. Thaw and drain spinach well, pressing between paper towels to absorb moisture. Whisk eggs, half and half, soup mix and pepper together. Stir in bacon, spinach, cheddar, and mozzarella. Pour into pie crust. Bake 40 – 45 minutes or until set.

6 servings

The "Stand" in Washington Park was dedicated in 2012 as a concession stand that was built as the final stage of the Iron Springs Restoration. Washington Park had been without a concession stand since the previous one closed in 1975. It was simply known as "The Stand," and the name has carried over.

## Sausage Spinach Swiss Strata

2 cups 1% low fat milk
4 large eggs
4 large egg whites
3/4 teaspoon salt
1/4 teaspoon cayenne pepper
1/4 teaspoon ground nutmeg
10 slices day-old whole-grain white bread, cut into 1/2 – inch cubes (about 9 cups)
16 ounces turkey breakfast sausage, crumbled

1 medium size onion, chopped
1 medium size red bell pepper, chopped
2 cloves garlic, minced
1 (10 ounce) package frozen chopped spinach, thawed and squeezed dry
1 cup shredded reduced fat Swiss cheese, divided

*Note: This can be refrigerated overnight before adding the topping. Remove from refrigerator and let rest at room temperature for 15 minutes before baking. Add the cheese. Additional baking time may be required.*

Preheat oven to 375°. Spray a 7 x 11 – inch baking dish with cooking spray. Whisk the milk, eggs, egg whites, salt, cayenne and nutmeg together in a large bowl. Add the bread and gently toss to combine. Let stand 5 minutes or until most of the liquid is absorbed. Meanwhile, spray a large non-stick skillet with cooking spray. Add sausage, onion, bell pepper and garlic to skillet and cook over medium high heat, stirring often, for 6 – 8 minutes or until sausage is no longer pink and vegetables are softened.

Stir the sausage mixture, spinach and 1/2 cup cheese into the bread mixture. Spoon into the prepared baking dish. Bake for 30 minutes. Remove from oven and top with the remaining cheese. Return to oven and bake 10 more minutes or until cheese melts.

8 servings

## Bountiful Breakfast Bake

1 cup diced fully cooked ham
1 (16 ounce) package frozen hash brown potatoes, thawed
1 medium green bell pepper, chopped (about 1 cup)
1 tablespoon chopped onion

2 cups shredded cheddar cheese, divided
1 cup Bisquick
3 cups milk
1/2 teaspoon pepper
4 eggs, lightly beaten

Preheat oven to 375°. Grease or spray a 9 x 13 – inch baking pan. Layer the baking dish with ham, potatoes, pepper, onion and 1 cup cheddar cheese. Stir Bisquick, milk, pepper and eggs together. Pour mixture over the baking dish. Sprinkle with 1 cup cheddar cheese. Cover and refrigerate at least 4 hours or overnight but no more than 24 hours. Bake uncovered for 30 – 35 minutes until light golden brown around edges and cheese is melted. Let stand 10 minutes before serving.

12 servings

## Scrambled Egg and Ham Bake

| | | | |
|---|---|---|---|
| 5 | tablespoons butter or margarine, divided | 1 | cup cubed fully cooked ham |
| 2 1/2 | tablespoons flour | 1/4 | cup chopped green onion |
| 2 | cups milk | 1 | dozen eggs, beaten |
| 1/2 | teaspoon salt | 1 | (4 ounce) can sliced mushrooms, drained |
| 1/8 | teaspoon pepper | 1/4 | cup melted butter |
| 1 | cup (4 ounces) shredded American cheese | 2 1/4 | cups soft bread crumbs |

Spray or grease a 9 x 13 – inch baking pan. Melt 2 tablespoons butter in a large sauce pan. Blend in flour. Cook for 1 minute. Gradually stir in milk and cook over medium heat until thick. Add salt, pepper and cheese. Stir until cheese melts. Set aside. In a large skillet, sauté ham and green onion in 3 tablespoons butter until onion is tender. Add eggs and cook over medium heat until eggs are set. Stir in mushrooms and cheese mixture. Spread mixture into baking pan. Combine melted butter and bread crumbs and sprinkle evenly over casserole. Cover and refrigerate overnight.

Preheat oven to 350°. Bake uncovered for 30 minutes or until heated through and lightly browned.

10 – 12 servings

## Capri Brunch

| | | | |
|---|---|---|---|
| 1 | pound Italian sausage | 1 | cup flour |
| 1 | cup sliced fresh mushrooms | 1/2 | cup Parmesan cheese |
| 1 | cup chopped onions | 1/2 | teaspoon seasoned salt |
| 1 | large roasted red pepper, chopped, divided | 1 | teaspoon basil leaves |
| 1 | package frozen chopped spinach, thawed | 8 | eggs |
| 2 | cups grated Provolone or mozzarella cheese, divided | 2 | cups milk |

Preheat oven to 375°. Grease a 9 x 13 – inch baking pan. Brown sausage in a skillet. Remove from pan, drain and crumble. Add mushrooms and onions to pan and cook until onions are translucent. Combine onions and mushrooms with sausage. Arrange sausage mixture in the baking pan. Sprinkle half of the red pepper, the spinach and 1 cup cheese over the sausage. In a large bowl, combine flour, Parmesan, seasoned salt and basil. In another bowl, combine eggs and milk and beat until smooth. Combine flour mixture and egg mixture and beat until well blended. Pour the flour mixture over the sausage mixture. Sprinkle remaining red pepper and cheese on top. Bake for 45 minutes or until set. Allow to stand 15 minutes before serving.

8 – 10 servings

## Spring Creek Crostini and Fonduta

| | |
|---|---|
| 1 | tablespoon unsalted butter |
| 1/4 | pound Italian Fontina cheese, rind discarded, and cut into 1/4 – inch dice (about 3/4 cup) |
| 1/2 | cup milk |
| 2 | egg yolks |
| 4 | 1/2 – inch thick slices from a large round crusty loaf of bread (about 8 - 9 – inches across) |
| 1 | large garlic clove, halved crosswise |
| 2 | tablespoons extra-virgin olive oil |
| | Salt, to taste |
| 1/4 | pound thinly sliced prosciutto |
| 1 | pound thin asparagus, trimmed and lower 2 – inches of stalks peeled |

*Note: Fontina is available at cheese shops and some supermarkets.*

Preheat broiler. To prepare fonduta, melt butter in a double boiler or a metal bowl set over a pan of simmering water. Add Fontina and milk. Heat, stirring with a whisk, until cheese begins to melt. Whisk in yolks. Cook, whisking constantly, until smooth and slightly thickened, about 7 minutes. Remove pan from heat and remove bowl from pan. Let the water cool slightly. Stir sauce for 1 minute while water in pan cools slightly. Return bowl to pan and keep sauce warm over hot water (off heat), whisking occasionally, to eliminate skin that forms on surface.

To prepare crostini, place bread on a baking sheet and toast about 3 – inches from broiler heat, turning until golden, about 1 to 2 minutes on each side. Rub tops of crostini with cut side of garlic. Brush with oil and season lightly with salt. Divide crostini among four plates and top with prosciutto.

In a deep 10 to 12 – inch skillet bring 1 1/4 – inches salted water to a boil. Add asparagus and cook until crisp tender, about 2 – 4 minutes. Transfer asparagus with tongs to a colander and drain. Divide asparagus among crostini. Pour fonduta over each serving.

4 servings

## Tomato Pie

| | |
|---|---|
| 3 | large ripe tomatoes, peeled and sliced |
| 1/2 | teaspoon salt |
| 1/2 | teaspoon basil |
| 1/2 | teaspoon oregano |
| 1 | tablespoon chopped chives |
| 1 | (9 – inch) pie crust |
| 4 | chopped green onions |
| 1 | cup mayonnaise |
| 1 | cup grated cheddar cheese |
| 1/2 | cup bacon bits |

*Note: Roma tomatoes are especially good in this recipe.*

A day before serving, peel and slice the tomatoes and put into a container with salt, basil, oregano and chives. Refrigerate.

Preheat oven to 350°. Place crust in baking pan and prick sides and bottom. Bake crust for 6 – 8 minutes. Drain the juices from the tomatoes. Layer the tomato slices and green onions on crust. Combine mayonnaise, cheese and bacon bits and spread on top. Bake for about 30 minutes.

8 servings

*Note: A family recipe used for many years.*

*Hint: The flavors will get better if the sausage sits overnight before cooking. This freezes well. Remember, if you use old spices and seasonings you do not get full flavors. Keep your pantry up-to-date.*

## Florentine Sausage

| | | | |
|---|---|---|---|
| 2 | pounds coarsely ground lean pork | 3 | cloves garlic, crushed |
| 1 | tablespoon coarsely ground fennel | 1/8 | teaspoon dried red pepper flakes |
| 2 | bay leaves, crushed | 1 | teaspoon salt |
| 1 | tablespoon dried parsley | 1/4 | teaspoon pepper |
| 1 | tablespoon fresh chives, chopped | 4 | tablespoons water |

Combine pork, fennel, bay leaves, parsley, chives, garlic, pepper flakes, salt, pepper, and water. Let them stand in a cool area to allow flavors to meld for at least an hour. Stir well and stuff into casings, make into patties or meatballs or use as base meat for a sauce.

2 pounds

## Onion Pie

| | | | |
|---|---|---|---|
| 1 | 9 – inch pie pastry | 2 | egg yolks |
| 3 | tablespoons butter | 1 | cup milk, more if needed |
| 5 | medium onions, very thinly sliced | 1/2 | cup heavy cream |
| 1 | cup grated Swiss or Parmesan cheese | 1 | teaspoon salt |
| 2 | eggs | | Cayenne pepper to taste |

To partially bake pie pastry, preheat oven to 400°. Line a 9 – inch pie pan with pastry. Trim the edges and flute. Prick tiny holes in the bottom and sides of the pastry with a fork. Bake for 3 minutes. Remove from oven, prick again with fork. Bake another 5 minutes.

Adjust oven temperature to 350°. Melt butter in a large heavy skillet. Add the onions and cook over medium low heat until they are limp and just beginning to turn golden. Arrange onions in the pastry. Cover onions with the grated cheese. Beat the eggs, yolks, milk and cream together. Season with salt and cayenne pepper. Pour egg mixture over the onions. Place the pie pan on lower shelf of oven and bake for 35 – 40 minutes until pie has puffed in middle and is golden brown.

8 – 10 servings

## Italian Breakfast Bread

|       |                                          |       |                                                          |
|-------|------------------------------------------|-------|----------------------------------------------------------|
| 3     | large eggs                               | 1     | crisp, juicy apple                                       |
| 1 1/3 | cups sugar                               | 1     | banana (you can use any mixture of the fruits but fruit should total nearly 4 cups) |
| 2     | tablespoons extra virgin olive oil       | 2     | tablespoons freshly squeezed lemon juice                |
| 1/4   | teaspoon salt                            | 2 3/4 | cups flour                                               |
|       | Grated rind of 2 oranges                 | 2 1/2 | teaspoons baking powder                                  |
| 1     | large pear or 2 small Anjou pears        |       |                                                          |

*Note: This is amazing and very tasty for a different sort of breakfast bread.*

Preheat oven to 375°. Generously butter a 10 – inch spring form pan. Beat the eggs and sugar until the mixture is light in color, about 5 – 6 minutes on high speed. Add the olive oil, salt and grated orange peel.

Peel and core pear, apple and banana and cut into very small pieces (less than 1/2 inch) and toss with the lemon juice. Whisk flour and baking powder together in a separate bowl. Add flour mixture to egg mixture and mix thoroughly. Fold in the fruit, mixing well to distribute fruit evenly. Pour the batter into the spring form pan. Bake on the center rack for 50 – 55 minutes or until the top of the bread is golden.

8 – 10 servings

## Cherry Coffee Cake

**Cake:**

|       |                                |
|-------|--------------------------------|
| 1     | cup unsalted butter            |
| 1 3/4 | cups sugar                     |
| 4     | eggs                           |
| 1     | teaspoon vanilla extract       |
| 1     | teaspoon almond extract        |
| 3     | cups flour                     |
| 1/2   | teaspoon salt                  |
| 1 1/2 | teaspoons baking powder        |
| 2     | (21 ounce) can cherry pie filling |

**Glaze:**

|   |                                                    |
|---|----------------------------------------------------|
| 1 | cup confectioners' sugar                           |
| 1 | teaspoon butter or margarine                       |
| 1 | teaspoon almond extract                            |
| 2 | teaspoons milk or amount needed for proper consistency |

Preheat oven to 350°. Grease an 11 x 15 – inch pan or use a non-stick pan. Cream butter and sugar. Add eggs, vanilla and almond extract to butter mixture. Combine flour, salt and baking powder and add to butter mixture. Spread 2/3 of the batter evenly into prepared pan. Spread cherry pie filling over batter. Place remaining batter by teaspoonfuls on the top. Bake 25 – 30 minutes or until golden and the cherry sauce bubbles. For the glaze, combine confectioners' sugar, butter and almond extract. Add milk as needed to create proper consistency. Let the cake cool slightly before drizzling with glaze.

20 – 24 servings

## Blueberry Lemon Pound Cake

| | |
|---|---|
| 2 cups granulated sugar | 1/2 teaspoon baking soda |
| 1/2 cup (1 stick) butter | 1/2 teaspoon salt |
| 1/2 (8 ounce) carton reduced fat cream cheese, softened | 1 (8 ounce) carton lemon low fat yogurt |
| 3 large eggs | 2 teaspoons vanilla extract |
| 1 large egg white | 2 teaspoons lemon extract |
| 3 cups flour, divided | 2 teaspoons grated lemon zest |
| 2 cups fresh or frozen blueberries | 1/2 cup confectioners' sugar |
| 1 teaspoon baking powder | 4 teaspoons lemon juice |

Preheat oven to 350°. Spray a 10 – inch tube or bundt pan with cooking spray. Beat sugar, butter and cream cheese at medium speed until well-blended (about 5 minutes). Add eggs and egg white, 1 at a time, beating well after each addition. Measure the flour by spooning lightly into a dry measuring cup and leveling top with a knife. Combine 2 tablespoons flour and blueberries in a small bowl and toss well. Combine remaining flour, baking powder, baking soda, and salt and lightly whisk to mix. Add flour mixture to sugar mixture alternately with yogurt, beginning and ending with flour mixture. Fold in blueberries, vanilla, lemon and lemon zest. Pour batter into prepared pan. Bake for 1 hour and 10 minutes or until a wooden pick inserted in center comes out clean. Cool cake in pan 10 minutes; remove from pan. Combine confectioners' sugar and lemon juice in a small bowl; drizzle over warm cake. Cut with a serrated knife.

16 – 20 servings

## Broiled Grapefruit

*Note: Good with a crisp cookie on the side.*

| | |
|---|---|
| 2 large grapefruit, preferably ruby red | **Mint leaves** |
| 4 teaspoons pure maple syrup | **Crisp cookie (optional)** |

Preheat broiler to at least 400°. Cut grapefruit in half and release the sections carefully, leaving in place. Place on a baking sheet. Spread 1 teaspoon syrup on the top of each half. Set under preheated broiler unit about 2 – 3 minutes, watching carefully until tops just begin to brown lightly. Remove and garnish with a mint leaf. Serve while warm with the cookie.

4 servings

## Peach Coffee Cake

1 3/4   cups flour
1 1/2   teaspoons baking powder
1/2   teaspoon baking soda
1/4   teaspoon salt
6   tablespoons butter, softened
2/3   cup granulated sugar
2   large eggs
1   teaspoon vanilla
1   cup sour cream
2   cups peaches (about 1 1/2 pounds) peeled, pitted, and cut into 1 – inch chunks
Confectioners' sugar for sprinkling (optional)

**Streusel:**
1/2   cup uncooked oats
2   tablespoons flour
1/2   cup firmly packed brown sugar
1/2   teaspoon cinnamon
3   tablespoons butter, chilled and cut into pieces
1/2   cup pecans, chopped (optional)

Preheat oven to 350°. Grease 9 – inch square baking pan. Combine flour, baking powder, baking soda, and salt in a medium bowl. Set aside. Combine butter and sugar and blend in a mixer until light and fluffy. Add eggs one at a time, mixing well. Add vanilla. Add sour cream alternately with flour mixture, beginning and ending with flour mixture. Mix until just combined.

For streusel, combine oats, flour, brown sugar and cinnamon in medium bowl. Cut in butter with pastry blender or 2 knives until mixture resembles coarse crumbs. Stir in nuts if using.

Spread batter over bottom of the prepared pan. Sprinkle half the streusel over the batter. Spread peaches on top streusel. Top with remaining streusel. Bake 50 – 60 minutes until toothpick inserted in center comes out clean. Sprinkle with confectioners' sugar.

16 servings

Opened June 4, 2007, Café Moxo was a Downtown Springfield splash. Their motto, "Always take care of the customer and everything else will fall into place" is a testament to why they are successful.

## Raspberry Almond Coffee Cake

**Coffee Cake:**
- 2 cups flour
- 1 cup milk
- 3/4 cup sugar
- 1/4 cup (1/2 stick) unsalted butter, softened
- 1 egg
- 2 teaspoons baking powder
- 1 1/2 teaspoons vanilla
- 1/2 teaspoon salt

- 2 cups raspberries
- 3 ounces almond paste, cut into pieces (not almond filling)

**Streusel Topping:**
- 1/3 cup flour
- 1/4 cup sugar
- 1/4 cup (1/2 stick) butter, softened
- 1/3 cup slivered almonds

Preheat oven to 350°. Lightly oil a 9 x 9 – inch baking pan. Combine flour, milk, sugar, butter, egg, baking powder, vanilla and salt in an electric mixer. Beat for 3 minutes, scraping bowl often. Pour half of the batter into the prepared baking pan and spread evenly. Sprinkle raspberries over batter. Drop bits of almond paste over raspberries. Pour remaining batter on top.

For the streusel, combine flour, sugar, butter and almonds. Sprinkle evenly over batter. Bake for 50 minutes or until lightly browned.

9 – 12 servings

## Healthy Granola

- 1 cup packed brown sugar
- 3/4 cup water
- 4 cups old fashioned whole oats
- 1 cup All Bran Buds cereal
- 1 cup nuts (choice of chopped pecans, chopped walnuts and/or sliced almonds)

- 1 teaspoon vanilla extract
- 1/4 teaspoon salt
- 3 – 4 tablespoons ground flax seed, wheat germ and/or steel cut oats (optional)

Preheat oven to 275°. Mix brown sugar and water in a microwave safe bowl and microwave 5 minutes. Meanwhile mix oats, cereal and nuts in a large bowl. Add vanilla and salt to brown sugar mixture. Drizzle sugar mixture over oats, cereal and nuts. Stir until oats are covered. Add optional ingredients, if you choose. Pour onto a large bar pan or cookie sheet. Bake 1 hour. Remove and cool completely before putting into an airtight container.

6 cups

*This popular bakery and café has been at its current location at the corner of 7th and Clay Streets since 1995. Patrick and Bitzy Groth opened* **Incredibly Delicious** *to bring a little taste of Europe to Springfield. Breakfast and lunch can be enjoyed in this quaint historic home.*

# A Touch of Green

*👑 The crown indicates a celebrity's recipe.*

*Note: Stilton is a type of English cheese known for its characteristic strong smell and taste. It is produced in two varieties: the well-known blue and the lesser-known white.*

## 5flavors
## Walnut and Stilton Salad with Pomegranate Vinaigrette

**Vinaigrette:**

| | |
|---|---|
| 1/2 | cup pomegranate vinegar |
| 1 | cup safflower oil |
| 1 | teaspoon sugar |
| | Salt and pepper to taste |

**Salad:**

| | |
|---|---|
| 8 | ounces mixed greens, romaine or artisan |
| 4 | ounces Stilton cheese |
| 2 | ounce walnuts, halved or crushed |

Vinaigrette: Mix the pomegranate vinegar, oil and sugar. Add salt and pepper to taste. Set aside.

For salad mix: Combine the mixed greens. Pour dressing over greens. Add blue cheese and walnuts. Toss and serve immediately.

4 servings

## Autumn Lettuce and Fruit Salad

**Dressing:**

| | |
|---|---|
| 1/2 | cup sugar |
| 2 | teaspoons celery seed |
| 1 | teaspoon dry mustard |
| 1 | cup canola oil |
| 1 | teaspoon salt |
| 3 | tablespoons grated yellow onion |
| 1/3 | cup white vinegar |

**Salad:**

| | |
|---|---|
| 10 | cups lettuce torn into bite sized pieces (romaine, Boston bibb, red and green leaf) |
| 1 | cup green grapes, sliced |
| 1/2 | cup red grapes, sliced |
| 1 | tart apple, diced |
| 1 | cup celery, diced |
| 1/2 | cup walnuts, chopped coarsely |
| 2/3 | cup crumbled blue cheese |
| 3/4 | cup seasoned croutons |

Dressing: Combine sugar, celery seed, mustard, canola oil, salt, onion and vinegar. Put into a container with a tight lid and refrigerate. Shake well before using.

Salad: Place lettuce in a large bowl. Toss lightly. Add green and red grapes, apple and celery. Pour a light coating of dressing onto the salad and toss. Add nuts, blue cheese and croutons just before serving.

12 servings

## Avocado Grapefruit Salad

**Vinaigrette:**

- 1 tablespoon Dijon mustard
- 1/4 cup freshly squeezed lemon juice
- 1 1/2 teaspoons kosher salt
- 1 teaspoon freshly ground pepper
- 1/2 cup good olive oil

**Salad:**

- 2 large grapefruits
- 4 ripe avocados
- 1 head Boston bibb lettuce

*Variations: Serve with cooked shrimp on a bed of butter crunch lettuce. It also makes a nice dip for blue corn tortilla chips when chopped into small pieces and sprinkled with freshly ground pepper.*

Vinaigrette: Combine mustard, lemon juice, salt and pepper; slowly add the oil, whisking until the vinaigrette is emulsified.

Cut the grapefruit in half and remove the seeds. Remove the peeling and the white pith; then cut between the membranes to release the whole segments. Set aside. Peel the avocados and slice each avocado into 8 – 10 slices, dipping them into the vinaigrette to prevent from browning.

Arrange lettuce on serving dish or on individual salad plates and arrange the grapefruit segments and the avocado slices in a pattern to suit. Spoon the vinaigrette over the top.

8 – 10 servings

## Julianne Glatz
## Lettuce Salad with Apples and Pecans

**Dressing:**

- 1 cup olive oil
- 5 tablespoons cider vinegar
- 4 tablespoons sour cream
- 1 1/2 teaspoons kosher or sea salt
- 1/2 teaspoon dry mustard
- 3 tablespoons sugar
  Coarsely ground black pepper to taste
- 2 tablespoons minced flat leafed parsley
- 1 tablespoon minced garlic

**Salad:**

- 2 medium red skinned tart/sweet apples, such as Jonathan, with skin
- 6 large handfuls mixed baby lettuces, washed and dried
- 1 cup pecans, lightly toasted
  Crumbled blue cheese (optional)

*Note: This makes much more dressing than needed for this recipe. It will keep refrigerated for several weeks.*

Dressing: Put oil, vinegar, sour cream, salt, mustard, sugar, pepper, parsley and garlic in a jar or bowl and whisk or shake to combine thoroughly.

Quarter and core the apples. Slice them thinly and put them in a large bowl. Add the lettuce. Add just enough dressing to lightly coat and toss to combine. Divide evenly among 6 salad plates and top with the pecans and blue cheese if desired.

Serves 6

## Romaine Apple Salad with Almonds

*Sugared Almonds:*
- 2 tablespoons butter
- 1 cup slivered almonds
- 1 tablespoon sugar

- 2 tablespoons sugar
- 1/2 cup olive oil
- Salt to taste
- Pepper to taste

*Dressing:*
- 1/4 cup finely minced onion
- 3 tablespoons apple cider vinegar
- 3 tablespoons white wine vinegar
- 2 tablespoons sesame seeds
- 1/4 teaspoon paprika

*Salad:*
- 1 (10 ounce) package or 1 large head romaine cleaned and torn
- 2 medium red-skinned apples, quartered, cored and thinly sliced

Melt butter in a large skillet over medium heat. Add almonds and stir until almonds begin to color, about 2 minutes. Sprinkle sugar over the almonds and stir until the sugar melts and begins to turn golden. Transfer almonds to a bowl and cool.

Dressing: Combine onion, apple cider vinegar, wine vinegar, sesame seeds, paprika and sugar in a small bowl. Gradually whisk in olive oil. Season the dressing to taste with salt and pepper.

Combine lettuce and apples in a large bowl. Toss with dressing to coat. Mix in the sugared almonds.

8 servings

## 24 Hour Fruit Salad

*Dressing:*
- 4 tablespoons cider vinegar
- 4 tablespoons sugar
- 2 eggs, beaten
- 2 tablespoons butter
- 1 cup whipping cream, whipped

*Salad:*
- 2 cups white cherries (Queen Ann), seeded and halved
- 2 cups diced fresh pineapple
- 2 oranges, peeled and cut into bite sized pieces
- 2 cups miniature marshmallows

Dressing: Combine vinegar and sugar and stir until sugar is dissolved. Add vinegar mixture to the eggs. Cook over low heat until thick and smooth, stirring frequently. Remove from heat and add butter. Let dressing cool before folding in whipped cream.

Salad: Combine cherries, pineapple and oranges. Fold fruit and marshmallows into the dressing. Cover and refrigerate overnight.

16 – 1/2 cup servings

# Baby Blue Salad

**Balsamic Vinaigrette:**
- 1/2 cup balsamic vinegar
- 3 tablespoons Dijon mustard
- 3 teaspoons honey
- 2 garlic cloves, minced
- 2 shallots, minced
- 1/4 teaspoon salt
- 1/4 teaspoon pepper
- 1 cup olive oil

**Sweet and Spicy Pecans:**
- 1 cup pecan halves
- 1/4 cup plus 2 teaspoons sugar, divided
- 1 cup warm water
- 1 tablespoon chili powder
- 1/8 teaspoon ground red pepper

**Salad:**
- 3/4 pound mixed greens (spring mix)
- 4 ounces blue cheese, crumbled
- 2 oranges, peeled and thinly sliced
- 1 pint strawberries or raspberries

*Variation: The blue cheese can be served on the side instead of tossed into the salad.*

Vinaigrette: Put vinegar, mustard, honey, garlic, shallots, salt, pepper and oil in a jar with a tight fitting lid. Shake thoroughly and set aside.

Preheat oven to 350°. Soak pecans in 1/4 cup sugar and water for 10 minutes. Drain. Coat pecans in 2 teaspoons sugar, chili powder and ground red pepper. Place on greased baking sheet. Bake for 10 minutes and set aside to cool.

Salad: Toss greens with blue cheese and vinaigrette. Place on plates. Arrange orange slices and berries on each salad, and top with the sweet and spicy pecans.

8 servings

# Fruit Salad with Limoncello

**Yogurt Topping:**
- 1/3 cup bottled lemon curd
- 7 ounces Greek yogurt, plus more for serving
- 1 tablespoon honey
- 1/4 teaspoon vanilla extract

**Fruit Salad:**
- 2 cups sliced strawberries
- 1 cup raspberries
- 1 cup blueberries
- 2 tablespoons sugar
- 3 tablespoons limoncello liqueur
- 1 banana, sliced (optional)
- Fresh mint sprigs

*Note: Lemon curd can be found in the jam section at most grocery stores, or see recipe on page 219.*

Yogurt topping: Whip the lemon curd. Slowly whisk in the yogurt. Whisk in honey and vanilla. Set aside at room temperature if serving soon or refrigerate if prepared ahead.

Fruit Salad: Carefully toss together the strawberries, raspberries, blueberries, sugar and limoncello. Allow to stand at room temperature for about 5 minutes for the berries to macerate in the sugar and liqueur. If using the banana, gently fold into the mixture just before serving. Serve bowls of fruit with a healthy dollop of yogurt on top. Dress with a sprig of fresh mint.

14 – 16 servings (1/2 cup)

## Grilled Romaine Salad

Note: When guests hear Grilled Romaine is on the menu, they groan – especially the men – until it's served.

**Buttermilk Chive Dressing:**
- 1/4 cup buttermilk
- 1/2 cup mayonnaise
- 2 tablespoons minced chives or green onion tops
- 1 clove garlic, minced
- 1/2 teaspoon salt
- 1/4 teaspoon freshly ground pepper

**Salad:**
- 4 bunches romaine
- 1 small red onion
- 2 tablespoons olive oil
- 1/2 cup freshly shaved Parmesan cheese
- Kosher salt to taste
- Freshly ground pepper to taste

Prepare the dressing by whisking buttermilk, mayonnaise, chives, garlic, salt and pepper until fully blended. Cover and chill until ready to use.

Coat the grill cooking grate evenly with cooking spray. Preheat grill to 300° – 350°. Pull off tough outer leaves of romaine and discard; cut bunches in half lengthwise, keeping leaves intact. Peel onion and cut in half vertically, keeping core (root end and top) intact. Cut each half into 4 wedges. Brush lettuce and onion evenly with olive oil. Place onion wedges on cooking grate and grill covered for 3 – 4 minutes on each side or to a desired appearance. Remove onion wedges. Place romaine halves, cut sides down, on cooking grate. Grill uncovered for 2 – 3 minutes or just until wilted. Divide grilled lettuce, cut sides up, evenly among serving plates. Top each with 1 onion wedge (separate into slices, if desired) and drizzle with dressing. Sprinkle evenly with shaved Parmesan cheese and salt and pepper to taste. Serve immediately.

8 servings

## Grape Salad with Cream Cheese

Alternate Directions: Combine the cream cheese, sugar, sour cream and vanilla. Combine grapes and mix with cream cheese mixture. Pat the brown sugar on top of the grapes. If using, sprinkle with Butterfinger bar crumbs on top. Sprinkle on nuts just before serving. Refrigerate to meld flavors.

Note: For a slightly different taste, use all white sugar. Splenda products may be substituted for sugars.

- 1 (8 ounce) package cream cheese of choice, softened
- 1 cup sugar
- 3/4 cup sour cream
- 3/4 cup brown sugar, packed
- 1 teaspoon vanilla extract
- 1 1/2 pounds green grapes
- 1 1/2 pounds red grapes
- 1 cup chopped pecans or walnuts
- 4 Butterfinger bars crushed (optional)

In a bowl, combine cream cheese, sugar, sour cream, brown sugar and vanilla; stir until smooth. Place the grapes in a serving bowl. Pour cream cheese mixture over grapes, tossing gently to coat. Cover and chill. To prevent nuts and crushed candy (if using) from becoming soft, add and toss just prior to serving.

12 servings

## Greek Tomato Salad

*Dressing:*
- 1/2 cup olive oil
- 1/3 cup red wine vinegar
- 1/4 teaspoon salt
- 1/4 teaspoon freshly cracked pepper
- 4 teaspoons sugar
- 1/2 teaspoon minced fresh basil
- 1 tablespoon minced fresh parsley

*Salad:*
- 6 medium tomatoes, sliced or wedged
- 1/4 pound crumbled feta cheese
- 1 small onion, thinly sliced
- 1 (3 1/2 ounce) can sliced ripe olives, drained

Dressing: Mix oil, vinegar, salt, pepper, sugar, basil and parsley thoroughly.

Layer the tomatoes, feta cheese, onion and olives alternately in a large serving bowl, sprinkling with the oil mixture. Lift gently to distribute.

6 servings

## Horiatiki Salata

*Salad:*
- 1 clove of garlic cut in half
- 4 – 5 firm ripe tomatoes
- 1 large cucumber, peeled and sliced
- 2 green peppers, seeded and sliced into thin rounds
- 3 – 4 scallions, green part included, sliced
- 18 pitted Greek olives
- 1/3 pound feta cheese, broken into small pieces

Salt and freshly ground black pepper

Chopped fresh parsley

Crumbled dried oregano for garnish

*Vinegar and Oil Dressing*
- 1 cup extra virgin olive oil
- 1/2 cup red wine vinegar
- 1/4 teaspoon salt
- 1/4 teaspoon sugar

*Variation: Use onion rings instead of scallions, dill leaves instead of oregano, and add capers.*

*Note: Horiatiki Salata is your basic big Greek Salad with Horiatiki meaning "village style."*

Rub a salad bowl with the cut garlic clove. Quarter the tomatoes and place in the bowl. Add the cucumber, green peppers, scallions, Greek olives and feta. Sprinkle with salt and pepper to taste. Just before serving, shake the dressing and drizzle over the salad; toss lightly. Sprinkle with parsley and oregano.

Dressing: Combine the olive oil and vinegar in a shaker jar. Add salt and shake well. Add additional salt to taste if needed. Add sugar, or more to taste if needed.

4 servings (yields: 1 1/2 cups dressing)

## Maroulosalata: Romaine Lettuce Salad

*Note: This Greek salad is traditional in late spring and early summer, when romaine lettuce, scallions and dill are at their peak. This salad should be light and crunchy. The amount of dressing needed depends on the amount of lettuce.*

| | |
|---|---|
| 2 | heads romaine |
| 1/4 | cup fresh dill, finely chopped (or 1 tablespoon dried dill weed) |
| 8 – 10 | spring onions, cleaned and finely chopped (bulb and stalk) |

**Dressing:**

| | |
|---|---|
| 3/4 | cup extra virgin olive oil |
| 1/4 | cup high quality red wine vinegar |
| 1 1/2 | teaspoons crushed oregano |
| 1 | teaspoon sea salt |
| | Pinch of freshly ground pepper |

Clean the lettuce, removing the stem and discarding damaged leaves. Separate and rinse leaves individually to remove any soil and debris. Pat lettuce dry with paper towels. Shred as thinly as possible. Refrigerate until ready to serve.

Combine lettuce, fresh dill and onions in a large salad bowl. Toss about half to three quarters of the dressing, adding more until the dressing coats the salad ingredients.

Dressing: Whisk together the oil and vinegar and add oregano, salt and pepper.

8 servings

## Tomatoes with Dressing

*Variation: Use feta or blue cheese for the cheese topping.*

**Salad:**

| | |
|---|---|
| 8 | medium tomatoes, sliced |
| 1 | red onion, thinly sliced |
| | Sliced green olives, to suit |
| | Sliced black olives, to suit |
| | Parmesan cheese, as needed |

**Dressing:**

| | |
|---|---|
| 3 | tablespoons red wine vinegar |
| 1 | tablespoon Dijon mustard |
| 1/2 | teaspoon salt |
| 1/2 | teaspoon pepper |
| 1/3 | cup olive oil |

Arrange tomato slices on a large platter; scatter onion rings over tomatoes and sprinkle with green and black olives.

Dressing: Combine vinegar, mustard, salt and pepper. Slowly whisk in olive oil to emulsify.

Drizzle dressing over salad ingredients and sprinkle with Parmesan cheese.

8 servings

## Walnut Street Salad

*Salad:*

- **5 ounce package spring mix greens**
- **6 ounce package dried cranberries**
- **2 ounces blue cheese**
- **1/2 cup walnuts**

*Sweet Balsamic Dressing:*

- **1 1/4 cup balsamic vinegar**
- **1/4 cup brown sugar, packed**

Wash and dry the greens. Combine the cranberries, blue cheese and walnuts. Add to greens and toss. Just before serving, lightly drizzle on the dressing and toss lightly. Serve additional dressing on the side.

Dressing: Combine vinegar and sugar in a small pan. Heat until the sugar is melted. Cook until volume is decreased by half. Can be stored for up to 7 days in the refrigerator.

4 servings

## The Feed Store
## Chicken Salad

- **1 pound cooked and boned chicken meat (both light and dark)**
- **1 1/2 cups mayonnaise**
- **1/3 cup finely chopped celery**
- **1 tablespoon lemon juice**
- **1/4 teaspoon white pepper**
- **1/2 teaspoon salt**

Process the chicken meat in a food processor. Add mayonnaise, celery, lemon juice, white pepper and salt. Mix thoroughly. Chill for several hours before serving.

8 servings

*The Feed Store, directly across from the Old State Capitol and close to most Lincoln sites, is a popular lunch spot with an interesting menu and fast service. The name is reminiscent of the day when people had horses and livestock in the city. In fact, pigs rooted in the dirt streets before they were paved and had sidewalks. It also recalls the expression for sitting at a table: "Putting on the feed bag." If you don't understand that one, consult an equine expert.*

## Grilled Chicken Pita Salad

*Variation: Use purchased frozen grilled chicken strips (thawed) or sliced rotisserie chicken. Either works well in the recipe.*

**Salad:**

- 2 boned, skinned chicken breast halves
  Olive oil, for rub
- 1 pound asparagus, ends trimmed, cut diagonally into 2 – inch pieces
- 4 ounces feta cheese, broken into chunks
- 2 cups halved grape tomatoes
- 1/2 cup pitted Kalamata olives
- 2 cups pita chips, slightly crushed
- 2 cups baby arugula or mixed greens

**Dressing:**

- 3 tablespoons fresh lemon juice
- 1/3 cup olive oil
- 1 tablespoon fresh oregano, chopped
- 1 clove garlic, minced (optional)
- 1/2 teaspoon freshly ground black pepper

Prepare grill for high heat (450° – 550°). Rub chicken breast halves with olive oil and grill, turning once, until no longer pink. Slice chicken into stripes.

Boil asparagus until just bright green, rinse with cold water, drain and place in a large bowl. Add sliced chicken, feta cheese, tomatoes, olives and pita chips. Toss gently with prepared dressing. Add arugula or lettuce and toss to combine.

Dressing: Whisk lemon juice, olive oil, oregano, garlic (if using) and black pepper together and set aside until ready to use.

4 servings

## Raspberry Chicken Salad

**Dressing:**

- 1/4 cup seedless raspberry jam
- 1/4 cup extra virgin olive oil
- 1/4 cup balsamic vinegar

**Salad:**

- 6 cups mixed greens
- 1/2 cup fresh raspberries
- 1/4 cup sliced, toasted almonds
- 1 rotisserie chicken or two cooked breasts, chopped in small pieces

Dressing: Combine raspberry jam, olive oil and balsamic vinegar in a screw-top jar and shake well.

Place greens in large salad bowl with raspberries and almonds. Spoon salad dressing over ingredients and toss lightly. Add chicken before serving.

4 servings

## Illini Country Club
# Chilled Chicken Curried Salad

**Chicken:**
- 10 chicken breasts
- 1 tablespoon curry
- 1/2 cup sugar
- 1 tablespoon turmeric
- Water to cover

**Sweet Curry Dressing:**
- 1 cup honey
- 1/2 cup apple cider vinegar
- 1 cup mayonnaise
- 1 tablespoon curry powder
- 1 tablespoon turmeric
- 1 teaspoon celery salt
- 1 tablespoon Dijon mustard

**Salad:**
- 1 cup dried apricots
- 3 cups cauliflower, pre-blanched
- 3 cups green peas
- 1/2 red onion, diced small
- 1 cucumber, diced small
- 3 cups garbanzo beans
- Mint (1 bunch)
- Cashews for garnish

Bring water to a simmer. Add chicken breasts, curry, sugar and turmeric and simmer until chicken is completely cooked, about 15 minutes. Strain off liquid and refrigerate chicken breasts until completely cool.

Dressing: Combine honey, vinegar, mayonnaise, curry, turmeric, celery salt and Dijon mustard.

To make the salad, cut the chicken into bite-sized pieces or slice into strips. Combine the apricots, cauliflower, peas, onion, cucumber, beans and mint in a salad bowl. Top the vegetables with the chicken. Add dressing and toss. Garnish with cashews.

## Fabulous Orzo Pasta Salad

- 1 1/2 cups (10 ounces) orzo
- 1/3 cup sliced sun-dried tomatoes packed in oil
- 2 (14 ounce) jars marinated artichokes, drained
- 1/4 cup good quality balsamic vinegar
- 1/4 cup (packed) sliced Kalamata olives
- 3 – 4 tablespoons good quality olive oil
- 2 large garlic cloves, minced
- 1/4 cup pesto, to taste
- 1/2 cup toasted pine nuts
- 1/2 cup shaved Parmigiano-Reggiano cheese
- 8 ounces cherry tomatoes, halved
- Salt to taste
- Pepper to taste

*Variations: You can add a variety of vegetables to this: peeled chopped cucumber, diced red pepper, al dente green beans, cauliflower or broccoli. Recipe can be made with fig and cherry balsamic. It is wonderful for a picnic or potluck.*

Cook orzo in boiling salted water until just tender. Drain well and transfer to a large bowl. Add sun-dried tomatoes, artichokes, vinegar, olives, oil, garlic and pesto and toss to blend. Let stand until cool, then cover and refrigerate. Mix in pine nuts, cheese and cherry tomatoes just before serving. Add salt and pepper to taste.

8 – 10 servings

## Margaret Garfield Orzo with Vegetables

*Hint: This can be made in advance and refrigerated prior to adding the scallions, pine nuts, feta and basil. Bring to room temperature and add those ingredients just before serving.*

*Note: Orzo is pasta shaped like rice grains.*

*Note: Cutting a vegetable into julienne means to cut long, thin strips. This technique is great for pasta salads, soups, or garnishes.*

| | | | | |
|---|---|---|---|---|
| 1 | small eggplant | | 1/2 | pound orzo |
| 1 | red bell pepper | | 1/3 | cup freshly squeezed lemon juice |
| 1 | yellow bell pepper | | 4 | scallions, green and white parts minced |
| 1 | red onion | | | |
| 2 | cloves garlic, diced | | 1/4 | cup pine nuts, toasted |
| 2/3 | cup extra virgin olive oil, divided | | 1/4 | pound feta cheese, cut in 1/2 – inch dice |
| 2 1/2 | teaspoons kosher salt, divided | | 15 | fresh basil leaves, julienned |
| 1 | teaspoon ground black pepper, divided | | | |

Preheat oven to 425°. Peel and dice eggplant into 3/4 – inch pieces. Seed peppers and cut into 1 – inch squares. Peel and cut onion into 1 – inch pieces. Combine the eggplant, red and yellow peppers, onion, garlic, 1/3 cup olive oil, 1 1/2 teaspoons salt and 1/2 teaspoon pepper and toss to cover vegetables with oil. Place mixture on a large, shallow baking sheet. Roast until browned, approximately 40 minutes. Turn once after 20 minutes. While vegetables are roasting, cook the orzo according to package directions. Drain and place in a large serving bowl. Combine lemon juice, 1/3 cup olive oil, 1 teaspoon salt and 1/2 teaspoon pepper. Mix vegetables with the orzo, stir in the dressing. Let cool to room temperature and add the scallions, pine nuts, feta and basil, stirring gently. Adjust seasonings if necessary. Serve at room temperature.

12 servings

##  Island Bay Yacht Club
## Spinach Flambé

| | | | | |
|---|---|---|---|---|
| 6 | bunches of spinach, about 10 – 12 ounces per bunch, washed and dried | | **Dressing:** | |
| | | | 12 | strips of bacon |
| 12 | button mushrooms, sliced | | 1 1/2 | ounces brandy |
| 1 | small red onion, thinly sliced | | 4 | teaspoons brown sugar |
| | | | 2 | tablespoons honey |
| | | | 1/2 | teaspoon Dijon style mustard |
| | | | 1/2 | cup red wine vinegar |

Tear the spinach into bite sized pieces and place in a large salad bowl. Add the mushrooms and red onion to the bowl and set aside.

Cut the bacon into small pieces and sauté in a heavy skillet until crispy (do not over cook the bacon). Discard the bacon grease and add the brandy to the hot skillet (be careful, a flame will be produced). Add the brown sugar, honey and Dijon mustard to the skillet, mixing thoroughly. Cook until the brown sugar caramelizes. Add the red wine vinegar and bring the ingredients to a boil. Remove from heat and pour dressing over the spinach mixture. Toss thoroughly and serve.

6 servings

## Leland Grove Spinach Salad

**Salad:**

| | |
|---|---|
| 8 | cups fresh spinach |
| 8 | cups lettuce of choice |
| 1 | (15 ounce) can mandarin oranges |
| 1 | small red onion cut into rings |
| 1 | avocado cut into chunks |
| 1 | (8 ounce) box of mushrooms, sliced |
| 6 | slices bacon, cooked and crumbled |
| | Croutons (optional) |

**Dressing:**

| | |
|---|---|
| 3/4 | cup sugar |
| 1 | tablespoons dry mustard |
| 1 | teaspoons salt |
| 1/3 | cup vinegar |
| 1 | cup oil |

*Note: This makes about 1 1/2 cups of dressing. Refrigerate extra for later use, using the microwave to reheat dressing.*

*Note: Crouton recipe see page 84.*

Tear spinach and lettuce into bite-sized pieces. Place spinach, lettuce, oranges, onion, avocado and mushrooms in a large salad bowl. Pour hot dressing over salad, using only enough to cover ingredients. Toss and top with bacon and croutons.

Dressing: Combine sugar, dry mustard and salt in a sauce pan. Add vinegar. Over low heat slowly add oil a small amount at a time, while stirring constantly so that it mixes well with the other ingredients as the sugar dissolves. After sugar has dissolved, remove from heat.

12 – 16 servings

## President's Choice Spinach Salad

**Dressing:**

| | |
|---|---|
| 3/4 | cup vegetable oil |
| 1/2 | cup sugar |
| 1/3 | cup catsup |
| 1/4 | cup vinegar |
| 1 | tablespoon Worcestershire sauce |

**Salad:**

| | |
|---|---|
| 2 | 10 ounce packages of spinach |
| 1 | cup bean sprouts |
| 1/2 | cup thinly sliced red onion |
| 2 | hard boiled eggs, sliced |
| 6 | pieces of cooked bacon, crumbled |

Dressing: Mix the oil, sugar, catsup, vinegar and Worcestershire sauce in a small jar. Shake well and refrigerate until ready to use. Bring to room temperature before tossing salad.

Combine spinach, bean sprouts and red onion. Add dressing and toss well. Garnish with eggs and bacon.

6 – 8 servings

# Spinach and Vidalia Salad

Tip: Double the crouton recipe. They make tasty snacks.

Variations: Any good croutons may be substituted, but it's a nice touch to make them fresh. See recipe below.

**Croutons:**

- 4 **cups bread crumbs, finely crumbled**
- 1/3 **cup Vidalia onion, finely chopped**
- 1 **tablespoon dried parsley**
- 2 **tablespoons margarine or butter, melted**
  **Vegetable oil for frying**

**Dressing:**

- 1/3 **cup Vidalia onion, finely chopped**
- 1/3 **cup white vinegar**
- 1 – 2 **teaspoons Frangelico (hazelnut liqueur)**
- 1 **teaspoon Dijon mustard**
- 1/3 **cup honey**
- 1 **cup safflower oil**
- 1 **teaspoon poppy seeds**

**Salad:**

- 1 **pound fresh spinach**
- 1 **cup Vidalia onions, sliced, rings separated**
- 12 **slices bacon, fried crisp and crumbled**

Croutons: Combine bread crumbs, onion, parsley and margarine. Using about 1 teaspoon of mixture, roll it into small balls. Fry in vegetable oil until browned.

Dressing: Combine onions, vinegar, Frangelico, mustard and honey. Slowly add the oil. Add poppy seeds and combine thoroughly.

Salad: Wash spinach and tear into bite-sized pieces. Place spinach, onion rings and bacon in a large serving bowl. Just before serving, lightly cover with the dressing and toss. Sprinkle generously with croutons and mix lightly. Place extra dressing and croutons on the table.

8 – 12 servings

# Capitol Croutons

Variation: Use 1/2 teaspoon garlic powder in place of fresh garlic. Mix rosemary, thyme, basil and oregano to total 1 teaspoon and use in place of Italian spice. Toss melted butter, oil and spices with the bread cubes and bake for 1 hour at 250° for crispier croutons.

Note: This is a good way to use leftover bread and make a salad great. These can be made a day or two ahead and stored.

- 4 **cups bread, dry or day old in 1/2 – inch cubes**
- 1 **teaspoon Italian spices**
- 1/2 **teaspoon salt**
- 1/2 **teaspoon pepper**
- 3 **tablespoons butter, melted**
- 3 **tablespoons olive oil**
- 2 **small cloves garlic, minced**

Let bread cubes dry for a few hours if bread is fresh. Mix the dry Italian spices, salt and pepper together in a small cup. Melt butter and oil in a deep skillet over medium heat. Add the garlic to the butter and sauté for 1 minute to release the flavor of the garlic. Quickly add the bread cubes. Sprinkle the herb mixture over the bread cubes and sauté stirring frequently for 3 – 5 minutes until the bread is browned and crispy.

4 cups

## Progress Party Salad

| | |
|---|---|
| 6 | cups diced chicken (4 1/2 – 5 pound roasted or baked chicken, or 5 breasts) |
| 3 | tablespoons lemon juice |
| 2 | cups water |
| 3 | apples with skin, diced (optional) |
| 1 1/2 | cups dried cranberries or cherries |
| 1 1/2 | cups diced celery |
| 3/4 | cup black walnut, walnut, pecan or almond pieces |
| | Little Gem lettuce leaves (or other decorative, crisp lettuce) |

**Dressing:**

| | |
|---|---|
| 1 1/2 | cups mayonnaise or salad dressing, more if needed |
| 3/4 | teaspoon salt |
| 1/2 | teaspoon pepper |
| 2 – 3 | teaspoons curry to suit |

*Tip: Great for entrée with or without curry. Better for sandwiches without apples. The black walnuts balance the curry extremely well.*

Remove chicken meat from bones and dice or chop in food processor. Combine lemon juice and water. Cut and dice apples and drop into the lemon water to prevent darkening. Drain lemon water from apples. Combine chicken, drained apples (if using), cranberries, celery and nuts.

Combine mayonnaise, salt, pepper and curry (if using). Combine mayonnaise mixture and chicken mixture. Refrigerate overnight for flavors to meld. Serve over lettuce leaves.

12 servings without apples; 20 servings with apples

## Shanghai Crunch Salad

| | |
|---|---|
| 3 | ounces uncooked whole wheat spaghetti |
| 1/2 | cup green onions, chopped |
| 1 | cup red bell pepper strips |
| 1/4 | cup fresh cilantro, chopped |
| 1 | (12 ounce) package broccoli slaw |
| 1/4 | cup unsalted dry roasted peanuts, chopped |

**Dressing:**

| | |
|---|---|
| 1/3 | cup seasoned rice vinegar |
| 2 | tablespoons sugar |
| 3 | tablespoons low-sodium soy sauce |
| 1 | tablespoon olive oil |
| 1 | teaspoon minced fresh garlic |

*Note: This is a good do ahead recipe because it's great the next day.*

Break pasta into 2 – inch pieces. Cook according to package directions. Drain well. Combine cooked pasta, onions, bell pepper strips, cilantro, broccoli slaw and peanuts. Add enough dressing to coat the pasta and vegetables. Cover and chill at least two hours, stirring occasionally.

Dressing: Combine vinegar, sugar, soy sauce, olive oil and garlic in large bowl. Whisk until sugar is dissolved.

8 servings

## Sangamon County Cole Slaw

| | |
|---|---|
| 12 cups shredded green cabbage | 1/2 cup chopped fresh parsley |
| 1/2 cup chopped or shredded green bell pepper | 1/2 cup dill weed |
| 1/2 cup chopped or shredded red bell pepper | 1/4 cup celery seed |
| 1 cup chopped onion | 1 cup shredded red cabbage (rinse and drain well to prevent bleeding) |
| 1 small carrot, chopped or shredded | **Dressing:** |
| 3 radishes, chopped | 2 cups vinegar |
| 2 – 3 stalks celery, chopped | 1 1/4 cups sugar |
| 2 tablespoons salt | 1 cup oil |
| 1 1/2 tablespoons pepper | |

Combine cabbage, red and green peppers, onion, carrot, radishes and celery in a large bowl. Add salt, pepper, parsley, dill weed and celery seed and toss. Add red cabbage to the green cabbage mix. Pour dressing over cabbage mix and toss. Refrigerate for several hours to permit flavors to meld

Dressing: Combine vinegar and sugar until sugar dissolves. Taste to determine if more sugar is needed. Slowly whisk oil into vinegar mix to emulsify.

16 – 20 servings

## Thai Shrimp Pasta

*Note: The sauce has a serious kick!*

*Al dente – See page 121.*

*Julienned – See page 82.*

| | |
|---|---|
| 1 package bowtie pasta | **Sauce:** |
| 1 tablespoon sesame oil | 1/2 cup chicken broth |
| 3 cups broccoli florets | 3 tablespoons soy sauce |
| 1 red bell pepper, julienned | 1 tablespoon sherry |
| 1 medium onion, quartered and sliced | 1 tablespoon sugar |
| 2 carrots, peeled and thinly sliced | 1 tablespoon cornstarch |
| 1 pound shrimp | 1/2 tablespoon chili paste |
| | 1 tablespoon hoisin sauce |
| | 1 tablespoon chopped fresh ginger |
| | 1/2 teaspoon salt |

Sauce: Combine chicken broth, soy sauce, sherry, sugar, cornstarch, chili paste, hoisin sauce, ginger and salt.

Boil water in a large pot and cook pasta to al dente. Drain and set aside. Heat sesame oil in a wok. Sauté broccoli, red pepper, onion and carrots until crisp and set aside. Sauté shrimp until just cooked. Return vegetables to wok with shrimp. Add pasta and sauce. Stir gently and cook until sauce thickens slightly. Serve immediately.

6 to 8 servings

## Willing Salad

**Salad:**

| | |
|---|---|
| 1 | pound linguine noodles |
| 1/2 | head of Napa cabbage |
| 1 | head purple cabbage, thinly sliced |
| 1 | (9 ounce) bag baby spinach |
| 1 | red bell pepper, thinly sliced |
| 1 | yellow bell pepper, thinly sliced |
| 1 | orange bell pepper, thinly sliced |
| 1 | bunch scallions, sliced |
| 1 | bunch cilantro, chopped |
| 1 | (16 ounce) can dry roasted skinless peanuts |

**Dressing:**

| | |
|---|---|
| 1 | lime, juiced |
| 6 | tablespoons soy sauce |
| 1/3 | cup brown sugar, packed |
| 3 | tablespoons ginger, finely chopped |
| 2 | cloves of garlic, finely chopped |
| 2 | jalapeños, seeded, finely chopped |
| 1 | bunch cilantro, chopped |
| 1/2 | cup olive oil |

*Note: This is a great make ahead "potluck" salad.*

Break the linguine noodles into 1 to 2 – inch lengths and cook according to package directions. Rinse, drain and cool. Combine the linguine, Napa cabbage, purple cabbage, spinach, red, yellow and orange peppers, scallions, cilantro and nuts in a large bowl. Lightly pour dressing over the salad and toss. Let salad set for 30 minutes for flavors to meld.

Dressing: Combine the lime juice, soy sauce, brown sugar, ginger, garlic, jalapeños and cilantro. Slowly add the olive oil, whisking until the mixture emulsifies.

24 servings

*The State Fair Main Gate, built in 1910, is an icon of both the state fair and the city of Springfield. Both in size and structure, the gate meets the neoclassical idea of what a grand entrance should look like. Renovated in 1985, the Main Gate was restored to its original grandeur as depicted on a 1911 postcard.*

## Caesar Salad with a Twist

*Dressing:*

- 1/4 cup lemon juice
- 3 tablespoons olive oil
- 2 tablespoons water
- 1 tablespoon Worcestershire sauce
- 1/4 teaspoon salt
- 1/4 teaspoon pepper

*Salad:*

- 1 (9 ounce) package cheese tortellini
- 1/2 pound asparagus, trimmed and cut into bite sized pieces
- 1 garlic clove
- 1 head romaine lettuce
- 1/4 cup Parmesan cheese

Dressing: Combine lemon juice, olive oil, water, Worcestershire sauce, salt and pepper. Blend well with a whisk.

Bring a pot of water to a boil. Add tortellini and asparagus and cook 4 minutes. Drain into a colander and rinse with cold water. Rub the serving bowl sides and bottom with garlic clove. Tear lettuce into bite sized pieces and place in the serving bowl. Add tortellini and asparagus. Drizzle with dressing. Add Parmesan cheese. Toss just before serving.

12 servings

## Summer Pasta Salad

- 1 pound bowtie pasta
- 1 (12 ounce) jar marinated artichokes, drained and chopped
- 1 (12 ounce) jar roasted red peppers, drained and cut into 1/4 – inch strips
- 1/2 pound mozzarella cheese, cut into 1/2 – inch cubes
- 2 cups cherry tomatoes, halved
- 1/2 cup Kalamata olives, pitted and chopped

*Dressing:*

- 2 garlic cloves
- 1 tablespoon Dijon mustard
- 1/3 cup red wine vinegar
- 2 tablespoons balsamic vinegar
- 1 tablespoon water
- 1/2 cup vegetable oil

  Salt and freshly ground pepper to taste

Cook pasta in a large pot of water according to the directions on the package. Drain, rinse under cold water and drain again. Transfer pasta to a large bowl.

Add dressing to pasta and toss well. Stir in the artichoke hearts, roasted red peppers, mozzarella, cherry tomatoes and Kalamata olives. Cover and chill salad for at least 1 hour and up to 1 day. Gently stir again before serving.

Dressing: In a blender or food processor, blend the garlic, mustard, red wine vinegar, balsamic vinegar, water and oil until emulsified. Season to taste with salt and freshly ground pepper.

8 – 10 servings

## Shrimp Salad

**Dressing:**
- 1 cup mayonnaise
- 1 tablespoon orange zest
- 1 tablespoon orange juice
- 1 tablespoon wine vinegar
- Salt to taste
- Pepper to taste

**Salad:**
- 2 pounds fresh shrimp, peeled and deveined
- 3 tablespoons olive oil
- Salt to taste
- Pepper to taste
- 1 tablespoon dried dill weed
- 2 tablespoons capers (optional)
- 1/3 cup red onion, finely chopped

Preheat oven to 350°. Mix mayonnaise, orange zest, orange juice, vinegar, salt and pepper and set aside.

Combine shrimp, olive oil, salt and pepper in a plastic bag and shake to coat shrimp. Place shrimp on a baking sheet and bake until shrimp turns pink, about 15 – 20 minutes. Remove from the oven and cool. Toss the shrimp, dill, capers and red onion together in a bowl. Add enough dressing to coat the salad. Reserve any leftover dressing for another use.

8 servings

*Dedicated in June of 1996, the Betty Mood Smith Rockery features a smorgasbord of plantings from perennials and annuals to trees and other woody plantings. The Rockery is situated among the numerous themed gardens on the grounds of the Washington Park Botanical Garden in Springfield.*

KING'S
DAUGHTERS
ORGANIZATION

# Warm Me Up, and more

*👑 The crown indicates a celebrity's recipe.*

## The Feed Store
## Chilled Strawberry Soup

*Note: This soup can be frozen.*

| | |
|---|---|
| 3 | **cups red wine, merlot or burgundy** |
| 6 | **cups water** |
| 1 | **teaspoon cinnamon** |
| 2 | **cups white sugar** |

| | |
|---|---|
| 1/2 | **cup lemon juice** |
| 12 | **cups (3 quarts) strawberries, washed and hulled** |
| 2 | **cups heavy whipping cream** |
| 1 | **cup sour cream** |

Combine the wine, water, cinnamon, sugar and lemon juice in a large stockpot. Bring to a boil and boil for 10 minutes.

Puree prepared berries in a food-processor or blender until they are mushy. Leave some small pieces of fruit for a hint of texture. Add pureed berries to the boiled liquid and simmer for at least 30 minutes. When simmering the fruit puree, watch the pot very carefully. When it begins to boil it wants to "explode" and will make a huge mess. Quickly lower burner heat at the first sign of boiling. For thicker soup, simmer a little longer. Pour berry mixture into a clean bowl and refrigerate for several hours.

Whisk the whipping cream and sour cream together, leaving no lumps. Add cream mixture to the chilled berries, mixing well, and return to refrigerator until serving.

Makes 4 quarts

## Augie's Front Burner
## Gazpacho

*Note: For homemade croutons, see page 84.*

| | |
|---|---|
| 3 | **cucumbers, diced** |
| 3 | **peppers, diced** |
| 4 | **tomatoes, diced** |
| 1/4 | **small onion, diced** |
| 2 | **garlic cloves, minced** |
| 1/4 | **cup olive oil** |
| 1/4 | **cup red wine vinegar** |
| | **Salt to taste** |
| | **Pepper to taste** |

| | |
|---|---|
| 1/2 | **tablespoon oregano** |
| 1/2 | **tablespoon basil** |
| 2 | **drops Tabasco sauce** |
| 2 | **drops Worcestershire sauce** |
| 4 | **cups tomato juice** |
| 2 | **cups V8 juice** |
| | **Croutons for garnish** |
| | **Avocado for garnish** |

Combine cucumbers, peppers, tomatoes, onion and garlic in a large container and add oil, vinegar, salt and pepper to taste, oregano, basil, Tabasco and Worcestershire sauce. Mix thoroughly. Add tomato juice and V8 juice and mix again. Refrigerate several hours. Serve chilled; topped with croutons and avocado pieces.

6 servings

## American Harvest
## Loaded Potato and Sweet Corn Chowder

1 **pound bacon, diced**
  **Oil for sautéing**
1 **onion, diced**
6 **cloves garlic, sliced**
1 **leek, diced and cleaned**
1 **cup sweet corn kernels**
1 **quart chicken broth**
2 **peeled and diced russet potatoes**

1 **cup heavy cream**
1/4 **cup corn starch slurry**
2 **cups sharp cheddar cheese**
2 **tablespoons Franks Red Hot sauce**
  **Kosher salt and freshly ground black pepper**
1 **cup chopped green onion**

*Note: Cornstarch slurry is a mixture of equal parts cornstarch and cold water.*

In a wide face stock pot, sauté the bacon in a small amount of oil over medium heat. Stir consistently and cook until crispy. Add the onion, garlic, leek, and corn; continue to sauté on low heat for about 10 minutes, stirring consistently until the vegetables are golden brown. Slowly add the broth, scraping the golden brown goodies from the bottom the pan. Add the potatoes and simmer on medium heat for about 20 minutes until the potatoes are tender. Add the cream, turn up the heat, and bring to a boil. Stir constantly.

Once the soup is boiling add the cornstarch slurry a little at a time until the soup thickens. The soup should not be too thick. Reduce the heat to low immediately after thickening. Fold in the cheese and hot sauce until the cheese is entirely melted. Season with salt and pepper to taste and add green onions at the very end.

## Asparagus Soup

4 – 6 **cups water, no salt added**
1/2 **pound fresh asparagus**
1 1/4 **cups onion, finely diced or to taste**
6 **tablespoons butter (3/4 stick)**
3 **tablespoons flour**
1 **tablespoon dried parsley**

1 1/2 **teaspoons garlic salt**
4 **cups chicken broth**
3/4 **cup sliced or diced mushrooms (optional)**
1 **cup milk (anything from 2% to cream)**

*Variation: Use chicken stock to cook asparagus and reserve it to add back in later.*

Bring water to simmer. Add coarsely cut asparagus, reserving the tips; cover and cook until almost tender; add tips to cook during the last few minutes. Drain and either mash asparagus or pulse a few times in a food processor. Sauté onions in butter until translucent. Blend in flour, parsley and garlic salt and cook over low heat for 2 – 3 minutes, stirring occasionally. Add chicken broth and mushrooms (if using) and cook until mixture is blended. Add asparagus to mixture. Add milk or cream and simmer for 3 – 5 minutes.

4 – 6 servings

## Pumpkin Amaretto Soup

*Variation: Substitute 2 pounds of butternut squash or 1 1/2 cups pure pumpkin puree (not pumpkin pie filling). However, it will not have the roasted flavor.*

*Note: Squash can be purchased peeled, cut and packaged.*

| | | | | |
|---|---|---|---|---|
| 1 | (3 pound) sugar or pie pumpkin or 2 pound butternut squash | | 1 | cup heavy cream |
| 1/3 | cup extra virgin olive oil | | 1/3 | cup Amaretto liqueur, preferably a good name |
| 1/4 | cup (1/2 stick) butter | | 1/2 | cup crushed plain Amaretto cookies |
| 1 | large onion, finely chopped Salt to taste | | 1/2 | cup walnuts, chopped and toasted |
| 6 | cups vegetable broth, divided; more if needed to vary consistency to suit taste | | | |

Preheat oven to 450°. Place rack in middle of oven. Line a shallow sided baking sheet with greased aluminum foil. Peel pumpkin and cut into 1 – inch pieces. Spread the pumpkin on the baking sheet in a single layer. Roast for 10 – 20 minutes or until tender, stirring frequently.

Heat the olive oil and butter in a large pot over medium heat. Add onion and salt; and sauté about 7 minutes until completely wilted. Add the roasted pumpkin and 4 cups broth to onion mixture. Simmer until pumpkin is soft, 13 – 20 minutes. Reduce heat to low and stir in cream, Amaretto, and Amaretto cookies and cook 15 minutes. Cool soup. Transfer in batches to food processor and puree. Return soup to pot and stir in 2 cups of broth. Add extra broth if you prefer a thin consistency. Taste and season with additional salt if needed. Garnish with a dollop of sour cream topped with chopped, toasted walnuts.

6 – 8 servings

## French Onion Soup

*Tip: If individual oven-proof bowls are not available, use a large, deep casserole and layer onion mixture; then top with bread and cheese. Bake until cheese melts. Ladle into individual serving bowls.*

| | | | | |
|---|---|---|---|---|
| 4 | tablespoons butter or margarine | | 1/2 | teaspoon salt |
| 8 | cups thinly sliced onions | | 1 | bay leaf |
| 1 | teaspoon sugar | | 1 | cup white wine |
| 1 | tablespoon flour | | 16 | thin slices of baguette bread |
| 8 | cups beef broth | | 5 | tablespoons butter, melted |
| 1 1/2 | teaspoons Worcestershire sauce | | 1 1/2 | cups shredded Swiss cheese |

Melt butter or margarine in a 4 quart pan. Add onions and sugar. Sauté about 30 minutes until onions become caramelized. Combine flour into onions. Stir beef broth, Worcestershire sauce and salt into mixture. Add bay leaf and wine. Return to simmer. Cover, reduce heat to low and simmer about 45 minutes. Remove bay leaf.

Preheat oven to 350°. Dip both sides of bread into melted butter and place on a jelly roll pan. Bake 10 minutes. Turn slices over and toast opposite side another 5 minutes.

To serve, place 1 cup of soup in each oven proof bowl and top with 2 slices of bread. Sprinkle with 3 tablespoons cheese. Put bowls in the oven for about 10 minutes or until the cheese has melted.

8 servings

## Julianne Glatz
## Butternut Squash and Apple Bisque

**Soup:**

| | |
|---|---|
| 1 | **large butternut squash, about 6 cups** |
| 3 – 4 | **tart apples such as Jonathan or Granny Smith** |
| 1 | **tablespoon butter** |
| 1 1/2 | **cups thinly sliced leeks (white part only) or onions** |
| 6 | **cups chicken or vegetable stock, plus additional if needed** |
| 1 | **cup heavy cream, plus additional to drizzle if desired** |
| | **Kosher or sea salt** |
| | **Freshly ground white pepper to taste** |

**Optional Garnishes:**

**Thinly sliced scallions**

**Croutons**

**Minced fresh herbs such as rosemary, thyme or marjoram**

**Fried sage leaves**

**Crisply fried crumbled bacon**

**Crumbled blue cheese**

**Diced fresh apple**

*Variation: This bisque lends itself well to several variations. Add a tablespoon of minced fresh ginger or ginger juice and/ or a tablespoon of curry powder, or a tablespoon of chili powder. Substitute yogurt for the cream. Do not boil the soup after adding yogurt. Sauté 2 tablespoons minced sage, rosemary, thyme, marjoram or winter savory with the leeks. This soup freezes well.*

*Note: Always cool a mixture before pureeing it in a blender or food processor. Hot ingredients can explode in them.*

Peel the squash and scoop out the seeds. Cut into 1 – inch chunks. You should have about 6 cups. Butternut squash vary a lot in size, so if you have less, cut back proportionately on the other ingredients. Peel, and core the apples and cut into chunks.

In a large Dutch oven, melt the butter over medium heat. Add the leeks or onions, stir to coat and cover the pan. Sweat the leeks until they are softened, about 5 minutes. Add the squash and apples and pour in the stock. Bring the mixture to a boil. Reduce the heat to a simmer, cover the pan and cook for 20 – 30 minutes or until the squash and apples are completely cooked. Cool the mixture. Purée the mixture with a hand held blender or food processor. Return the mixture to the pan, whisk in the cream and season to taste with the salt and freshly ground pepper. Serve the soup with or without garnishes, as desired.

6 servings

*Julianne Glatz's daughter, Ashley Meyer, helps prepare Thanksgiving dinner in her mom's kitchen. Ashley is carrying on her family's love of cooking with her RealCuisine catering business.*

## Tasty Tortilla Soup

*Note: If using avocado, sprinkle with lime juice to retain green color.*

2   tablespoons vegetable oil, divided

1   green pepper, diced

2   garlic cloves, divided

1   medium onion, halved

1   (4 ounce) can green chiles, drained

1   tablespoon chili powder

1   (14 1/2 ounce) can fire roasted diced tomatoes

1   jalapeño pepper, seeds and ribs removed

3   teaspoons minced chipotle peppers in adobo sauce, divided

1/8   teaspoon salt

8   cups low-sodium chicken broth

1   (14 1/2 ounce) can no-salt added diced tomatoes

1   (14 1/2 ounce) can black beans, drained and rinsed

1   (15 1/2 ounce) can corn, drained

Shredded meat of 1 rotisserie chicken, or 4 chicken breasts cooked and shredded

2   tablespoons lime juice, more if needed

1   ripe avocado, cut into chunks

Sour cream, tortilla chips and grated Mexican cheese for garnish

Heat 1 tablespoon oil in a skillet over medium heat. Add green pepper, 1 minced garlic clove, 1/2 onion (chopped) and green chiles to pan; cook for 7 minutes, stirring often. Stir in chili powder and cook for 1 minute, stirring occasionally, . Set aside. While vegetables are cooking, puree the fire roasted tomatoes, remaining onion, 1 whole garlic clove, jalapeno, 1 1/2 teaspoons of chipotles and 1/8 teaspoon salt in a food processor until smooth. In a large Dutch oven, heat 1 tablespoon oil over high heat for about 1 minute. Add pureed mixture and cook, stirring frequently, until the mixture has darkened in color, about 10 minutes. Stir in cooked vegetables, broth, diced tomatoes, black beans, corn, chicken, remaining chipotles (to taste) and lime juice. Bring to a boil. Reduce heat to low and simmer to blend flavors, about 15 minutes or longer if desired. Ladle soup into bowls. Garnish with avocado, sour cream, tortilla chips and cheese as desired.

12 servings

## Friendship Chili

3   pounds lean ground hamburger

1   pound ground pork

1   large white onion, chopped

4   cans (16 ounces) light red kidney beans

1/2   cup chili powder or to taste

1   teaspoon ground oregano

3/4   cup brown sugar, packed

1/4   teaspoon ground red pepper

9   drops Tabasco sauce, or to taste

1   bottle tomato juice (64 ounce)

2   cups water

Brown the hamburger, pork and onion together. Drain excess fat. In a 12 quart stock pot combine meat and onion mixture with beans, chili powder, oregano, brown sugar, pepper, Tabasco sauce, tomato juice and water. Bring ingredients to a boil. Reduce heat to low and simmer for about 2 hours.

10 servings

## The Feed Store
## Mushroom Bisque

| | | | | |
|---|---|---|---|---|
| 1 | pound fresh mushrooms | 1/2 | cup (1 stick) unsalted butter | |
| 1 | medium yellow onion | 1/2 | cup flour, more if needed | |
| 5 | cups chicken broth | 4 | cups whole milk (1 quart) | |
| 1 | teaspoon salt | 1 | cup heavy whipping cream | |
| 1/2 | teaspoon white pepper | 2 | tablespoons sherry (optional) | |
| 1/4 | teaspoon Tabasco sauce | | | |

Wipe mushrooms carefully, trim the stems and thinly slice (a food processor works well for this). Peel and finely dice the onion. Bring the chicken broth to a boil, add the mushrooms and onion. Return to a boil; reduce heat to maintain a steady, slow simmer. Add salt, pepper and Tabasco sauce and allow the mushroom mixture to simmer 30 – 40 minutes.

Slowly melt the butter, using a pan large enough to hold the flour and milk. As soon as the butter is melted, beat the flour into it with a wire whisk, a little at a time. Leave the heat on, as you want to cook the flour and butter together gently for about two minutes to make a roux. As you are making the roux, bring the milk to a boil in another pan. As soon as the milk reaches a boil, pour it into the roux all at once. Immediately begin beating the milk and roux with the wire whisk. Steady consistent strokes are more important than speed or force. The sauce will at first look curdled, then lumpy, but the longer you beat it, the smoother it will get. It will take 2 – 4 minutes of steady beating to produce a creamy white sauce.

Finally, combine the smooth white sauce with the mushroom broth and then add the cream. Sherry may be added, but not until just before serving.

Yield: 3 quarts

*Note: This is the first soup The Feed Store offered when it opened in the autumn of 1977, and it's made daily in either 26 or 40 quart quantities. We've sold well over 1 1/2 million cups of this particular soup and it remains one of our most popular.*

## Sebastian's Hideout
## Potato Bleu Cheese Soup

| | | | |
|---|---|---|---|
| 3 | tablespoons vegetable oil | 10 | cups chicken broth |
| 3 | yellow onions, finely chopped | 12 | ounces crumbled blue cheese (or Gorgonzola) |
| 5 – 6 | stalks celery, finely chopped | 2 | cups heavy whipping cream |
| 3 | tablespoons minced fresh garlic | 1 | cup half and half |
| 5 | pounds red potatoes, quartered | | salt and pepper to taste |

Add vegetable oil to 6 quart or larger warmed stock pot. Add onions, celery and garlic and sauté until soft. Add potatoes and chicken broth. Simmer on medium-high heat until potatoes are fork tender. Add scalded heavy cream 1 cup at a time to stock pot. Stir in half and half and cheese. Add salt and pepper.

Working in small batches, slightly puree soup mixture in stand blender or an emersion blender directly in stock pot until desired consistency is reached. Blend longer for smoother creamier soup or less for heartier chunky potato style. Continue to adjust salt and pepper to taste. Taste soup throughout process. Cheeses differ in their depth of flavor and can change saltiness.

## Carol Jean's Fine Cuisine
## Oyster and Lettuce Soup

| | |
|---|---|
| 1 medium onion, diced | 2 heads Boston bibb, washed and chopped |
| 1/4 cup (1/2 stick) butter, plus more for serving | 1/4 cup chopped parsley |
| 1/2 cup flour | 1 pint chopped oysters with their liquid |
| 1 teaspoon grated nutmeg | |
| 3 cups chicken stock | 1/2 cup dry sherry |
| 1 cup milk or light cream | Salt to taste |
| 1 tablespoon chicken base | Pepper to taste |

Sauté the diced onion in butter until it becomes transparent. Add flour and stir until mixed. Add nutmeg, stock, cream, chicken base and lettuce. Stir and bring to boiling point. Reduce heat and simmer 30 – 40 minutes. Puree the soup in small batches in a food processor. Return to heat and add parsley, oysters and sherry. Bring just to boiling point. Stir in salt and pepper to taste. Serve with an extra bit of butter.

8 servings

## Pasfield Potato Soup

*Variation: A dollop of sour cream can be placed on top of the soup when served. Green onions or chives may be used as a garnish.*

| | |
|---|---|
| 4 large baking potatoes | 1 cup sour cream (optional) |
| 2/3 cup (1 stick plus 3 tablespoons) butter or margarine | 4 green onions, sliced thinly including green part (optional) |
| 2/3 cup flour | 12 ounces bacon, cooked and crumbled (optional) |
| 6 cups milk, divided (milk of choice) | 1 1/4 cups shredded Monterey Jack, cheddar or Provolone cheese, shredded (optional) |
| 3/4 teaspoon salt | |
| 1/2 teaspoon pepper | |
| 1 tablespoon chicken base | |

Preheat oven to 400°. Wash potatoes, prick with a fork and bake for one hour until soft when gently squeezed. Cool. Cut into 1/2 – inch pieces either retaining skin or removing it. Melt butter in a large saucepan. Add flour, stirring until smooth. Cook 1 – 2 minutes, stirring constantly. Add four cups of milk quickly, stirring continuously. Add remaining milk. Cook over medium heat stirring continuously until mixture is thick and bubbly. Add potato cubes, salt, pepper and chicken base. Cook until heated through. Additional milk may be added if soup becomes too thick. Stir in sour cream and/or onions if desired. Garnish with bacon and cheese.

8 servings

## Cheesehead Soup

1 quart water
4 chicken broth cubes or 4 teaspoons chicken base
2 1/2 cups diced potatoes
1 cup diced celery
1/2 cup diced onion
1 (16 ounce) bag mixed cauliflower, broccoli, and carrots

2 (10 3/4 ounce) cans cream of chicken soup
1 (1 pound) package Velveeta cheese, cubed into 1 – inch squares

*Tip: This soup freezes well. Vary amount of vegetables to suit your taste.*

Combine the water and chicken broth cubes or base over medium heat until cubes/ paste have dissolved. Add potatoes, celery and onion and cook 20 minutes. Add the cauliflower, broccoli, and carrots; cook 10 minutes. Add cream of chicken soup and stir until the soup dissolves. Add the cheese and cook over low to medium heat until cheese melts. Continue cooking over low heat or place pan on diffuser, stirring frequently, until vegetables are done; about 20 minutes.

12 servings

## Wild Rice Soup

1/2 cup (3 ounces) wild rice
2 1/2 cups water
1 teaspoon salt, divided
2 tablespoons butter
2 tablespoons chopped onion
1/4 cup flour

4 cups chicken broth
1/3 cup shredded carrots
3 tablespoons slivered almonds
2 cups half and half
2 tablespoons dry cooking sherry minced parsley or chives to suit

*Tip: It is best to make the day before.*

Rinse rice thoroughly in a strainer. Combine rice, water and 1/2 teaspoon salt; cook covered until most of the water is absorbed. Set aside. Melt butter in a sauce pan and sauté onions. Blend in the flour and gradually add the broth whisking until mixture thickens. Stir in cooked rice, salt, carrot and almonds. Simmer about 5 minutes. Combine half and half and sherry and blend into the rice mixture. Refrigerate overnight. Remove from refrigerator and place over medium heat until warm. Add parsley and/or chives to suit.

12 servings

# Creamy Leek Soup with Brie

*Variation: Sauté 2 peeled, diced potatoes along with the leeks and stir in 1/3 cup bacon crumbles after adding the cheese.*

| | |
|---|---|
| 1/2 cup (1 stick) unsalted butter, divided | 1 1/2 pounds mild, creamy Brie cheese, trimmed of rind and cut in 1 – inch cubes |
| 8 large leeks, white part only, sliced and washed well | 1/2 cup dry white wine |
| 4 cups chicken broth (regular or low-sodium) | Salt to taste |
| 1/2 cup flour | White pepper, to taste |
| 4 cups half and half | Chopped fresh chives for garnish |

Melt 1/4 cup of the butter in a large, heavy sauté pan. Add leeks and sauté over medium-low heat until soft. Add chicken broth and increase the heat to bring soup to a boil. Reduce heat, cover and simmer 25 minutes. Cool slightly and puree leeks in food processor or blender. In a soup pot, melt remaining butter and add flour, stirring to incorporate well. Gradually add half and half, whisking until smooth. Add cheese (about 1/4 at a time) and stir until melted and smooth. Add wine, chicken broth and pureed leeks. Add salt and pepper to taste. Heat through. Serve garnished with fresh chives.

6 servings

# Augie's Front Burner
# Scallop Rockefeller Soup

*Note: Roux is a thickening agent made with equal parts of butter and flour. Use 4 ounces butter (8 tablespoons) and 4 ounces (4 tablespoons) of flour. Melt the butter over medium heat. Add flour slowly but all at once, whisking vigorously. When it begins to bubble, reduce the heat to low and lessen whisking. Cook until it offers a toasty aroma and then continue cooking 2 more minutes.*

| | |
|---|---|
| 2 cups chopped bacon | 2 – 3 tablespoons roux |
| 1 large onion, diced | 1 ounce (1 tablespoon) pernod (absinthe flavored liquor) |
| 1 clove minced garlic | 1 cup Parmesan cheese |
| 2 quarts (8 cups) chicken or fish stock | 1 (10 ounce) package chopped spinach, thawed and well drained |
| 2 cups heavy cream | 2 cups baby bay scallops |
| Salt | |
| Pepper | |
| Nutmeg | |

In a large soup pot, sauté bacon until crisp. Add onion and garlic and stir for a few minutes. Add stock, cream, salt, pepper and nutmeg to taste. As this reaches boiling, thicken with a little roux.

The soup should come to a soft boil. Slowly add pernod, cheese, spinach and scallops. Cook for another 5 – 10 minutes. Adjust to taste with additional salt and pepper if needed.

8 – 10 servings

## Lobster Bisque

6 tablespoons (3/4 stick) butter, divided

4 tablespoons green pepper, finely chopped

4 tablespoons onion, finely chopped

1 scallion, finely chopped

2 tablespoons parsley, finely chopped

1 1/2 cups fresh mushrooms, sliced

2 tablespoons flour

1 cup milk

1 teaspoon salt

1/8 teaspoon white pepper
   Dash of Tabasco sauce

1 1/2 cups half and half

1 1/2 cups cooked lobster meat (canned or frozen)

3 tablespoons dry sherry

*Note: An elegant first course for formal dining or a wonderful main course with a green salad of your choice.*

Heat 4 tablespoons of the butter in skillet. Add green pepper, onion, scallion, parsley and mushrooms. Sauté until vegetables are soft (about 5 minutes). In a saucepan, heat remaining 2 tablespoons of butter. Stir in flour. Add milk and cook over medium to medium-high heat, stirring constantly until thickened and smooth. Stir in salt, pepper and Tabasco to taste. Add sautéed vegetables and the half and half. Bring to a boil, stirring constantly. Reduce heat and add the lobster meat. Simmer uncovered for 5 minutes. Just before serving, stir in the dry sherry.

4 servings

## Shrimp Coconut Soup

1 tablespoon vegetable or coconut oil

2 tablespoons grated fresh ginger

1 stalk lemongrass, thinly sliced white part only

2 teaspoons red curry paste, minced

4 cups chicken broth

3 tablespoons fish sauce

1 tablespoon light brown sugar

3 (13 1/2 ounce) cans coconut milk

1/2 pound fresh shitake mushrooms, sliced

1 pound medium shrimp, peeled and deveined

2 tablespoons fresh lime juice
   Salt to taste

1/4 cup fresh cilantro, chopped

*Note: Chicken can be substituted for the shrimp. For less spice, reduce the amount of the red curry paste. If whole lemongrass is not available, substitute 2 tablespoons of lemongrass paste. Fresh or frozen corn makes a nice addition.*

Heat the oil in a large pot over medium heat. Cook and stir the ginger, lemongrass and curry paste in the heated oil for 1 minute. Slowly pour the chicken broth over the mixture, stirring continuously. Stir in the fish sauce and brown sugar; simmer for 15 minutes. Stir in the coconut milk and mushrooms; cook and stir until the mushrooms are soft, about 5 minutes. Add the shrimp; cook until shrimp is no longer translucent, about 5 minutes. Remove from heat; stir in the lime juice; season with salt; garnish with cilantro.

8 servings

# Vegetable Beef Soup

*Variation: For vegetables, use one diced onion, 2 diced medium potatoes, 1 (32 ounce) package frozen soup vegetables and 1 cup pearl barley.*

*Note: If you choose not to use oxtails substitute beef broth.*

**Soup Base:**

| | |
|---|---|
| 1/3 | cup flour |
| 1 | tablespoon salt |
| 1/2 | teaspoon freshly ground black pepper |
| 1/4 | teaspoon thyme or marjoram |
| 4 | pounds oxtails |
| 3 – 4 | tablespoons olive or canola oil |
| 1 | cup beef broth or 1 cup water and 1 teaspoon of beef base or bouillon |
| 1 | cup Burgundy wine |
| 1 | leek, sliced, white only |
| | Water to cover |
| 1 | tablespoon sugar |
| 2 | cloves garlic, minced |
| 1 | bay leaf |
| 2 | cups tomatoes, diced or 1 (8 ounce) can tomato sauce |

**Soup:**

| | |
|---|---|
| 3 | pounds stew meat or chuck roast cut into pieces |
| 64 | ounces tomato or V8 juice or 16 ounces of tomato sauce and broth to make 8 cups |
| 6-8 | cups oxtail broth or beef broth |
| 4 | celery stalks, chopped |
| 6 | carrots, chopped |
| 3 | medium onions, chopped |
| 3 | medium potatoes, chopped |
| 1 | cup shredded cabbage (optional) |
| | Salt to taste |
| | Pepper to taste |

For the stock, combine flour, salt, pepper and thyme or marjoram. Coat the oxtails with seasoned flour. Brown the oxtails on all sides in oil in a stock pot or Dutch oven. Add broth, Burgundy and leek. Add just enough water to barely cover the oxtails. Cover the pot and bring to a boil. Skim and add sugar, garlic, bay leaf and tomatoes or sauce. Simmer 2 – 2 1/2 hours. Skim off fat as oxtails cook. Remove oxtails and bay leaf from broth base. Can be made up to two days ahead and refrigerated until ready to use.

For the soup, brown the stew meat. Add the soup base to the meat. Add the tomato juice, celery, carrots, onions, potatoes and cabbage. If you prefer to add other vegetables, reduce the amount of carrots, onions and potatoes and replace that amount with vegetables of your choice (corn, peas, lima beans, etc.) Bring to a boil; lower heat and simmer about 25 minutes. Test for flavor and add salt and pepper to taste. Simmer another 30 minutes.

10 – 12 servings

*This block print, entitled* The Coal Miners' Lunch, *hangs in the Sangamo Club Grill Room. It reminds us of the black gold under our land and the men who labor to provide us with the fuel to warm our homes and to create electricity.*

## Tuscan Chicken Stew

| | |
|---|---|
| 1 **pound boneless, skinless chicken breast or tenders** | 1 **(14 ounce) can chicken broth** |
| 1/2 **teaspoon crushed, dried rosemary** | 1 **(16 ounce can) cannellini beans, rinsed and drained** |
| 1/2 **teaspoon salt** | 1 **(7 ounce) jar roasted red peppers, drained and coarsely chopped** |
| 1/4 **teaspoon ground pepper** | 3 1/2 **cups torn spinach** |
| 2 **teaspoons olive oil** | |
| 2 **teaspoons minced garlic, can use bottled** | |

*Note: If preparing in advance, wait to add the spinach after it is reheated and piping hot.*

Cut chicken into 1 – inch pieces. Combine the rosemary, salt and pepper. Season the chicken pieces with the seasonings. Heat the oil in a large, nonstick skillet over medium heat. Add chicken and cook for about 3 minutes. Add garlic and sauté one minute. Add chicken broth, beans and roasted red peppers and bring to a boil. Reduce heat and simmer for 10 minutes until chicken is cooked through. Stir in spinach and simmer one more minute.

4 servings

## Jambalaya Soup

| | |
|---|---|
| 1 **tablespoon olive oil** | 2 **(15 ounce) cans diced tomatoes (fire roasted are good)** |
| 1/2 **pound sliced, spicy Andouille or Italian sausage** | 2 **cups chicken broth** |
| 1 **cup diced onion** | 1 1/2 **cups finely chopped cauliflower** |
| 3/4 **cup chopped green pepper** | 1/2 **pound raw shrimp** |
| 1/2 **cup chopped celery** | **Dash of cayenne pepper (optional for heat)** |
| 1 1/8 **teaspoons Cajun seasoning, divided (optional)** | |
| 1 **bay leaf** | |

*Variation: Substitute shredded cooked chicken for sausage.*

In a large sauce pan, heat olive oil. Add sausage, onion, green pepper and celery. Sauté for about 5 minutes. Add 1 teaspoon of Cajun seasoning and bay leaf; cook for another minute. Add tomatoes, chicken broth and cauliflower. Bring to boil; reduce heat and simmer for 20 minutes. Remove bay leaf.

In another skillet sauté shrimp, 1/8 teaspoon Cajun seasoning and a dash of cayenne, if using, and sauté for about 2 minutes until shrimp is done. Do not overcook shrimp. Add shrimp to the soup and serve.

4 – 6 servings

# Chatty Cathy Chili

**Chili:**
- 1 tablespoon vegetable oil
- 2 pounds lean ground beef or turkey or mixture
- 2 tablespoons chili powder
- 2 tablespoons cumin
- 1 tablespoon paprika
- 2 teaspoons salt
- 2 teaspoons ground coriander
- 2 teaspoon ground cinnamon
- 2 teaspoon cocoa powder
- 1 teaspoon garlic powder
- 1/2 teaspoon cayenne pepper
- 1 large yellow onion, diced
- 6 cloves garlic, diced
- 3 cups diced sugar pumpkin, butternut squash or 1 1/2 cups pumpkin puree
- 1 (28 ounce) can diced, fire roasted tomatoes
- 1 (7 ounce) can diced, roasted green chilies
- 1 (15 ounce) can tomato sauce
- 1 cup chicken or beef stock

**Avocado Cream:**
- 2 avocados, peeled and pitted
- Zest of 1 orange
- Juice of 2 oranges
- 1 teaspoon ground coriander
- 1/2 teaspoon salt

Heat the oil in a large soup pot over medium high heat. Add the meat and cook until no longer pink. While the meat browns, combine chili powder, cumin, paprika, salt, coriander, cinnamon, cocoa powder, garlic powder and cayenne in a medium bowl. Using a slotted spoon remove the beef and place in the spice mixture bowl, leaving the fat in the pot. Add diced onion and garlic to pot and sauté for 3 – 4 minutes stirring occasionally or until onions have softened. Add the spice mixture and stir well. Add diced pumpkin and sauté for another 5 - 6 minutes. Add tomatoes, green chilies, tomato sauce and stock and bring to a low boil. Cover and cook another 10 - 12 minutes, stirring occasionally, until the pumpkin is fork tender. Continue cooking at a simmer until the consistancy is to your liking.

For the avocado cream, blend avocados, orange zest, orange juice, coriander and salt in a food processor until smooth. Serve chili with a dollop of the avocado cream.

10 – 12 servings

In 1935 Island Bay Yacht Club was incorporated, providing lake enthusiasts a place to gather with family and friends. It began with a tiny building where hamburger cuisine and drinks were served and there were a few boat tie-ups. It has become a key dining spot with greatly expanded facilities.

## Mary Vienna White Bean Soup

| | |
|---|---|
| 1 pound quality sausage | 3/4 cup macaroni noodles |
| 2 medium onions, chopped | 2 tablespoons pesto (optional) |
| 1 cup sliced carrots | Salt to taste |
| 4 cloves garlic, minced | 1 teaspoon freshly ground pepper |
| 1 (28 ounce) can diced tomatoes | |
| 2 (14 1/2 ounce) cans white beans, drained and rinsed | 2 cups of chopped kale or spinach (optional) |
| 8 cups chicken broth | Water or chicken broth as needed |
| Piece of Parmesan cheese rind (optional) | |

Crumble sausage and sauté with onion and carrots in a large soup pot until the sausage is cooked through. Add garlic and sauté for another 2 – 3 minutes. Drain grease if necessary. Add tomatoes; beans, chicken broth and cheese rind (if using). Simmer 30 minutes or until flavors meld. Add macaroni noodles, pesto (if using), salt and pepper and cook an additional 10 minutes until the noodles are tender. Add kale or spinach (if using) and cook for a few additional minutes. Add additional water if the soup is too thick for your taste. Adjust seasonings. Remove cheese rind (if used) before serving. Serve with freshly grated Parmesan cheese and crusty French bread.

10 – 12 servings

## Pasta Fagioli

| | |
|---|---|
| 1 pound ground beef | 1 (15 ounce) can tomato sauce |
| 1 cup diced onion | 1 (12 ounce) can V8 juice |
| 1 cup julienned or chopped carrot | 1 tablespoon white vinegar |
| 1 cup chopped celery | 1 1/2 teaspoon salt |
| 2 cloves garlic, minced | 1 teaspoon oregano |
| 2 (14 1/2 ounce) cans diced tomatoes | 1 teaspoon basil |
| | 1/2 teaspoon pepper |
| 1 (15 ounce) can red kidney beans (with liquid) | 1/2 teaspoon thyme |
| 1 (15 ounce) can great northern beans (with liquid) | 1 1/2 cups ditali pasta or other small grain pasta |
| | Chicken broth as needed |

*Tip: This can be made in a crock pot.*

Brown beef over medium heat and drain off most of the fat. Add onion, carrot, celery and garlic and sauté for 10 minutes. Add tomatoes, kidney beans, northern beans, tomato sauce, V8 juice, vinegar, salt, oregano, basil, pepper and thyme; simmer 1 hour. Add pasta to the soup and simmer about 10 minutes until cooked. If soup is too thick, add chicken broth as needed and heat through.

12 – 14 servings

## Unstuffed Pepper Soup

| | |
|---|---|
| 1 1/2 | **pounds lean ground beef or turkey** |
| 1 | **large onion, chopped** |
| 4 | **garlic cloves, crushed** |
| 4 | **peppers, diced (green or mixture of colors)** |
| 2 | **(14 1/2 ounce) cans beef broth** |
| 2 | **(10 1/2 ounce) cans condensed tomato soup** |
| 1 | **(28 ounce) can crushed or diced tomatoes** |
| | **Tabasco sauce to taste** |
| | **Freshly ground pepper to taste** |
| 1 1/2 | **cups of cooked rice** |
| 2 1/2 | **cups of fresh or frozen corn (optional)** |
| | **Sour cream or shredded cheddar cheese for garnish** |

Cook meat, onion, garlic and diced pepper in a large sauce pan or Dutch oven over medium heat until meat is no longer pink. Drain fat as needed. Stir in broth, soup, tomatoes, Tabasco sauce and pepper. Bring to a boil. Reduce heat. Cover and simmer for at least 30 minutes, stirring occasionally. Add rice and corn (if using) and heat through. Add a dollop of sour cream or a sprinkling of cheddar cheese when serving, if desired.

8 servings

*The delectable food and elegant presentation is not all that Carol Jean's Fine Cuisine offers their patrons. Your experience is enhanced in their country gardens with the melody of birdsong, a breeze humming through chimes and the gurgle of a waterfall.*

## Beaver Dam Beef Stew

1/4 cup vegetable oil

1 1/4 pounds beef stew meat, cut into 1 – inch pieces

1 large onion

6 large garlic cloves, minced

4 cups carrots, peeled and cut into 1/2 – inch pieces

6 large garlic cloves, minced

6 cups beef stock or canned beef broth

1 cup red wine

2 tablespoons tomato paste

1 tablespoon sugar

2 teaspoons dried thyme

1 teaspoon salt

1 teaspoon black pepper

2 tablespoons Worcestershire sauce

2 bay leaves

1/4 cup flour

1/2 cup water

*Variation: Add 2 1/2 pounds russet potatoes, peeled and cut into 1/2 – inch pieces.*

Heat oil in a heavy large pot over high heat. Add beef and sauté until brown on all sides. Remove from pot. Add onion and sauté for a few minutes. Add garlic and sauté for a minute, then add carrots for 5 – 6 additional minutes. Return beef to the pan, adding beef stock, wine, tomato paste, sugar, thyme, salt, pepper, Worcestershire sauce and bay leaves. Stir to combine. Bring mixture to a boil. Reduce heat to medium low; cover and simmer for 1 1/2 – 2 hours until vegetables and beef are tender. Remove bay leaves and tilt pan to spoon off any fat. Mix flour and water. Add to the beef and boil until thickened. Add additional salt and pepper to taste. Serve with mashed potatoes.

Serves 4 – 6

*The grounds of the Fraase Farm are ideal for all types of gatherings. They can serve partygoers throughout the year, be it in their gardens or under the canopy of a heated tent.*

# Main Event

*— continued on next page*

 *The crown indicates a celebrity's recipe.*

*The wine glass indicates The Corkscrew Wine Emporium's recommendation.*

# Main Event

The crown indicates a celebrity's recipe.

 The wine glass indicates The Corkscrew Wine Emporium's recommendation.

## Naples Chicken

| | | | | |
|---|---|---|---|---|
| 8 – 10 | chicken breast halves | 1 | cup imported pitted kalamata olives | |
| 6 | cloves garlic, minced | | | |
| 1 | tablespoon dried thyme | 2 1/2 | cups mixture of dried apricots, dried small figs, dates and/or prunes, chopped | |
| 2 | teaspoons ground cumin | | | |
| 1 1/2 | teaspoons ground ginger | 1/4 | cup brown sugar, packed | |
| 1/2 | teaspoon salt | 3/4 | cup dry white wine | |
| 1/2 | cup red wine vinegar | | Grated zest of 2 lemons (optional) | |
| 1/2 | cup extra virgin olive oil | | | |
| 4 | teaspoons capers with a little juice | | | |

Combine chicken, garlic, thyme, cumin, ginger, salt, vinegar, olive oil, capers, olives and selected dried fruits in a large bowl or plastic zipper bag. Cover and refrigerate at least 4 hours or overnight.

Preheat oven to 350°. Grease or spray a large baking dish. Arrange chicken and marinade in a single layer in a large baking dish. Sprinkle with brown sugar and pour wine between the chicken breasts. Cover the pan with aluminum foil and bake for 20 minutes. Remove foil and continue baking; baste frequently with pan juices until chicken is tender, about 40 more minutes. Use a slotted spoon to remove the chicken, olives, apricots and figs to a large serving platter. Top with a few spoonfuls of pan juices and sprinkle with grated lemon zest. Serve immediately. Pan juices may be served in a gravy boat.

8 – 10 servings

*Note: This goes well with Lemon Rice Pilaf, see page 168.*

*Recommended wine – A full bodied, fruit-forward wine, such as Pinot Grigio or Argentine Chardonnay, marries well with the fruit flavors displayed here.*

## Rustic Rosemary Chicken

| | | | | |
|---|---|---|---|---|
| 3 – 4 | pound whole chicken | 2 | teaspoons dried rosemary, crumbled | |
| 3 | tablespoons soy sauce | | | |
| 2 | tablespoons lemon juice | 2 | cloves garlic, pressed | |
| 2 | tablespoons olive oil | 1 | lemon, cut in half | |

Preheat oven to 350°. Place chicken, breast-side up, on rack in a shallow roasting pan. Blend soy sauce, lemon juice, olive oil, rosemary and garlic. Reserve half of the mixture for basting. Brush chicken cavity and skin thoroughly with half the mixture. Place lemon halves in cavity. Roast for 1 hour and 45 minutes. Baste with reserved soy mixture every 30 minutes. Remove from oven and let rest 10 minutes before carving.

4 – 6 servings

*Recommended wine – Italian Vernaccia or California Sauvignon Blanc. Both of these wines are dry, crisp and clean which balance the aromatic dish.*

## Chicken Artichoke Casserole

*Tip: Use delicatessen roasted chicken. If Gruyère cheese is not available substitute any good Swiss type cheese.*

*Recommended wine – Gruner Veltliner from Austria. Not many wines pair with artichoke, but this super-dry white is always perfect.*

4   **cups cooked chicken**

2   **(8.5 ounce) cans artichoke hearts, drained and chopped**

1   **cup (2 sticks) plus 2 tablespoons butter, divided**

1/2   **cup flour**

1/4   **teaspoon cayenne pepper**

1   **teaspoon salt**

1   **clove garlic, crushed**

3 1/2   **cups milk**

1   **cup grated sharp cheddar cheese**

1   **cup shredded Gruyère cheese**

8   **ounces mushrooms, chopped**

1   **cup bread crumbs**

Preheat oven to 350°. Spray or grease a 3 quart oven-proof dish. Spread chicken in prepared dish. Top with artichokes. Melt 1 cup butter in a saucepan; add flour, cayenne pepper, salt and garlic and stir until smooth. Cook 1 minute to cook flour, stirring constantly. Gradually stir in milk. Cook over medium heat until thick and smooth. Add cheddar and Gruyère and stir until melted. Add mushrooms. Pour sauce over chicken and artichokes. Melt remaining butter and combine with bread crumbs. Spread evenly on casserole. Bake for 60 minutes or until the casserole is set and not loose when the pan is moved.

12 – 16 servings

## Chicken in Orange Sauce

*Hint: Serve with a fruit plate of fresh pineapple, strawberries and white and red grapes.*

*Recommended wine – White Cotes du Rhone from France. This is usually a blend of Roussane and Marsanne grapes. The richness of the wine contrasts with the citrus flavors.*

**Chicken:**

8   **boneless, skinless chicken breast halves**

1/2   **teaspoon pepper**

1/2   **teaspoon paprika**

1/2   **teaspoon garlic powder**

**Sauce:**

1   **cup concentrated frozen orange juice, thawed**

10   **tablespoons (1 stick plus 2 tablespoons) butter, melted**

1   **teaspoon ground ginger**

**Rice:**

1   **cup rice; white, brown or mixture**

1/2   **cup golden raisins, preferably soaked in water for an hour for plumping (optional)**

1/2   **cup slivered almonds (optional)**

Preheat oven to 375°. Grease or spray a 9 x 13 – inch baking pan. Wash chicken and dry with paper towels. Combine salt, pepper, paprika and garlic powder. Sprinkle on each piece of chicken. Place in prepared pan. Bake uncovered for 40 minutes. Mix concentrated orange juice, butter and ginger and spoon evenly over chicken. Bake an additional 20 minutes.

While the chicken is baking, prepare the rice. Cook rice according to the directions on the package. Remove from heat and add raisins and almonds just before serving. Serve chicken over the rice and top with a small amount of the orange sauce.

8 servings

## Illini Country Club
## Chicken Pad Thai

**Peanut Sauce:**

- 1 can coconut milk
- 2 cups smooth peanut butter
- 2 tablespoons minced garlic
- 2 tablespoons sugar
- 1/4 teaspoon cayenne pepper
- 1 cup lime juice
- 1 cup soy sauce
- 1 cup vegetable oil
- 1 cup water

**Stir Fry:**

- 1 package (16 ounce) dry packet flat rice noodles
- 6 (6 ounce) boneless, skinless chicken breasts
- 2 tablespoons minced ginger
- 2 tablespoons minced garlic
- 2 stalks lemongrass, cleaned and chopped

- 2 tablespoons sesame seeds
- 1/2 tablespoon sesame oil
  Zest of 1 lime
- 1/2 cup teriyaki sauce
- 1/4 cup chopped cilantro
- 1/4 cup vegetable oil, extra for wok
- 1/3 cup diced shallots
- 1/2 cup sliced carrots
- 1 cup cabbage, thinly sliced
- 1 cup broccolini, thinly sliced
- 1/2 cup bean sprouts
- 1 cup pea pods, cut into 1/2 – inch pieces
- 2 limes, juiced
- 2 cups chicken stock
- 1/2 cup teriyaki sauce
- 1/4 cup soy sauce
- 1/2 bunch cilantro
  Salt

For the peanut sauce, combine coconut milk, peanut butter, garlic, sugar, cayenne, lime juice, soy sauce, oil and water; warm over medium-low heat, whipping until smooth. Cool.

For the stir-fry, place a medium sized pot of water on the stove and bring to a boil. Add rice noodles and cook until tender, about 5 minutes. Drain and chill. Cut chicken breasts into thin strips and place in a bowl. Combine ginger, garlic, lemongrass, sesame seeds, sesame oil, lime zest, teriyaki sauce, cilantro and oil. Pour over chicken breasts. Heat wok or sauté pan until very hot. Add oil to wok. Drain chicken and sear in wok until brown. Add shallots, carrots, cabbage, broccolini, bean sprouts and pea pods and stir fry until vegetables are tender crisp. Add rice noodles, lime juice, chicken stock, teriyaki sauce, soy sauce, cilantro, salt to taste and the peanut sauce.

8 servings

*For over 100 years, Illini Country Club has been enriching the lives of its members and families by providing the finest in dining, social and recreational activities.*

# Chicken Vesuvio

*Recommended wine – Vermentino from Italy or Sardinia. This aromatic, medium-bodied white wine from Sardinia will perfectly complement the herbaceous flavors in this dish.*

| | |
|---|---|
| 1/3 cup flour | 3 pound fryer chicken cut into 8 pieces |
| 1 1/2 teaspoons dry basil | 3 large russet potatoes, scrubbed and cut into lengthwise wedges |
| 3/4 teaspoon dry oregano | 3 tablespoons minced fresh parsley |
| 1/4 teaspoon dry thyme | 3 cloves garlic, minced |
| 1/4 teaspoon pepper | 3/4 cup dry white wine |
| 1/2 teaspoon salt | |
| Pinch of rosemary | |
| Pinch of sage | |
| 1/2 cup olive oil | |

Preheat oven to 375°. Mix flour, basil, oregano, thyme, pepper, salt, rosemary and sage in a shallow dish. Coat chicken lightly with flour mixture, shaking off excess. Heat oil in heavy frying pan and fry chicken until brown all over. Remove to paper towel and blot off excess oil. Add potato wedges to pan and fry until light brown. Drain on a paper towel. Pour about 2 – 3 tablespoons of pan drippings into an oven safe roasting pan. Arrange potatoes on the bottom of the roasting pan and lay chicken pieces over potatoes. Sprinkle with parsley and garlic. Pour wine over all. Bake covered with foil for 20 minutes. Remove foil and bake for an additional 20 minutes. Serve with pan juices.

4 servings

# Comfort Chicken Casserole

*Recommended wine – The New Zealand Sauvignon Blanc's grassy, zingy, crisp wine contrasts with the creaminess of this casserole.*

| | |
|---|---|
| 1 cup sour cream | 1 (4 ounce) can chopped green chilies, drained |
| 1/3 cup milk | 2 – 3 cups cubed cooked chicken |
| 1/4 cup chopped onion | 4 ounces shredded Monterey Jack cheese |
| 1/2 teaspoon garlic salt | 2 ounces shredded cheddar cheese |
| 1/4 teaspoon cumin | Prepared biscuit dough of choice |
| Dash hot pepper sauce | Paprika to taste |
| 1 (10 3/4 ounce) can cream of chicken soup | |
| 1 (9 ounce) package chopped spinach, thawed and drained | |

Preheat oven to 375°. Lightly grease a 9 x 13 – inch pan. In a large bowl, combine sour cream, milk, onion, garlic salt, cumin, hot pepper sauce, soup, spinach and green chilies. In another bowl, combine and lightly toss chicken, Monterey Jack and cheddar cheese. Spoon half of the spinach mixture into prepared pan. Sprinkle half of chicken mixture on top. Repeat layers. Prepare your favorite biscuits and place small spoonfuls on top of pan. Sprinkle with paprika. Bake for 45 minutes or until biscuits are golden brown.

6 - 8 servings

## Gourmet Chicken Breasts

6 **boneless, skinless chicken breasts**
1 **(8 ounce) container chive onion soft cream cheese**

6 **slices prosciutto or thin sliced ham**
12 **slices bacon**

*Recommended wine – New World Pinot Noir will stand up to the bacon flavors, as will Dolcetto.*

Preheat over 350˚. Pound chicken breasts until they are even in thickness. Spread thin layer of cream cheese on chicken. Place prosciutto/ham over cream cheese. Roll up chicken and wrap 2 slices bacon around the roll. Bake uncovered 1 – 1 1/2 hours until completely cooked. Serve with rice and salad.

6 servings

## Grilled Chicken Kebabs

4 **tablespoons extra virgin olive oil**
4 **minced garlic cloves**
1/2 **teaspoon dried mint**
1/2 **teaspoon dried oregano**
1 **teaspoon salt**
1 **teaspoon cracked ground black pepper**
4 **tablespoons fresh lemon juice**

1 1/2 **pounds skinless boneless chicken breast, cut into 1 – inch pieces**
1 **red onion, cut into 1 – inch pieces**
2 **small zucchini squash thinly sliced**
8 **12 – inch metal skewers or soaked wooden skewers**

*Recommended wine – California Rhone Style Red. The smoke fruit flavors in this syrah blend is well-suited to grilled fare.*

Combine oil, garlic, mint, oregano, salt, pepper and lemon juice in a small bowl or measuring cup. Place chicken, onion and zucchini in a zipper bag and add marinade. Refrigerate a minimum of 4 hours or overnight.

Prepare grill to medium high heat. Alternate the chicken, zucchini and onion on skewers. Grill until chicken is cooked through, turning several times.

8 servings

*The Illinois State Library is the principal information resource for state government. The library has a collection of more than 5 million items. It serves as regional federal documents depository and maintains an authoritative collection of historic and contemporary Illinois documents.*

## Grilled Margarita Chicken

*Variation: Add 1 tablespoon minced fresh cilantro to the marinade, and if you like a bit of sweetness, also add 1 – 2 tablespoons of honey.*

*Recommended wine – Both Riesling and Gruner Veltliner have a citrus backbone that will bridge the lime/ orange flavors of the chicken.*

1/2 cup gold tequila

1 cup freshly squeezed lime juice (5 or 6 limes)

1/2 cup freshly squeezed orange juice (1 or 2 oranges)

1 tablespoon chili powder

1 tablespoon minced fresh jalapeño pepper

1 tablespoon minced fresh garlic

3 whole boneless skin-on chicken breasts

2 teaspoons kosher salt

1 teaspoon freshly ground black pepper

Combine the tequila, lime juice, orange juice, chili powder, jalapeño pepper and garlic in a large bowl. Split the chicken breasts and add to the bowl, stirring to thoroughly coat chicken. Cover and refrigerate overnight.

Heat the grill to medium and brush the rack with oil to prevent the chicken from sticking. Remove the chicken breasts from the marinade, sprinkle evenly with salt and pepper and grill skin side down for about 5 minutes until nicely browned. Turn the chicken and cook for another 10 minutes or until done. Serve hot or at room temperature.

6 servings

##  Caitie Girl's Honey Glazed Sweet Tea Brined Fried Chicken

**Brine:**

2 cups kosher salt

1 cup sugar

1 small jar pickling spice

1 cup vinegar

1 gallon warm water

2 gallon sized tea bags

2 whole frying chickens, each cut into 8 pieces (backs set aside for broth)

**Chicken Breading:**

Egg wash (1 egg and 2 tablespoons milk or water)

Flour (for coating)

Seasoned salt, to taste

**Glaze:**

1 bottle Frank's Hot Sauce

1 medium bottle of honey

1/2 cup water

Combine the salt, sugar, pickling spice, vinegar, water and tea bags. Completely submerge chicken in brine and let sit at least 24 hours.

Preheat oil to 325°. To make egg wash, whisk together egg and milk or water. Set aside. Remove chicken from the brine and dry thoroughly. Combine flour and salt. Dip into egg wash and flour mixture, shaking off the excess. Fry chicken in the oil for 10 – 12 minutes or until golden. Use a candy thermometer to help maintain the oil temperature.

Preheat oven to 375°. Combine hot sauce, honey and water. Bring to a boil and cook until the consistency of chocolate sauce. Place fried chicken on a sheet pan. Drizzle liberally with glaze. Bake in oven for 10 – 15 minutes until glaze is slightly caramelized. Serve.

8 servings

# Hungarian Chicken Paprika

**Chicken:**

| | |
|---|---|
| 1 | large frying chicken, 8 pieces |
| 2 | tablespoons butter |
| 1 | large onion, chopped |
| 1 | teaspoon paprika |
| 1 | teaspoon salt |
| 1 | cup sour cream |

**Galushka Dumplings:**

| | |
|---|---|
| 1 | cup flour |
| 1/2 | teaspoon baking powder |
| 1/4 | teaspoon salt |
| 2 | eggs, beaten |
| 1 | tablespoon milk |

Cook chicken in butter. When slightly browned, add onion, paprika and salt. Cook for two minutes; then add just enough water to cover. Simmer 20 minutes or until chicken is about 3/4 done. Stir in sour cream and cook until tender.

While the chicken is cooking, bring a pan of salted water to a boil. Sift flour, baking powder and salt together. Add eggs and milk; mix just until blended. Drop into boiling water from the tip of a spoon or from a pastry bag fitted with a round tube, cutting the paste about an – inch long each time. Boil slowly with the pan covered about 10 minutes. Lift out and top with the chicken and pan sauce.

4 servings

*Variation: Substitute 4 boneless, skinless chicken breast halves.*

*Recommended wine – Austrian Blaufrankisch is a medium-bodied spicy red. Perfect with paprika.*

# Parmesan Herb Chicken Bake

| | |
|---|---|
| 1/2 | cup flour |
| 1/4 | cup grated Parmesan cheese |
| 1/4 | cup finely chopped, blanched almonds |
| 2 | tablespoons finely chopped parsley |
| 1 | teaspoon salt |
| 1/2 | teaspoon paprika |

| | |
|---|---|
| 1/4 | teaspoon marjoram |
| 1/8 | teaspoon pepper |
| 1/2 | cup (1 stick) butter |
| 1 | clove garlic, minced |
| 3 | pounds boneless, skinless chicken breast halves and/or thighs |

Preheat oven to 350°. Mix flour, Parmesan, almonds, parsley, salt, paprika, marjoram and pepper in a 9 – inch pie pan. Melt butter in a 9 x 13 – inch baking pan. Stir garlic into butter. Dip chicken pieces into melted butter and garlic; then coat them with the flour mixture. When all pieces are coated, arrange in the baking pan, turning once to coat the flour mixture with butter. Bake for 65 – 75 minutes, or until fork-tender and nicely browned. Baste occasionally.

6 – 8 servings

*Note: Use additional butter for more rich and crispy chicken. This can be prepared ahead of time and refrigerated before baking. Allow extra baking time.*

*Recommended wine – The US Sauvignon Blanc's crisp, citrus base contrasts well with this rich, buttery dish.*

### Café Moxo
# Moxie Potpie

**Crust:**
- 2 pie crusts, room temperature
- 1 large egg, whisked

**Filling:**
- 1 sweet onion, diced
- 1 clove garlic, minced
- 2 stalks celery, sliced
- 1 tablespoon olive oil
- Salt and pepper, to taste
- 1 tablespoon butter
- 3/4 cup red potatoes, diced
- 1 cup chicken stock
- 2 sprigs fresh sage
- 1/2 cup white wine
- 1/2 cup whole milk
- 2 tablespoons half and half
- 2 1/2 tablespoons flour
- 1/2 teaspoon parsley
- 1/4 teaspoon thyme
- 1/8 teaspoon nutmeg
- 3 cups frozen mixed vegetables
- 2 cups rotisserie chicken, pulled

Preheat oven to 400°. Sauté onion, garlic and celery in olive oil about 5 minutes. Add salt and pepper. Remove from pan and set aside. In the same pan, melt butter and add potatoes, chicken stock and sage. Cover and cook about 15 minutes or until potatoes are softened. Adjust seasoning. Add white wine, milk, half and half, flour, parsley, thyme and nutmeg to mixture. Whisk to combine and cook to thicken for 5 minutes. Remove from heat and add frozen vegetables, chicken and onion, garlic and celery. Discard springs of sage. Taste and add additional salt and pepper, if needed.

Using a 5 – inch biscuit cutter, cut 8 circles out of dough. Place a round of dough into each of 4 individual pie pans. Fill with potpie filling. Cover with remaining dough rounds and seal edges with a crimp. Place pies on a baking sheet and brush crust with egg wash. In a conventional oven bake 30-35 minutes. In a convection oven, bake 20 minutes.

Makes 4 potpies

## Poppy Seed Chicken Casserole

*Tip: This can be frozen before applying crackers, poppy seeds and butter for use at a later date.*

*Recommended wine – Dry Riesling. Yes, there are dry Rieslings! Try one from Austria, New Zealand or Germany.*

- 12 bone-in chicken breast halves
- 2 stalks of celery in chunks
- 1 small onion, sliced
- Salt to taste
- Pepper to taste
- 2 (10 1/2 ounce) cans cream of chicken soup
- 3 cups (24 ounces) sour cream
- 1/4 cup sherry
- 1 full cylinder Ritz crackers, crumbled
- 3 tablespoons poppy seeds
- 6 tablespoons butter, melted

Preheat oven to 350°. Cook chicken in water with celery, onion, salt and pepper. Leave in broth to cool. When cool, remove from broth and debone. Place in ungreased 9 x 13 – inch baking dish. Combine cream of chicken soup, sour cream and sherry and pour over chicken. Sprinkle crackers and poppy seed over chicken and drizzle with melted butter. Bake 30 minutes.

8 – 10 servings

## Hot Chicken Artichoke Bake

4 tablespoons butter, divided use

2 boxes herb or chicken long and wild rice (cooked according to directions)

10 slices thick bacon fried and crumbled

2 1/2 cups of carrots in 1 – inch julienne strips

8 ounces mushrooms, sliced

1 bunch of scallions both white and green chopped

2 cans cream of chicken soup

1 cup heavy cream

1 cup of sherry

1 teaspoon salt

1/2 teaspoon pepper

3 whole boneless chicken breasts, cooked and diced (approximately 4 cups)

2 cans (14 ounce) artichoke hearts drained and quartered

3 cups grated mozzarella cheese

1/2 cup of freshly grated Parmesan cheese (topping)

*Note: Excellent choice for potluck dinners.*

Grease 9 x 13 casserole with two tablespoons of butter and spread the cooked rice over bottom. Layer the crumbled bacon on top of the rice.

In a large sauce pan sauté the carrots in the remaining 2 tablespoons of butter until almost cooked then adding the mushrooms and scallions. When this mixture is tender add the soup, cream, sherry, salt and pepper mixing well. Then add the chicken, artichokes, and mozzarella again stirring just until mixed. Layer this mixture on the bacon, sprinkling the top with Parmesan cheese.

Bake at 350° for 45 minutes, covered for 30 minutes, uncovered for the final 15 minutes until hot and bubbly.

10-12 servings

*The Great Western Railroad depot, located at 10th and Monroe Streets, is where Lincoln made his famous farewell address as he left for his inauguration. He paid high tribute to the kindness of his friends.*

*"I now leave, not knowing when, or whether ever, I may return…"*

*When he did, it was on the funeral train.*

## New Salem Chicken and Noodles

Tip: To store noodles longer, use powdered cow or goat milk and powdered eggs to prevent spoilage and dry them thoroughly.

Recommended wine – A rich buttery Chardonnay (US or Australia) pairs perfectly with this classic comfort food. Avoid overly-oaked ones, however.

**Chicken:**

| | |
|---|---|
| 1 | (4 – 5 pound) chicken |
| 1 – 2 | stalks celery, chunked |
| 1 | medium onion, quartered |
| 1 | tablespoon salt |
| 6 | black peppercorns |
| 2 – 3 | tablespoons paste chicken base |
| | Water |

**Milk Noodles:**

| | |
|---|---|
| 4 – 5 | cups flour, divided |
| 1 | teaspoon salt |
| 1 | teaspoon baking powder |
| 1/2 | cup shortening |
| 7 | ounces evaporated milk |
| 4 | eggs |

Place chicken, celery, onion, salt, peppercorns and chicken base into a 6 – 8 quart pan. Cover with water. Cover pan and bring to a boil. Skim top as chicken cooks. Simmer for 45 – 60 minutes until chicken is done. Remove chicken from the pan and set aside to cool. Remove the skin and bones and tear into pieces. Set aside. While chicken is cooling strain the broth into another pan. Remove as much fat as possible or refrigerate chicken and broth until the fat hardens and can be removed. After fat is removed, heat broth to boiling and add noodles. Cook until they are almost done, to your taste. Add chicken and heat through.

For the noodles, combine 2 cups of flour, salt and baking powder. Cut in shortening until the mixture is pea-like. Make a hole in the flour and add the milk and eggs to the flour mix. Add additional flour until the dough forms a soft ball. Refrigerate for one hour before rolling out. Remove from refrigerator and roll noodles to 1/8 to 1/4 – inch thickness. Cut noodles 1/2 – inch wide and 2 to 3 – inches long. If not using immediately, dry noodles on a pasta drying rack or place on parchment paper. Best if cooked within a week.

Serves 24 – 30

## White Chicken Fricassee

Recommended wine – Pinot Grigio or Aussie Verdelho: Both of these white wines are light, crisp and refreshing and won't overpower the chicken.

| | |
|---|---|
| 2 | tablespoons butter |
| 2 | tablespoons flour |
| 1 1/2 | cups hot chicken broth |
| 3 | pounds chicken cut into pieces, bone-in or boned |
| 1 | large onion, sliced or diced (optional) |
| 1 | teaspoon salt |

| | |
|---|---|
| 1/2 | teaspoon pepper |
| 1/2 | teaspoon mace |
| 1 | tablespoon sage or marjoram |
| 2 | egg yolks |
| 1/4 | cup cream |
| 1/4 | teaspoon nutmeg |
| | Juice of 1/2 lemon |

Melt butter in pan and stir in the flour. Cook 1 minute stirring constantly. Add hot broth, stirring until it thickens. Add chicken, onion, salt, pepper, mace and sage or marjoram. Simmer uncovered, stirring frequently, for 30 – 45 minutes. Beat egg yolks. Add cream and nutmeg. Remove a small amount of broth from the pan and whip the egg mixture into it. You may choose to strain this to guarantee that no cooked egg lumps have developed. Return mixture to the pan, carefully mixing it into the remaining chicken and sauce. Squeeze lemon over top; heat through.

8 – 10 servings

# Nonna's Tetrazzini

**Nonna's Seasoning:**

2 1/2 tablespoons paprika
2 tablespoons salt
2 tablespoons garlic powder
1 tablespoon black pepper
1 tablespoon onion powder
1 tablespoon cayenne pepper
1 tablespoon dried oregano
1 tablespoon dried thyme

**Chicken:**

7 tablespoons unsalted butter, divided
12 ounces bow tie pasta or pasta of choice
2 tablespoons olive oil
1 1/2 cups chopped onions
1/2 cup chopped red bell peppers
1 teaspoon minced garlic
1 pound white button mushrooms, ends trimmed, sliced

1 1/2 teaspoons Nonna's seasoning
1/2 teaspoon freshly chopped thyme leaves
1/4 cup flour
1/4 cup dry white wine
2 cups chicken stock or low-sodium canned chicken broth
1 3/4 cups heavy cream
4 cups chopped rotisserie chicken (4 pound chicken)
1 tablespoon freshly chopped parsley leaves
1 1/2 teaspoons salt
3/4 teaspoon freshly ground black pepper
1/3 cup freshly grated Parmesan
1 (5 1/2 ounce) bag potato chips, crushed

*Note: Al dente – an Italian phrase meaning "to the tooth," used to describe pasta or other food that is cooked only until it offers a slight resistance when bitten into, but which is not soft or overdone.*

*Recommended wine – What better than a rich Italian white, such as Gavi or Soave, with a rich Italian dish?*

Preheat oven to 375°. Coat a 9 x 13 – inch baking dish with 1 tablespoon butter. Prepare the seasoning by combining paprika, salt, garlic powder, black pepper, onion powder, cayenne, oregano and thyme. Store the extra seasoning in a glass jar in a dark place to keep for other uses.

Bring a large pot of salted water to a boil and cook the pasta al dente, about 10 minutes. Drain in a colander; place in a bowl and add the olive oil, coating the pasta. Set aside. Sauté the onions and bell peppers in remaining butter in a large skillet over high heat until soft, about 4 minutes. Add garlic and cook for 2 minutes, stirring. Add the mushrooms, Nonna's seasoning and thyme and cook, stirring occasionally, until the mushrooms are soft and have released their liquid, about 6 minutes. Sprinkle with the flour and cook, stirring, for 2 minutes. Add the wine and chicken stock and cook, stirring, until smooth and thick, about 2 minutes. Add the heavy cream and bring to a boil. Immediately reduce the heat to medium and simmer, stirring occasionally, until the sauce is thick enough to coat the back of a spoon and is very flavorful, 15 – 20 minutes.

When the sauce has thickened, add the noodles, chicken, parsley, salt, black pepper and Parmesan to the skillet and stir until thoroughly combined. Transfer mixture to the prepared baking dish and top with potato chips. Bake uncovered until bubbly and golden brown, about 30 – 40 minutes. Serve immediately.

12 servings

## Scaloppini al Limone

*Recommended wine – Italian Vernaccia or Gavi. The crisp, citrus tone of this white wine will complement the lemon in the sauce.*

| | | | |
|---|---|---|---|
| 2 | tablespoons olive oil | 1/2 | teaspoon black pepper |
| 1/4 | cup (1/2 stick) butter, divided | 2 | tablespoons freshly squeezed lemon juice |
| 1 | pound chicken breasts, thinly sliced and pounded flat | 2 | tablespoons parsley |
| 3/4 | cup flour | 1/2 | lemon, thinly sliced (optional) |
| 1/2 | teaspoon salt | | |

Combine oil and 2 tablespoons of the butter in a skillet over medium high heat. Flour both sides of chicken and shake off the excess. Carefully place a single layer of chicken in the pan. Cook until lightly browned on one side, about 1 minute. Turn and brown the other side. Remove chicken from pan. Season with salt and pepper and set aside. Cook remaining chicken in the same manner. Remove the skillet from heat and add the lemon juice, scraping loose the crusty remains in the bottom of the pan. Add remaining butter, coating the pan lightly. Add the parsley. Return the cooked chicken to the pan, coating pieces on both sides with the sauce. Lower heat to medium and warm sauce and meat to serving temperature. Warming it too long will toughen the meat. Transfer the scaloppini to a serving platter and pour sauce over them. These cool quickly, so serve immediately garnished with twisted lemon slices.

4 servings

## Szechwan Chicken

*Recommended wine – Chinese food always lends itself to a slightly sweet white, such as Riesling.*

| | | | |
|---|---|---|---|
| 1 | tablespoon cornstarch | 1 | teaspoon vinegar |
| 3 | tablespoons soy sauce, divided | 1/4 | cup oil |
| 2 | large chicken breasts, boned, skinned in 1/2 – inch cubes | 1/4 | teaspoon crushed red pepper |
| 1 | tablespoon dry sherry | 2 | scallions, sliced |
| 2 | tablespoons chicken broth or white wine vinegar | 2 | teaspoons freshly grated ginger or 1/2 teaspoon ground ginger |
| 2 | teaspoons sugar | 1/2 | cup salted peanuts |

Combine cornstarch and 1 tablespoon soy sauce in a bowl. Add chicken and stir to thoroughly coat. Set aside. Combine 2 tablespoons soy sauce, sherry, chicken broth, sugar and vinegar. Set aside.

Heat the oil in a wok. Add red pepper and cook until black. Add chicken and cook 2 – 3 minutes. Remove chicken and set aside. Add scallions and ginger. Stir fry for 1 minute. Return chicken to wok and cook 2 minutes, stirring constantly. Add soy sauce mixture. Cook and stir 1 minute. Fold in peanuts and continue to cook long enough for them to warm. Serve over rice.

4 servings

## Southwest Chicken Lasagna

| | | | |
|---|---|---|---|
| 1 | (10 ounce) package lasagna noodles | 2 | (10 3/4 ounce) cans of condensed tomato soup |
| 4 | egg whites, lightly beaten | 1 | (10 ounce) can enchilada sauce |
| 3 | cups cottage cheese, low fat | 1 | tablespoon chili powder |
| 1/3 | cup chopped parsley | 1/4 | teaspoon pepper |
| 1 | (4 ounce) can diced green chili peppers, drained | 3 1/2 | cups cooked chicken breasts cut into bite-sized pieces |
| 2 | tablespoons olive oil or 1 tablespoon coconut oil | 1 1/2 | cups finely shredded sharp cheddar cheese, divided |
| 1 | cup chopped onions | 1 | cup finely shredded Monterey Jack cheese, divided |
| 1 | red pepper, chopped | | |
| 2 | cloves minced garlic | | |

Cook the noodles according to the directions on the box. Drain and set aside.

While the noodles are cooking, stir together the egg whites, cottage cheese, parsley and chili peppers in a medium bowl. Set aside.

Heat the oil in a skillet. Add onions, chopped pepper and garlic. Cook and stir over medium heat until tender. Stir in the soup, enchilada sauce, chili powder and pepper. Bring to a boil. Reduce heat and simmer uncovered for 10 minutes, stirring often.

Preheat oven to 375°. Lightly spray a 9 x 13 – inch baking pan. To assemble the lasagna, place 4 of the noodles in the pan. Spread half of the cottage cheese mixture over the noodles. Top with half of the sauce mixture, half of the chicken and half each of the cheddar and Monterey Jack cheeses. Repeat layers in the same order. Bake uncovered for 45 minutes or until bubbly. Let stand 15 minutes before cutting.

8 servings

## Beef Romanov

| | | | |
|---|---|---|---|
| 2 | pounds sirloin or beef tenderloin | 1/2 | teaspoon pepper |
| 1/4 | cup butter | 2 | teaspoons Worcestershire sauce |
| 1 | cup finely minced onions | 1/3 | cup flour |
| 2 | cans beef broth | 1/3 | cup cold water |
| 2 | cloves garlic, finely minced | 1 | tablespoon sour cream per serving for garnish |
| 1/4 | cup catsup | | |

*Slurry: A thin paste of water and flour, which is stirred in as a thickener.*

*Recommended wine – California Cabernet or Red Bordeaux from France. The tannins in these dry full-bodied reds are softened by the fats and proteins of this rich beef dish.*

Cut meat into bite sized pieces and brown in melted butter with the minced onions and garlic. Add beef broth. Add the catsup, pepper and Worcestershire sauce to the meat. Cover and simmer for at least one hour. Combine the flour and water to make a slurry. Add slurry to meat mixture and bring to a boil to thicken sauce. Serve immediately over cooked rice or cooked noodles. Top with garnish if desired.

6 servings

*Note: Serve with pan roasted vegetables or pecan smashed potatoes. For information on roasting vegetables, see page 241.*

## Augie's Front Burner
## Barbeque Flank Steak with Mango & Sweet Chili Glaze

**Steak:**

- 2 cups soy sauce
- 1 cup rice vinegar
- 1 tablespoon sesame oil
- 1 cup sugar
- 4 (6 ounce) flank steaks

**Glaze:**

- 1 cup rice vinegar
- 1/2 cup sugar
- 1 cups orange juice
- 4 mangos, peeled, cored and diced
- 1 tablespoon chipotle in adobo chili
- 1 bunch cilantro picked and chopped
- 1/2 cup extra virgin olive oil
- 1 tablespoon ground cumin
- Salt and pepper

Combine soy sauce, vinegar, sesame oil and sugar; bring to a boil and boil for 5 minutes. Allow to cool. Pour over flank steaks and marinate 4 – 6 hours.

For the glaze, boil vinegar and sugar together for 5 minutes. Add orange juice and cook to reduce volume by 2/3. Cool slightly. In food processor, combine mango, chipotle and cilantro. Puree to rough paste. Pour orange reduction into processor and combine with mango puree. With machine running, drizzle in olive oil and season with cumin, salt and pepper.

Heat grill. Remove steaks from marinade. Grill 3 – 4 minutes per side. Brush on mango glaze. Slice thinly on bias.

4 servings

## Quick Chicken and Pasta

*Note: For helpful tips on oven roasting vegetables, see page 241.*

- 1/2 cup extra virgin olive oil
- 1/4 cup balsamic vinegar
- 2 tablespoons sugar
- 2 tablespoons Dijon mustard
- 1 pinch cayenne (more or less to taste)
- 3 cloves garlic
- 1/4 cup water
- 4 boneless skinless chicken breast halves
- 8 ounces penne or other pasta
- Salt to taste
- Pepper to taste
- Freshly grated Parmesan cheese
- Grilled or oven roasted vegetables (optional)

Combine olive oil, vinegar, sugar, mustard, cayenne, garlic and water. Transfer to shallow bowl and add chicken breasts, turning to coat. Marinate at least 2 hours. Take chicken out of marinade (saving marinade) and grill or broil until done and cut into bite size pieces. Cook pasta according to package directions. Bring reserved marinade to a boil in a small saucepan. Combine pasta, chicken pieces and marinade in large bowl or pasta plate. Sprinkle with freshly grated Parmesan cheese. Add vegetables if desired for a complete meal.

4 - 6 servings

## BBQ Beef Roast

1/4   cup finely chopped onion
1   clove garlic, crushed
1/4   cup (1/2 stick) butter, melted
1   cup tomato catsup
1   tablespoon brown sugar
1/2   cup dry sherry
1   teaspoon dry mustard

1   tablespoon lemon juice
1/2   cup white vinegar
1   tablespoon Worcestershire sauce
1/2   cup water
6 – 8   pound beef rib roast

*Hint: I like to partner this dish with a Rice Pilaf, see page 168.*

*Recommended wine – A California Cabernet is always a good choice for beef dishes.*

Prepare BBQ sauce for roast the day before making the roast. Sauté onion and garlic in butter until soft, but not brown. Add catsup, brown sugar, dry sherry, dry mustard, lemon juice, vinegar, Worcestershire sauce and water. Bring to a boil, stirring frequently. Reduce heat and simmer, uncovered for 1 hour. Stir occasionally to prevent scorching. You may add more water if needed. Strain sauce and store in refrigerator.

Preheat oven to 325°. Grease or spray a shallow roasting pan. Place roast fat side up in pan. Brush generously with bbq sauce and insert thermometer near center, making sure not to touch bone. Place in oven. Baste with sauce several times during the cooking process. Cook until thermometer registers 150° for medium-rare or 170° for well-done. Estimate about 15 minutes per pound. Ovens vary, so rely on the thermometer for perfect results. Remove from oven, strain sauce and remove fat. Let roast rest 15 minutes before carving. Reheat sauce and serve in a gravy boat with the roast.

8 – 12 servings

## German Beef Rouladen

1/4   cup Dijon mustard
8   (4 ounce) pieces round steak, pounded to 1/4 – inch
1/2   cup minced onion
2   teaspoons paprika
2   teaspoons salt
2   teaspoons freshly ground black pepper

8   slices bacon
3   tablespoons canola oil
1   (12 ounce) can beef broth
1 1/2   cups water
2   tablespoons cornstarch
1   cup cold water
1/4   cup sour cream

*Recommended wine – German Spatburguner or Austrian Zweigelt. What could be a better match with German cuisine than a red wine from the same area?*

To prepare, spread 1 - 2 tablespoons mustard on one side of each piece of steak. Combine onion, paprika, salt and pepper and sprinkle mixture over steaks. Place a slice of bacon over the steak. Roll steaks in a jelly roll manner. Fasten closed with toothpicks. Heat oil in a skillet over medium heat. Brown meat on all sides. Add the beef broth and water to the pan and bring liquid to a boil. Reduce heat to medium, cover and simmer until tender, about 30 minutes. Remove the rolls from the pan and set aside. Strain the broth and return to the pan. Mix cornstarch with the cold water and slowly pour it into the skillet. Cook over medium heat until the sauce thickens, about 2 – 3 minutes. Stir in the sour cream. Return rolls to the pan coating them with the sauce and serve.

4 servings

## Italian Poor Boy

*Note: Leftovers freeze well.*

*Variation: If you prefer, put the ingredients into a crock pot and cook on high setting for 6 – 8 hours. Remove meat. Cool and shred. Return meat to the pot, reduce heat to low and cook until ready to serve.*

*Recommended wine – Italian Barbera with high acidity, lots of fruit and low tannins is the dream wine for Italian fare.*

| | | | |
|---|---|---|---|
| 5 | pound rump roast or beef sirloin tip roast | 1/4 | teaspoon black pepper |
| 1 | bay leaf | 1/4 | cup Italian seasoning |
| 2 | (12 ounce) cans beer | 2 | tablespoons beef paste |
| 2 | (11 1/2 ounce) jars pepperoncini peppers, drained, stems removed | 1 | cup water |
| 1 | medium onion, chopped | | Hoagie buns (hearth-baked rolls are best) |
| 4 | cloves garlic | | Yellow mustard (if desired, to taste) |
| 1/4 | teaspoon salt | | |

Preheat oven to 350°. Place roast, bay leaf, beer, pepperoncini, onion, garlic cloves, salt, pepper, Italian seasoning, beef paste and water in a roasting pan and bake for 3 – 3 1/2 hours. Remove beef from pan and let cool. When cool, shred it with two forks or fingers. Place shredded meat in a sauce pan with part of the juices and keep warm until ready to serve. Serve with hoagie buns and mustard.

20 – 24 servings

## Simply Lasagna

*Note: May be made ahead and refrigerated. Let rest at room temperature for 30 minutes before cooking. If necessary adjust cooking.*

*Use your favorite jar of marinara or make your own, see page 230.*

*Recommended wine – Italian Dolcetto is a soft medium bodied red from the Piedmont region of Italy.*

| | | | |
|---|---|---|---|
| 1 | pound lean ground beef | 1 | cup grated Parmesan cheese, divided |
| 1 | large yellow onion, diced | 1 | pound ricotta cheese |
| 1 | (16 – 20 ounce) jar marinara | 1 | pound grated mozzarella cheese |
| 1 | (8 ounce) can tomato sauce | 1 | pound lasagna noodles |
| 1 | tablespoon sugar | | |
| 1 | teaspoon oregano leaves | | |

Preheat oven to 350°. Grease or spray a 2 x 9 x 13 – inch pan. Brown ground beef. Add diced onion and cook until clear. Add marinara, tomato sauce, sugar, oregano and 1/4 cup of Parmesan cheese. Simmer for 30 minutes. Combine ricotta, mozzarella and 1/2 cup of Parmesan. Cook lasagna noodles according to package directions. Rinse and leave in cold water. Arrange 1/3 of the meat sauce in the prepared pan, a single layer of DRAINED noodles overlapping lengthwise and trimmed to fit crosswise over any exposed meat. Begin layering. Layer 1/2 of cheese mixture over noodles and cover with 1/3 of meat sauce. Repeat the last 3 layers in the same order: noodles, cheese, and meat sauce. Sprinkle with last 1/4 cup of Parmesan cheese. Bake 30 minutes or until bubbly.

8 servings

## Sweet and Sour Ribs

| | | | | |
|---|---|---|---|---|
| 3 | pounds boneless country style ribs | 1/2 | cup brown sugar, packed | |
| 4 | cloves garlic, minced | 1/4 | cup soy sauce | |
| 1/2 | cup cider vinegar | 2 | tablespoons cornstarch | |
| | | 6 | ounces pineapple juice | |

In a large skillet or Dutch oven, brown ribs on all sides. Combine garlic, vinegar, brown sugar and soy sauce and add mixture to ribs. Bring to a boil; reduce heat and simmer for 45 minutes. Mix together cornstarch and pineapple juice. Pour over browning ribs. Simmer until tender, 2 hours. The longer they simmer the more tender they become.

6 – 8 servings

*Recommended wine – Austriav Zweigelt or Aussie Shiraz. These big spicy reds will complement both the sweet and sour flavors of the ribs.*

## Carol Jean's Fine Cuisine
## Tenderloin of Beef with Walnut & Port Stuffing

| | | | |
|---|---|---|---|
| 1 | medium onion, chopped | | Kosher salt to taste |
| 2 | cloves garlic, chopped | | Cracked pepper to taste |
| 1/4 | cup butter (1/2 stick) | | Garlic powder to taste. |
| 1/2 | cup port wine | | |
| 1/2 | cup chopped parsley | | *Saga Blue Cheese Sauce:* |
| 1 | cup bread crumbs | 3/4 | cup dry white wine |
| 1/2 | cup chopped walnuts | 1 | cup heavy cream |
| 1 | tablespoon leaf thyme | 4 | ounces Saga blue cheese |
| 2 | tablespoons orange zest | 1/2 | cup (1 stick) butter |
| 1 | egg | | White pepper to taste |
| | Salt to taste | | Salt to taste |
| | Pepper to taste | | |
| 1 | whole tenderloin of beef, trimmed | | |

*Butterfly: See Pork Roast with Apricot/ Onion Dressing page 132.*

Preheat oven to 500°. Grease or spray a roasting pan with a rack. Sauté onion and garlic in butter. Add port wine and reduce by half. Remove from heat and stir in parsley, bread crumbs, chopped walnuts, thyme, orange zest, egg, salt and pepper. Butterfly the tenderloin and fill with the stuffing. Tie with string and season top of roast with kosher salt, cracked pepper and garlic powder. Place on rack and roast for 40 – 50 minutes, or until internal temperature reaches 140°.

While the meat is roasting, cook white wine in a sauce pan until reduced to 2 tablespoons. Add cream and continue cooking until cream is reduced by half. Combine cheese and butter in a bowl until well blended. When ready to serve, reheat cream and whisk in the cheese mixture. Season sauce with white pepper and salt. Slice roast and serve with the sauce.

## Ashikaga Pork Tenderloin

| | | | | |
|---|---|---|---|---|
| 9 | strips bacon | 1 | tablespoon vinegar |
| 3 | pork tenderloins | 1 | tablespoon honey |
| 1/2 | cup soy sauce | 1/4 | teaspoon cayenne pepper |
| 1 | tablespoon grated onion | 1/4 | cup brown sugar |
| 1 | clove garlic | | |

*Ashikaga – Springfield's sister city is a medium sized city about 80 km north of Toyko, Japan.*

*Recommended wine – The spicy California Syrah or gamey French Cotes du Rhone are both good matches for the Asian spice and bacon influence of this dish.*

Wrap 3 strips of bacon evenly spaced around each tenderloin and fasten with wooden picks. Place meat in a baking dish. Combine soy sauce, onion, garlic, vinegar, honey, cayenne pepper and brown sugar. Mix well and pour over the meat. Cover and refrigerate 4 – 5 hours or overnight. Turn meat occasionally. When ready to cook, remove roasting pan from the refrigerator and let rest on the counter for 30 minutes. Meanwhile, preheat the oven to 300°. Bake 1 1/2 hours, basting occasionally, or until meat thermometer inserted into the roast reaches 170°. Serve pan juices separately to spoon over meat.

8 to 10 servings

## Bridgette's Pulled Pork and Beef

| | | | | |
|---|---|---|---|---|
| 4 | pounds beef bottom round | 2 | tablespoons salt |
| 5 | pounds pork shoulder or butt | 1 1/2 | teaspoons freshly ground black pepper |
| 5 | cloves garlic, crushed | 8 | ounces horseradish |
| 1 | large onion, chopped | 4 – 6 | ounces Worcestershire sauce |
| 2 | stalks celery, large chunks, with leaves | | |

*Tip: If the meat is to be frozen, omit the horseradish and add it when heating to serve.*

*Variation: Add a little hot sauce during last simmering.*

*Recommended wine – Zinfandel or South African Pintoage. Both Zinfandel and Pintoage pair well with spicy food. Beer pairs well with horseradish.*

Combine beef, pork, garlic, onion, celery, salt and pepper in a large pan. Add water to cover meat. Bring to a boil and simmer until pork will pull apart. Remove meat from pan. Cool just enough to permit shredding with two forks or fingers. If some chunks are extremely long, cut them in half crosswise to keep shreds more consistent. Strain broth. Skim most of the fat from the broth. Mash vegetables and return to broth if you wish to use them. Put meat back into pan. There should be enough liquid to almost cover meat. Add horseradish and Worcestershire sauce. Simmer for 2 hours. Serve on crusty buns or bread. Serve with sides of catsup, mustard, horseradish, peppers, dill pickles, provolone cheese, bbq sauce and/or marinara sauce if you like.

20 – 24 servings

## Illini Country Club
## Braised Pork Shoulder Roast

Olive oil for browning
1   4 – 5 pound pork shoulder roast
    Salt
    Pepper
1   pound bacon, apple wood
15  cloves garlic
2   yellow onions, diced
2   green peppers, diced
2   yellow peppers, diced

2   red peppers, diced
1   jalapeño pepper, sliced
3   stalks celery
6   fresh tomatoes
1   bunch fresh garden herbs
    (sachet bouquet garni)
3   quarts (12-cups) chicken stock
3   tablespoons olive oil

*Note: Bouquet garni includes thyme, parsley and bay leaf.*

Preheat oven to 300°. Place a large oven proof sauté braising pot on high heat. Add olive oil. Season pork shoulder to taste with salt and pepper. Sear pork until golden brown on all sides. Remove pork from pan. Add bacon to the pan and render for a few minutes. Add garlic, onion, green, yellow and red peppers, jalapeño and celery; sauté 5 minutes. Add tomatoes and fresh herb sachet. Continue to sauté. Deglaze with chicken stock and bring to a simmer. Add pork roast back to the pot and cover with aluminum foil. Bake for 3 hours. Check for tenderness and seasoning before serving.

4 – 6 servings

## Buttermilk Marinated Pork Roast

2   cups buttermilk
1   onion, sliced or chopped
2   tablespoons salt
3/4 cup maple or apple syrup
    (sugarfree may be used)
3/4 tablespoon thyme

2   tablespoons bacon grease
1/2 cup Dijon mustard
4   pounds lean, boneless pork
    loin roast
    Olive oil

*Recommended wine – A red Beaujolais (Gamay grape) has a natural earthiness and bacon-like flavor.*

Combine buttermilk, onion, salt, syrup, thyme, bacon grease and mustard; mix well. Place roast in zipper plastic bag, preferably, double bag. Pour marinade over roast. Seal and refrigerate for 48 hours. Turn meat occasionally.

Preheat oven to 300°. Remove meat from refrigerator. Remove the roast from the marinade, drain and dry thoroughly. Heat olive oil in a skillet until quite hot. Brown roast until all sides are brown. Place meat in a roasting pan and bake for 20 minutes per pound or until the meat reaches 165° on a meat thermometer. Let rest for 20 minutes.

12 servings

## Pork Loin Adobo

*Note: Indirect grilling is a barbeque cooking technique in which the food is placed to the side of the heat source instead of directly over the flame as is more common.*

2   cups canned tomatoes (excess juice drained off)
6   tablespoons ancho chile powder
1   canned chipotle pepper, seeded
1   tablespoon honey

1   tablespoon dark brown sugar
3   tablespoons red wine vinegar
1/4   teaspoon cayenne
6   cloves garlic, chopped
1/4   cup olive oil
4 – 5   pound boneless pork loin

*Recommended wine – A good hearty Zinfandel or Syrah with forward berry fruit will stand up to these lovely flavors.*

Puree the tomatoes, ancho chile powder, chipotle pepper, honey, brown sugar, vinegar, cayenne, garlic and olive oil in a blender or food processer. Pour the marinade into a plastic zipper bag. Add the pork loin and refrigerate 12 - 24 hours.

If using a charcoal grill, arrange charcoal for indirect cooking. When the coals are ready or the gas grill is heated, place the pork loin on the center of the grill. Cover and cook for 45 – 60 minutes or until the internal temperature reaches 150°. Remove from heat and rest for 10 - 15 minutes. Slice thinly to serve.

8 – 10 servings

## Hearty Boy Ribs

*Note: Asian sweet chili sauce may be found in the Asian aisle of supermarkets or Asian specialty markets.*

**Sauce:**
3   tablespoons minced garlic
1   cup cilantro leaves, coarsely chopped (optional)
2   tablespoon sugar
2   cups reduced sodium soy sauce
1   cup Asian sweet chili sauce

1/2   teaspoon cayenne pepper (optional)
1/4   cup vegetable oil

**Ribs:**
3   pounds pork ribs, cut into 2 racks
    Barbeque sauce (optional)

*Recommended wine – US Syrah or French Gigondas. These full-bodied spicy reds are perfect with grilled red meat.*

Combine the garlic, cilantro, sugar, soy sauce, sweet chili sauce, cayenne (if using) and vegetable oil. Place ribs in a large glass, plastic or stainless steel container. Pour sauce over the ribs, turning ribs to coat. Cover and refrigerate at least 6 hours or overnight.

Preheat oven to 250°. Preheat grill. Remove ribs from the sauce, shaking off any excess. Reserve the remaining sauce. Place the ribs on the grill meaty side down for 8 minutes. Flip and grill another 4 minutes. Transfer ribs to a large baking dish and pour reserved sauce over ribs. Cover with foil and bake 3 hours if you are not using barbeque sauce. If you are using barbeque sauce, remove ribs from oven after 2 1/2 hours, pour off excess sauce from pan and liberally brush ribs with the barbeque sauce. Cover with foil and bake another 30 minutes.

4 servings

## Honey Glazed Pork

| | |
|---|---|
| 2 | pork tenderloins |
| 2 | tablespoons Dijon mustard |
| 1/4 | cup honey |
| 2 | tablespoons coarse brown mustard |
| 2 | cloves garlic, crushed |
| 1 1/2 | teaspoons kosher salt |

**Herb mixture:**

| | |
|---|---|
| 1 | teaspoon rosemary |
| 1 | teaspoon thyme |
| 1 | teaspoon oregano |
| 1 | teaspoon marjoram |
| 1 | teaspoon basil |
| 1/2 | teaspoon tarragon (optional) |
| 1/2 | teaspoon savory (optional) |

*Variation: Use other herbs of your choice. Add a few crushed almond slices.*

*Note: Leftovers make great sandwiches.*

*Recommended wine – Southern French Red from Côtes Du Rousillon ar Minervois. If possible, use wine that comes from the same region as your food.*

Preheat oven to 375°. Line a baking sheet with foil. Trim fat and silver skin from tenderloins if needed. Combine Dijon, honey, brown mustard, garlic, salt and herb mixture. Rub over tenderloins, covering well. Bake for 25 minutes for rare or until the internal temperature reaches 150°. Let rest for a few minutes before slicing to serve.

4 – 6 servings

## Caitie Girl's Grown-Up Mac-n-Cheese

| | |
|---|---|
| 1 | pound cooked bowtie pasta |
| 1 | pound pepperjack cheese |
| 1 | pound Velveeta cheese |
| 1 1/2 | quarts heavy cream |

| | |
|---|---|
| 1 | (16 ounce) tub prepared pork barbeque |
| | Dried bread crumbs |
| | Melted butter |

*Note: Serve with fried chicken.*

Preheat oven to 350°. Prepare pasta according to package directions. Melt pepperjack cheese and Velveeta. Add the cream and whisk until smooth. Add pasta and barbeque and mix well. Pour into a sprayed glass baking dish. Top with bread crumbs, drizzle with butter and bake for 20 – 25 minutes until golden and bubbly.

6 – 8 servings

*"Lincoln in Springfield" by native Charles Houska is meant to portray Lincoln's close association with both the old state capital and the Tinsley building which housed his law office with William Herndon. It is the only work done by Charles which depicts Lincoln and the sites that helped shape this great American.* Copyright 2005. The Gift Source Inc. All rights reserved.

# Pork Roast with Apricot and Onion Dressing

| | |
|---|---|
| 1 | cup dried apricots |
| 1 | cup onions, chopped |
| 1 | tablespoon bacon drippings |
| 1/2 | cup bread crumbs |
| 2 | eggs |
| 4 – 5 | pound pork loin, boneless |

Ginger, chopped or ground (optional)
Cinnamon (optional)
Salt and pepper
1 cup apple cider or apple juice

*Variation: Try this with and without the ginger and cinnamon for entirely different flavors.*

*Note: Have the butcher butterfly the roast. To do it yourself, hold your knife horizontally to the roast. Beginning about 1/2 – inch from the end of the roast; cutting to 1/2 – inch from the other end of the roast, make a lengthwise cut about 3/4 through the roast. Do not cut it through the other side. Open the sides like a book. Pound the flattened roast gently with a meat mallet to an even thickness. Spread dressing evenly and not too thickly over the roast leaving the edges clean so the dressing will not escape during cooking. Roll the roast from side to side like a jelly roll and fasten the closure with tooth picks until you can tie it according to the directions.*

Cut apricots into small pieces. Soak dried fruit overnight in water to cover. Drain well. Preheat the oven to 325°. Sauté onions in bacon drippings. Combine apricots, onions, bread crumbs and eggs. Set dressing aside. Butterfly the roast. Sprinkle with ginger, cinnamon, salt and pepper. Spread roast with dressing leaving enough space from the edge of the meat to roll the roast lengthwise like a jelly roll. Tie the roll in several places with string. Place on a baking rack in a roasting pan. Baste with apple cider. Bake for about 25 minutes per pound or until meat reaches 165° on a meat thermometer. Baste with apple cider every 10 minutes until the roast begins making its own juices. Then baste every 20 minutes. Remove from oven and let sit for 15 minutes. Carve into slices.

16 – 20 servings

# Julianne Glatz
## Sage Marinated Roast Pork with Braised Apples and Onions

| | |
|---|---|
| 3 – 4 | pound pork roast, such as a loin or tied shoulder roast, or substitute six 1 1/2 – inch thick loin pork chops |

**For the marinade:**

| | |
|---|---|
| 2 | cups buttermilk |
| 1/2 | cup thinly sliced or diced onion |
| 6 | garlic cloves, crushed |
| 2 | tablespoons kosher or sea salt |
| 1/2 | cup dark brown sugar |
| 1/4 | cup minced sage leaves |

**For the braised apples, onions and celery root:**

Kosher or sea salt and freshly ground pepper to taste

| | |
|---|---|
| 6 | tablespoons bacon fat or vegetable oil, divided, plus additional if needed |
| 4 | cups onions, sliced 1 – inch thick |
| 4 | cups peeled celery root, cut into 1 – inch cubes |
| 4 | cups cored apples, unpeeled, cut into 1 – inch thick slices |
| 1 | cup thinly sliced sage leaves |
| 1/2 | cup unpasteurized cider |

Sage sprigs for garnish, optional
Cider Sauce (recipe follows)

*Recommended wine – US Chardonnay or South African Chenin Blanc. A fruit driven Chardonnay or Chenin Blanc will complement the apricots and spices.*

1 – 2 days before you plan to serve the pork, combine the buttermilk, thinly sliced onion, crushed garlic, salt, brown sugar and sage leaves in a large sealable plastic bag. Squish the bag with your hands to combine the ingredients and dissolve the sugar.

*(continued on next page)*

Place the meat in the bag. Remove as much air as possible and seal. Refrigerate the meat, turning the bag occasionally. Remove the bag from the refrigerator 2 – 3 hours before cooking to allow the meat to come to room temperature.

Preheat the oven to 375°. Heat 2 tablespoons of the bacon fat or oil in a large skillet over high heat. Sprinkle onions and celery root with salt and pepper. When the fat is hot but not smoking, add the thickly sliced onions and sauté until lightly browned, about 5 minutes. Transfer the onions to a baking dish large enough to hold the pork roast. Add another tablespoon of bacon fat to the skillet and add the celery root cubes. Brown them lightly and transfer them to the baking dish. Add another tablespoon of the bacon fat to the skillet and repeat with the apples. Stir the apples, onions and celery root to combine.

Pour off any fat remaining in the skillet. Return the skillet to the heat and add the sage leaves. Stir fry for about a minute, then pour in the cider and deglaze the skillet, scraping up any browned bits into the liquid, then pour over the apples, onions and celery root. Stir to combine and sprinkle lightly with salt and pepper. Place the baking dish in the oven for 15 minutes. After 15 minutes, reduce the oven temperature to 300°. Remove the pork from the marinade, pat dry with paper towels and sprinkle generously with pepper. Wipe the skillet clean and heat the remaining 2 tablespoons bacon fat in it over medium high heat. Brown the pork well on all sides then transfer it to the baking dish. Set the skillet aside to make the cider sauce. Bake the pork until a meat thermometer inserted halfway into it registers 150°. Baking time will depend on the size and type of roast. If using pork chops, begin checking them after 45 minutes. Begin checking roasts after 1 hour and 15 minutes.

While the pork is roasting, make the cider sauce (recipe follows). When the roast is done, remove from the oven. Let it rest for 20 – 30 minutes, then slice. Spread the vegetable/apple mixture onto a large platter and top with the sliced pork. Drizzle with some of the cider sauce, and pass the rest separately at the table. Garnish with sprigs of sage leaves if desired.

6 servings

*Variations: Whisk in 1/2 cup heavy cream or remove from the heat and whisk in 4 tablespoons chilled butter cut into bits, or use both cream and butter. You may also add 1 – 2 tablespoons cracked black peppercorns.*

*Note: Celeriac, listed under its more commonly known name, celery root, is a variety of celery grown for its edible roots. It is also called turnip-rooted celery or knob celery. It tastes like celery but has somewhat a potato consistency.*

### Cider Sauce:

- **1/2 cup minced shallots or onions, not super-sweet**
- **1 tablespoon bacon fat or unsalted butter or the fat and browned bits left in the skillet from sautéing the pork**
- **1/2 cup applejack or Calvados**
- **4 cups unsalted chicken stock**
- **2 cups unpasteurized apple cider**
  **Salt, freshly ground pepper and cider vinegar to taste**

If using the skillet or pan in which the meat was cooked, pour off any excess fat so that only a thin film remains. Otherwise, melt the bacon fat or butter in a medium to large skillet over medium high heat. Add the shallots and stir until softened. Pour in the applejack and increase the heat to high. Add the cider and chicken stock and boil until the mixture is reduced to a syrupy glaze, 15 – 20 minutes. Season to taste with salt, pepper and cider vinegar.

Makes about 1 1/2 cups.

# Southern Pulled Pork

*Note: This is a great dish for large groups of people. Serve with small rolls, such as Hawaiian rolls. Great if put in the oven at bedtime and cooked overnight.*

*Recommended wine – Red Zinfandel or Petite Sirah. Hot, sweet foods like this pair well with a fruit forward red wine.*

**Pork:**

2   untrimmed boneless pork shoulder halves or Boston butt, about 6 pounds total

**Dry Rub:**

3   tablespoons coarsely ground black pepper

3   tablespoons brown sugar (packed)

3   tablespoons paprika

2   tablespoons coarse salt

1   teaspoon cayenne pepper.

**Liquid Mop:**

1   cup apple cider vinegar

1/2   cup water

2   tablespoons Worcestershire sauce

1   tablespoon black pepper

1   tablespoon salt

2   tablespoons olive oil or vegetable oil

Mix pepper, brown sugar, paprika, salt and pepper in a bowl. Place pork fat side up on a work surface. Cut each piece lengthwise in half. Place on a large baking sheet. Sprinkle dry rub evenly over pork and press it in. Cover with plastic and refrigerate at least 2 hours or overnight.

For the mop, combine vinegar, water, Worcestershire, pepper, salt and oil in a bowl. Refrigerate until ready to use.

Preheat the oven to 400°. Grease or spray a deep roasting pan. Place the pork in the prepared pan and pour mop sauce over it. Cover pan tightly with foil and place in oven. Immediately lower oven temperature to 250° and cook the roast for 7 – 8 hours. Increase oven temperature to 350° and cook one more hour. Let stand until cool enough to handle and shred into bite-size pieces. Mound onto a platter with raised sides, and pour any juices left in pan over the pork.

16 servings

Lincoln's Home is one of the many exhibits in a four-block neighborhood near downtown Springfield which recreates the atmosphere of life at the time Abraham Lincoln and his family lived here.

# Orecchiette with Broccoli and Sausage

| | | | | |
|---|---|---|---|---|
| 1 1/4 | pounds hot or sweet Italian sausages | | 1 1/2 | pounds orecchiette pasta |

1 1/4  pounds hot or sweet Italian sausages
   4  tablespoons olive oil, divided
   4  garlic cloves, peeled and chopped
   2  pounds broccoli florets cut into bite-size pieces (about two heads)
1 1/2  cups chicken stock, divided
   1  tablespoon salt

1 1/2  pounds orecchiette pasta
      Juice of 1/2 lemon
 1/2  cup dry sherry
      Red pepper flakes to taste
 1/4  cup (1/2 stick) butter
   1  cup reserved pasta water
      Freshly grated Parmesano-Reggiano cheese for serving

Remove casings from sausages. In a large sauté pan or wok heat 2 tablespoons of olive oil over medium high heat. Add sausage and sauté. Use a wooden spatula to break the sausage into bite-size pieces. Transfer cooked sausage to a large bowl lined with paper towels to drain. Drain the oil, leaving 2 tablespoons of the remaining fat in the bottom of the pan. Add garlic to pan and sauté for about one minute. Steam the broccoli florets in the pan with 1/4 cup chicken stock for 5 minutes. Remove from heat. Bring a large pot of water to a rapid boil. Add remaining olive oil, salt and orecchiette. Cook according to package directions until al dente, stirring occasionally. Drain cooking water, reserving 1 cup. While orecchiette is cooking, reheat the broccoli pan to medium. Add the lemon juice, sherry and remaining chicken stock to the steamed broccoli to deglaze the pan. Add red pepper flakes to taste. Simmer until it thickens a little. Add the butter and stir until melted to incorporate the flavors. Add the reserved pasta water and simmer until the sauce will coat the back of a spoon. Add sausage to reheat. Toss with hot orecchiette and serve with freshly grated Parmesano-Reggiano cheese.

4 servings as a main course or 6 servings as a pasta course

*Variation: Substitute broccoli rabe for the florets. Remove any tough or outer leaves from 2 bunches of broccoli rabe. Cut off the stems and tear the leaves into large pieces, about 3 to 4 – inches. Rinse well in a colander under running water. Place in a deep saucepan with cold water to cover by about 2 – inches. Bring to a simmer over high heat. As soon as bubbles appear at the sides of the pan. remove it from the heat. Drain cooking water, reserving 1 cup. Immediately place the broccoli rabe in cold water to cover. When it is cooled, drain well and transfer to the large sauté pan or wok. Proceed with the recipe as with broccoli florets.*

*Recommended wine – Italian Primitivoan Aglianico. Full-bodied, fruit forward reds from Southern Italy pair well with spicy sausage.*

*Our 16th President rests at a peaceful setting in the dignified tomb designed by Larkin Mead. The bronze reproduction of Abe's head at the entrance is from Gutzon Borglum's heroic statue at the Lincoln Monument in Washington, D.C. The shine on Abe's nose is from the myriad of hands which have rubbed it for good luck. Flag-lowering ceremonies are performed weekly during the summer by Civil War infantry re-enactors.*

**Main Event**

---

# Tipsy Glazed Ham

*Recommended wine – Your choice here. Both white Riesling or the red Pinot Noir pair well with ham.*

**1  (10 pound) ham, uncooked or partially cooked
Whole cloves
2 1/2  cups white wine**

**1  cup honey
1  cup brown sugar, packed**

Preheat oven to 300°. Remove any rind from the ham, leaving a thin layer of fat. Score the fat into diamonds. Place a clove in each of the diamond points. Place meat, fat side up, on a rack in a roasting pan. Pour the wine over the ham. Spread the honey over the ham and sprinkle with brown sugar. Bake 1 hour. Increase oven temperature to 325°. Cover and bake 3 hours longer, until ham is tender or reaches 360° on a meat thermometer. Remove from oven and let cool before cutting.

20 – 24 servings

---

# Lamb Chops

*Variation: Place the chops on a griddle over hot coals or on the grid of a charcoal grill. For either method, the olive oil may be combined with the seasonings to make a moist rub or marinade.*

**8  lamb chops
2  tablespoons olive oil
1/2  teaspoon black pepper
1/4  teaspoon rosemary**

**1/4  teaspoon dry mustard
1/4  teaspoon salt
1 – 4  tablespoons shortening**

Rinse lamb chops and pat dry. Rub chops with olive oil. Combine pepper, rosemary, dry mustard and salt and use as a rub to coat the chops. Melt shortening in frying pan and cook lamb chops about 5 minutes on each side.

4 – 8 servings

*Recommended wine – Red Bordeaux. The gameness of lamb matches well with Old World style reds with higher tannins.*

*The gazebo in the Union Station Park across from the Abraham Lincoln Presidential Library and Museum provides a place for visitors to rest while visiting our historic city. This backdrop is a perfect setting for The Historic Preservation Agency to sponsor many events.*

## Tortilla Pork Tenderloin

| | | | |
|---|---|---|---|
| 1 | cup yellow tortilla chips, crushed | 4 | (4 – 5 ounce) slices of pork loin, fat removed |
| 1 | cup blue tortilla chips, crushed | 2 | eggs beaten (use more if needed) |
| 1 | cup plain corn flakes, crushed | 1/4 | cup peanut oil |
| 1/4 | teaspoon black pepper | | |

Preheat oven to 450°. Coat a 9 x 9 – inch baking pan with cooking spray. Blend yellow tortilla chips, blue tortilla chips, cornflakes and pepper in a food processor until they are finely ground. Dip the pork loin rounds in the beaten eggs and coat heavily with the crumb mixture. Let rest for coating to set. Heat the peanut oil in a large skillet on high. Sauté the pork loin rounds about one minute on each side until nicely browned. Place them in the baking pan and roast them for 5 – 6 minutes or until done.

4 servings

*Note: These are good served with fresh salsa.*

*Recommended wine – Rich, fruity California Red Zinfandel is the perfect match for Southwestern or Tex-Mex fare.*

## Sangamo Club
## Herb Roasted Rack of Lamb

| | | | |
|---|---|---|---|
| 3/4 | cup fresh bread crumbs | 3 | tablespoons olive oil |
| 4 | teaspoons fresh rosemary, chopped | 2 | racks of lamb, trimmed and frenched |
| 4 | teaspoons fresh thyme leaves | 2 | teaspoons salt |
| 3 | tablespoons minced garlic | 2 | teaspoons freshly ground black pepper |
| 1 | teaspoon salt | | |
| 1/2 | teaspoon freshly ground black pepper | 2/3 | cup olive oil |
| | | 3 | tablespoons Dijon mustard |

Preheat oven to 450° with oven rack in the middle position. Combine bread crumbs, rosemary, thyme, garlic, salt and pepper. Add 3 tablespoons olive oil and lightly mix together. Set aside.

Season lamb with the remaining salt and pepper. Heat 2/3 cup olive oil in skillet over high heat. Sear lamb on all sides until browned. Remove from skillet. Brush the lamb with Dijon mustard. Pat crumb mixture evenly over lamb. Roast bone side down until a thermometer inserted in the center of the thickest part of the meat registers 125° – 130° for medium rare, approximately 18 – 20 minutes. Remove from oven, loosely cover with foil and let rest 10 minutes before carving.

Serves 8

*Note: Your butcher can trim and french the racks of lamb.*

*The Sangamo Club, located near the heart of downtown, has for over 100 years included in its membership key community, political, charity, social, business and educational leaders from across the state of Illinois. This window was an integral part of the original building, a power station for the city's early street cars.*

# Lamb Souvlaki with Tzatziki

*Recommended wine – A Greek red like St. George is a perfect match.*

**Tzatziki (Cucumber Sauce):**
- 1 medium English hot house cucumber
- 1/2 teaspoon salt
- 1 cup Greek-style plain yogurt
- 1 tablespoon olive oil
- 1/2 teaspoon dry mint leaves
- 2 cloves of garlic minced (use more or less according to taste)

**Lamb:**
- 2 pounds boneless leg of lamb, trimmed of fat and cut into 1 – inch strips
- 1/4 cup fresh lemon juice
- 4 tablespoons plus 2 teaspoons olive oil, divided
- 1/2 teaspoon salt
- 1/2 teaspoon freshly ground pepper
- 1 1/2 tablespoon dry oregano
- 2 teaspoons minced garlic
- 1/4 cup grated onion
- 1 large white onion, thinly sliced
- 8 pita bread rounds

For the Tzatziki, peel, slice in half, seed and grate the cucumber. Sprinkle salt over cucumber and let sit 3 hours or overnight. Strain the cucumber, discarding the juice. Combine the cucumber and yogurt in a bowl with the olive oil, mint leaves and garlic. Stir well. Cover and chill for at least 2 hours before serving.

For the lamb, place in a nonreactive bowl. Mix together the lemon juice, 4 tablespoons oil, salt, pepper, oregano, garlic and grated onion. Pour over the meat. Cover and chill at least 3 hours or overnight.

Preheat grill for direct cooking. Cook sliced onion in 2 teaspoons olive oil until clear. Thread the meat onto 8 metal or bamboo skewers. Place skewers on the grill and cook turning occasionally, until brown on all sides. Remove from the grill. Quickly heat the pita bread on the grill until just warmed through and pliant. Holding a pita in the one hand and the skewer in the other hand, pull the contents from the skewer into the pita bread. Repeat with the remaining skewers. Divide the cooked onions among the pitas and top with Tzatziki. Serve immediately.

8 servings

The Cathedral of the Immaculate Conception was built in the Greek revival style and dedicated in 1928. It is home of the Diocese of Springfield in Illinois and serves 130 parishes. The complex includes the Bishop's residence.

## Maldaner's Restaurant
## Osso Buco

**Shanks:**

6 – 7 **pounds veal shanks,**
**2 1/2 – inch pieces**
**Salt and freshly ground pepper**
**Flour for dredging**
6 **tablespoons olive oil**

**Vegetables:**

2 – 4 **tablespoons butter**
1 1/2 **cups finely diced onions**
1/2 **cup finely diced carrots**
1/2 **cup finely diced celery**
1 – 2 **garlic cloves minced**

**Sauce:**

1 **cup dry white wine**
3/4 **cup beef stock**
2 **bay leaves**
1/2 **teaspoon thyme**
3 **cups canned tomatoes,**
**coarsely chopped**
1 1/2 **tablespoons chopped parsley**

**Gremolata:**

1 **tablespoon grated lemon rind**
1 **teaspoon minced garlic**
3 **tablespoons finely chopped**
**fresh parsley**

*Note: A traditional accompaniment to Osso Buco is Risotto a la Milanese but plain buttered orzo or mashed potatoes are great substitutions. This is a Maldaner's favorite, served generally in the coldest months of the year. When it's really cold outside this dish will warm up your soul from the inside. Be sure to eat the marrow.*

*Note: Flour can be deleted to make this gluten free.*

Preheat oven to 350°. Season veal pieces with salt and pepper and dredge in flour. Heat oil in skillet until a haze forms on it. Brown the veal over moderately high heat, adding more oil if needed. Remove shanks from oil and set aside. Add 2 – 4 tablespoons butter to olive oil in skillet and heat until melted. Add onions, carrots, celery and garlic cloves and cook until lightly browned. Transfer vegetables to casserole or Dutch oven with tight cover. Place the veal shanks side by side on top of the vegetables. The casserole should be just large enough for the veal shanks to stand up in one layer.

Discard most of the fat from the skillet, leaving a thin layer on the bottom. Pour in wine and boil over high heat until reduced by about half. Scrape up any browned bits from sides of pan. Stir in stock, thyme, parsley, bay leaves and tomatoes and bring to a boil. Pour all over the veal. If the mixture does not come halfway up the side of the veal, add more stock. Bring the casserole to a boil on top of the stove, cover and place in oven, basting occasionally. Adjust the oven to keep casserole gently simmering. Cook 1 1/2 hours, until tender. In the meantime prepare the Gremolata, mixing lemon, garlic and parsley together.

Arrange shanks on a heated platter if available. Spoon sauce and vegetables around them. Sprinkle Gremolata over the top.

*Michael Higgins, the fifth owner and chef of Maldaner's Restaurant, is proud to be associated with one of Springfield's oldest operating businesses. He has been credited for being a leader in using locally produced products in his kitchen, which he began in 1983.*

## Veal Saltimbocca

*Variation: Use 6 ounce boneless chicken breast halves in place of veal.*

*Recommended Wine – Italian Nebbiolo is a tannic, medium bodied red wine that pairs well with veal or beef.*

4   **veal cutlets (about 1 pound), pounded to an even thickness**
    **Salt to taste**
    **Freshly ground pepper to taste**
1/2  **cup flour**
2   **tablespoons unsalted butter, divided**
1   **tablespoon extra virgin olive oil**
2   **teaspoons chopped fresh sage or scant 1 teaspoon dried sage**

    **Sage leaves for garnish**
4   **slices prosciutto, cut and trimmed to fit the veal**
1/4  **pound fresh mozzarella, thinly sliced and trimmed to fit the veal**
3/4  **cup dry white wine (Pinot Grigio or Savignon Blanc)**

Season the veal with salt and pepper. Place flour in a bowl and dredge cutlets in flour, shaking off excess flour. Melt 1 tablespoon butter in a frying pan over medium high heat and brown veal in the butter until golden brown, about 5 minutes on each side. Reduce heat and sprinkle sage on top of meat. Place a piece of prosciutto then a slice of cheese on top of each piece of meat. Cover the pan and cook about 1 1/2 minutes or until cheese is melted. Place meat on serving dish and tent with foil. Raise the heat to high. Add the wine to the pan and deglaze the pan. Boil liquid until it is reduced to 1/4 cup, about 3 minutes. Whisk in the other tablespoon of butter. To serve, spoon 1/4 of the sauce over each piece of meat and garnish with a sage leaf.

4 servings

## Baked Stuffed Fish

*Tip: For whole fish, the head may be removed. To use fish fillets, place stuffing on the flat fillet, roll up and secure with a tooth pick.*

*Recommended wine – The richness of this dish would be complemented by a full bodied California unoaked Chardonnay.*

1   **2 1/2 to 3 pound firm whole white-fleshed fish**
    **Salt and pepper to taste**
3/4  **cup chopped onion**
3   **cups grated bread crumbs**
1/8  **teaspoon cayenne pepper**
1   **teaspoon thyme**

1/4  **teaspoon salt, plus salt to taste**
1   **egg, lightly beaten**
2   **tablespoons butter, melted**
2   **tablespoons flour**
1/2  **cup water**
1/2  **cup white wine**

Preheat oven to 400°. Grease or spray a baking pan. Wash fish and pat dry. Sprinkle inside and out with salt and pepper. Set aside.

Combine onion, bread crumbs, cayenne, thyme, salt, egg and butter. Add water, if necessary, to obtain the proper consistency for dressing. Stuff the cavity of the fish and secure with a skewer. Sprinkle fish with flour and place in a greased baking pan. Combine water and wine and pour over fish. Cover and bake 20 – 25 minutes. Baste occasionally. Strain the wine sauce and boil for 5 minutes or until slightly reduced. Season to taste. Serve this sauce with the baked fish.

6 servings

## Bourbon Glazed Salmon

| | |
|---|---|
| 1 cup packed brown sugar | 1/4 teaspoon freshly ground black pepper |
| 6 tablespoons bourbon | 2 crushed cloves of garlic |
| 1/4 cup low sodium soy sauce | 8 (5 ounce) salmon fillets (about 1 – inch thick) |
| 2 tablespoons fresh lime juice | |
| 2 teaspoons peeled grated fresh ginger | 4 teaspoons sesame seeds |
| 1 1/2 teaspoon salt | 1/2 cup thinly sliced green onions |

*Tip: Cooking the fish directly on the foil creates a very easy cleanup! The marinade is also good on pork tenderloin or boneless chicken breasts.*

In a large zip-top plastic bag combine the sugar, bourbon, soy sauce, lime juice, ginger, salt, pepper and garlic. Add the salmon fillets and seal bag. Marinate in refrigerator at least 30 minutes, turning the bag occasionally.

Cover a cookie sheet with aluminum foil and place the filets directly on the foil, skin side down. Discard the marinade. The cookie sheet is used to carry the fish to and from the grill. When grilling, place the foil directly on the grates. Cook until the fish flakes easily when tested with a fork. Do not turn the fish during the cooking process. Remove each fillet from the foil with a spatula carefully placed between the skin and the fish. The skin will remain adhered to the foil. Sprinkle each fillet with 1/2 teaspoon sesame seeds and 1 tablespoon onions.

*Recommended wine – Salmon with an Oregon Pinot Noir is the perfect pairing. Why serve anything else?*

8 servings

## Island Bay Yacht Club
## Crab Cakes

| | |
|---|---|
| 1/4 cup (1/2 stick) of lightly salted butter | 1/4 cup of Grey Poupon mustard |
| 1/2 chopped red pepper | 1 egg |
| 1/2 chopped yellow onion | 1 cup of Japanese panko bread crumbs |
| 1/4 bunch chopped celery | |
| 1/2 tablespoon of minced garlic | 1/2 tablespoon of blackening seasoning |
| 1/2 pound of backfin crabmeat | 1 ounce heavy cream |
| 1 cup mayonnaise | extra butter for sautéing |

Melt butter in a sauté pan. Cook the pepper, onion, celery and garlic until soft. Remove from heat and place the mixture in a bowl. Combine the crabmeat, mayonnaise, egg and mustard and add to the sautéed vegetables. Slowly blend in the bread crumbs. After the bread crumbs are combined, slowly add the heavy cream to soften the mixture. When the desired texture is achieved, add the blackening seasoning. Form into 3 ounce size patties and cook in a little butter until lightly brown on each side and warm in the middle.

8 crab cakes

# Goat Cheese Smoked Salmon Quesadilla

*Variation: Roast peppers on the grill or purchase jarred roasted peppers.*

*Recommended wine – California Pinot Noir will taste delicious with the tangy yet smoky combo.*

1   **poblano pepper**
1   **red bell pepper**
2   **tablespoons olive oil**
2   **ounces smoked salmon, cut into narrow strips**
1/4   **cup fresh goat cheese (room temperature)**

1/4   **cup cream cheese (room temperature)**
3   **(8 – inch) flour tortillas**
1   **avocado, peeled, pitted and cut into thin slices**
1/4   **cup minced shallots**

Preheat oven to 450°. Cut the poblano and bell pepper in half vertically and place on a sheet of waxed or parchment paper. Add olive oil to a small mixing bowl. Use a basting brush to coat both sides of the pepper halves with oil. Arrange the oiled pepper halves on a baking sheet and roast for 30 – 40 minutes, turning occasionally with metal tongs, until the skin is charred and blackened. Remove the baking sheet from the oven and carefully transfer the peppers to a brown paper bag. Fold the top of the bag closed and allow the peppers to sit for 5 – 10 minutes to loosen the charred skin. Remove from the bag and place them on a cutting board. Use a paring knife to remove the charred skins, stems and any seeds from the peppers. Cut into thin strips. This can be done up to 3 days in advance. Refrigerate until ready to use.

Mix the goat cheese and cream cheese in a small bowl until smooth and creamy. Spread 1/3 of the cheese mixture over one half of each of the tortillas. Divide the poblano and red pepper strips evenly over the cheese. Place salmon over cheese and layer the avocado slices over the peppers and sprinkle with the shallots. Fold the tortillas in half and press the edges to seal.

Heat a heavy non-stick skillet over medium high heat. Toast the tortillas on each side until golden brown. Cut each tortilla into 4 wedges and serve immediately.

6 servings

# 5flavors
# Pan Roasted Salmon

*Variation: Substitute spinach or brocollini for escarole.*

1   **tablespoon olive oil**
1   **pound salmon cut into 4 portions**
    **Salt and pepper**
1   **tablespoon butter**
1/4   **pound bacon, diced**
1/4   **cup shallots, finely chopped**

1/2   **cup chicken stock**
1   **10 – 12 ounce can cannellini beans, drained**
8   **ounces escarole, cut into strips**
    **Salt and pepper to taste**
    **Olive oil (optional)**

Heat a sauté pan and add olive oil. Season salmon with salt and pepper and sear salmon to medium; remove from pan and rest on a plate. In a separate pot, add butter, bacon and shallots. Lightly sweat. Add chicken stock, cannellini beans and escarole. Simmer until tender, about five minutes. Season with salt and pepper. Once the beans are done, place them on top of the plated salmon. Garnish with olive oil if desired.

4 servings

## Mike Aiello
## Lobster with Browned Butter Risotto

| | |
|---|---|
| 1 | **pound (about 2 medium) frozen lobster tails, thawed** |
| 4 1/2 | **cups reduced sodium chicken stock** |
| 4 | **tablespoons (1/2 stick) butter, at room temperature, divided** |
| 1 | **cup finely chopped onion** |
| 1 1/2 | **cups Arborio rice** |
| 2 | **teaspoons salt** |
| 3/4 | **cup brandy** |
| 1 | **cup grated Parmesan cheese** |
| 1/4 | **cup chopped fresh chives, divided** |
| | **Kosher salt to taste** |
| | **Freshly ground black pepper to taste** |

Bring a medium saucepan of salted water to a boil over medium high heat. Add the lobster tails and boil for 8 – 10 minutes until the shells curl and the lobster meat turns opaque. Drain, transfer to a cutting board and cool for 15 minutes. Using kitchen shears or a sharp knife cut through the top shell lengthwise. Remove the meat and cut into 1/2 – inch pieces. Set aside.

In a medium saucepan, bring the chicken stock to a boil. Keep hot over low heat. In a large saucepan, melt 3 tablespoons of butter over medium heat. Cook until the butter begins to foam and turn brown, about 1 – 1 1/2 minutes. Add the onion and cook 3 minutes. Stir in the rice and salt until rice is coated with butter. Add brandy and simmer until the liquid has almost evaporated, about 3 minutes. Add 1/2 cup of stock and stir until almost completely absorbed, about 2 minutes. Add 1/2 cup of stock at a time, stirring constantly and allowing each addition of stock to absorb before adding the next. Continue cooking until the rice is tender but still firm to the bite, about 20 minutes. Remove from heat and stir in the cheese, remaining butter and 2 tablespoons chives. Taste rice and season with additional salt and pepper if necessary.

Place the rice on a platter or large serving bowl. Arrange the lobster meat on top and garnish with the remaining chives.

4 servings

*Variations: Substitute 2 1/2 cups Barolo wine for 2 1/2 cups of the chicken stock. Substitute shrimp, crab or scallops for the lobster. Asparagus, mushrooms and roasted butternut squash are very good substitutes or additions.*

*Recommended wine – A full-bodied White Burgundy (Chardonnay) from France adds a matching richness to this buttery lobster risotto.*

## Scallops with Cider Gewürztraminer and Sage

| | |
|---|---|
| 1 | **cup apple cider** |
| 1/2 | **cup gewürztraminer wine** |
| 6 | **tablespoons unsalted butter, divided** |
| 1 | **pound sea scallops** |
| | **Salt to taste** |
| | **Pepper to taste** |
| 1 | **Granny Smith apple, unpeeled, cored and cut into matchstick size pieces** |
| 16 | **small sage leaves** |
| 2 | **tablespoons fresh lemon juice** |

In large heavy skillet, boil the cider and wine, skimming occasionally, until reduced to 3 tablespoons. Pour this into a small bowl and set aside. Wipe out the skillet. Add 2 tablespoons of butter and melt over high heat. Season the scallops with salt and pepper and cook in the butter until browned. This should take about 2 minutes per side. Transfer scallops to a serving plate and cover with foil. Add remaining butter to skillet and melt. Add the cider mixture, apple, sage and lemon juice. Cook this until the apple is tender and sauce is slightly thickened. This should take about 3 – 5 minutes. Spoon the sauce over scallops. Serve with mashed potatoes or cooked pasta of choice.

4 servings

*Note: The wine is a semi-dry, slightly spicy-tasting German white wine.*

*Recommended wine – Dry Gewürztraminer. Use the same dry Gewürztraminer in the recipe and for drinking.*

## Nut Crusted Halibut with Oriental Vinaigrette

*Recommended wine – A white wine balanced with fruit and acid either semi-dry like a German Riesling or dry like a French (Burgundy) Chardonnay, pairs well with Asian inspired seafood.*

**Vinaigrette:**

- 6 tablespoons rice vinegar
- 2 tablespoons sesame oil
- 3 tablespoons canola oil
- 2 tablespoons creamy peanut butter
- 3 tablespoons soy sauce
- 1 1/2 tablespoons brown sugar
- 1 tablespoon minced garlic cloves
- 2 tablespoons fresh ginger, peeled and minced

**Halibut:**

- 1/2 cup crushed roasted peanuts
- 1 cup panko (Japanese bread crumbs)
- 4 (4 – 6 ounce) halibut fillets
- 5 tablespoons canola oil, divided
- Salt and white pepper
- 4 cups shredded cabbage
- Green onion slices for garnish, optional
- Red pepper slices for garnish, optional

Preheat oven to 350˚. Combine rice vinegar, sesame oil, canola oil, peanut butter, soy sauce, brown sugar, garlic and ginger in a small bowl and set aside.

Combine peanuts and panko in medium bowl. Rub fillets with 2 tablespoons vegetable oil and season with salt and white pepper. Heat 3 tablespoons oil in oven-safe skillet over medium-high heat until hot. Add coated fillets, skin-side up. Cook on one side for about 5 minutes, until brown. Flip fish and place skillet in oven for 5 – 10 minutes, until fish breaks apart when pressed. Mound 1 cup cabbage on individual serving plates. Pour 1/4 cup of vinaigrette over the cabbage and place fillet on top. Garnish with green onion and red pepper slices, to make a nice presentation.

4 servings

## Salmon or Halibut Steaks with Lemon Dill Dressing

*Recommended wine – Unoaked Chardonnay with the halibut, US Pinot Noir with the salmon.*

**Fish:**

- 6 salmon or halibut steaks 1 to 1 1/2 – inches thick
- 1 1/2 cups water
- 1/4 cup lemon juice
- 1 medium onion, sliced
- 10 whole black peppercorns
- 3 sprigs fresh parsley
- 2 bay leaves
- 1/2 teaspoon salt

**Lemon-Dill Dressing:**

- 3/4 cup mayonnaise
- 3 tablespoons buttermilk
- 2 tablespoons fresh dill
- 1 tablespoon chives, snipped or 2 teaspoons dried dill weed
- 1/2 teaspoon lemon peel, finely shredded
- 2 teaspoons lemon juice

Wash fish and pat dry with paper towels. Set aside. Combine water, lemon juice, onion, peppercorns, parsley, bay leaves and salt in a skillet. Bring to a boil. Add fish. Return to a boil and reduce heat. Cover and simmer 8 – 12 minutes or until fish flakes. Remove fish from pan. Cover and chill about 2 hours. Make the dressing when you put the fish in to chill. Combine mayonnaise, buttermilk, dill, chives, lemon peel and lemon juice. Cover and chill for at least 1 hour. Serve with the fish.

6 servings

## Shrimp Brie Pasta

1 *pound large shrimp, grilled or boiled and peeled*

4 *large tomatoes cut into bite size pieces*

1/2 *pound Brie cheese, rind removed and cut into small pieces*

1 *cup fresh basil leaves, cut into small pieces just before using*

3 *cloves garlic, minced*

1/2 *cup good olive oil (or less, if desired)*

1/2 *teaspoon salt*

1/2 *teaspoon pepper*

1/4 *teaspoon crushed red pepper*

3/4 *pound fusilli or bowtie pasta*

*Note: Substitute 1 (28 ounce) can whole tomatoes, chopped.*

*Recommended wine – French Sancerre is a crisp, acidic Sauvignon Blanc from the Lorre Valley which is prefect with seafood.*

Combine cooked shrimp, tomato, Brie, basil, garlic, olive oil, salt, pepper and crushed red pepper and refrigerate overnight or at least 2 hours. Let the marinade sit at room temperature for a least one hour before serving. Just before serving, cook the pasta and immediately toss it with the shrimp and marinade. Fold together and heat slightly until the cheese is melted.

6 servings

*Frank Lloyd Wright's first carte blanche assignment was this home for Susan Lawrence Dana, a leading Springfield socialite. Completed in 1904, now a museum, it contains all the original extravagant art glass, including the famous butterfly window and hanging lamps at the entrance and dining room, plus almost all of the original furnishings designed by Wright specifically for this remarkable home.*

*Susan Lawrence was well-known for her interest in causes for women, and the first fundraiser she held at her newly-designed home was for the King's Daughters!*

## Seafood Lasagna

*Recommended wine – The full-bodied, buttery wine, such as US Chardonnay or White Burgundy, will enhance the richness of this dish.*

- 12 lasagna noodles
- 1 cup chopped onions
- 1/4 cup plus 2 tablespoons butter, divided
- 1 (8 ounce) package cream cheese, softened
- 1 1/2 cups cottage cheese
- 1 egg, beaten
- 2 teaspoons dried basil
- 1/2 teaspoon salt
- 1/8 teaspoon pepper
- 1/4 cup flour
- 2 cups milk
- 2/3 cup dry white wine
- 1 pound shelled, cooked shrimp, cut in half lengthwise
- 2 (7 1/2 ounce) cans crabmeat, drained and flaked
- 3/4 cup grated Parmesan cheese, divided

Preheat oven to 350°. Grease or spray a 9 x 13 – inch pan. Cook noodles in boiling water according to package directions. Drain, rinse with cold water and drain again. Sauté onion in 2 tablespoons melted butter until tender. Blend in softened cream cheese. Add cottage cheese, egg, basil, salt and pepper. Mix thoroughly and set aside. Blend flour into 1/4 cup butter over medium low heat. Gradually add milk, stirring constantly until smooth. Continue stirring over medium heat until thickened. Add wine and stir in shrimp and crabmeat. Place two layers of three noodles on bottom of prepared pan. Spread half of the cream cheese mixture over noodles. Spread half of the shrimp and crab mixture over cream cheese mixture. Repeat the three layers. Sprinkle top with 1/2 cup Parmesan cheese. Bake uncovered for 40 minutes. Sprinkle with remaining 1/4 cup Parmesan cheese and bake for 5-10 minutes more. Let stand 15 minutes before serving.

12 servings

## Island Bay Yacht Club
## Shrimp Madagascar

- 1/4 cup lightly salted butter, more if needed
- 6 ounces fresh button mushrooms, sliced
- 12 medium shrimp (peeled and deveined)
- 1 ounce Anisette liqueur
- 1 cup of heavy cream, more if needed
- 2 tablespoons chopped green onion
- Freshly ground pepper
- Angel hair pasta or rice

Put approximately 1/4 cup of butter into a 12 – inch heavy skillet. Allow to melt and get hot. Add mushrooms and sauté until about half done. Make a well in the skillet and add shrimp. Add more butter if needed. Sauté until the outer surface of the shrimp turns white. Do not overcook shrimp. Remove mushrooms and shrimp and set aside.

Deglaze pan with Anisette liqueur. This might flame up. Add 1 cup of cream. Reduce until thickened. Add more cream if needed. When thickened, return the mushrooms and shrimp to the pan and add the onions. Heat until hot. Serve over angel hair pasta or rice. Top with freshly ground pepper.

2 servings

## Shrimp with Feta Cheese and Tomatoes

| | | | | |
|---|---|---|---|---|
| 1 | pound jumbo shrimp, peeled and deveined | 2 – 3 | large ripe tomatoes, peeled, seeded and chopped |
| 2 | tablespoons olive oil | 1/2 | teaspoon oregano, crumbled |
| 2 | cloves garlic, minced | 4 | ounces feta cheese, crumbled |
| 1/4 | teaspoon crushed red pepper (optional) | | Salt to taste |
| 1/2 | cup dry white wine (optional) | | Pepper to taste |

*Variation: Use 1 or 2 cans of diced tomatoes (fire-roasted, Italian or plain) in place of fresh tomatoes. If using 2 cans, drain the juice from one can and reserve for use if needed.*

In a skillet, sauté shrimp in olive oil for 4 – 5 minutes until they start to turn pink. Add garlic and crushed red pepper (if using) and sauté another 1 – 2 minutes. If using wine, drain approximately the same amount of juice from the tomatoes, reserving for use if additional liquid is needed. Add wine, if using, tomatoes, oregano and cheese to the sauté pan. Stir over medium heat for 5 minutes. Add salt and pepper to taste. Serve over rice or fresh pasta.

2 – 3 servings

*Recommended wine – A dry Greek white, perhaps from Santorini, is the perfect match for Greek-inspired cuisine.*

## South Grand Shrimp Scampi

| | | | | |
|---|---|---|---|---|
| 1 | box (16 ounces) linguine | | Kosher salt to taste |
| 4 | tablespoons butter, divided | | Freshly ground pepper to taste |
| 4 | tablespoons olive oil, divided | 1/2 | cup dry white wine |
| 1 | large shallot, finely diced | 1 | lemon, juiced |
| 5 | cloves garlic, sliced or minced | 1/2 | cup parsley leaves, finely chopped |
| 1 | pinch red pepper flakes, to taste | | Olive oil for drizzling, optional |
| 1 | pound large shrimp, peeled and deveined | | Freshly grated Parmesan cheese (optional) |

*Recommended wine – French Muscadet is a light-bodied wine from the Loiare Valley with hints of citrus, green apple and salt.*

Cook linguine according to the directions on the box. Drain the pasta reserving 1 cup of water. In a large skillet, melt 2 tablespoons butter in 2 tablespoons olive oil over medium-high heat. Sauté the shallots, garlic and red pepper flakes until the shallots are translucent, about 3 to 4 minutes – do not burn! Season the shrimp with salt and pepper and add them to the pan. Cook until they have turned pink, about 2 – 3 minutes. Remove shrimp from the pan and set aside. Add wine and lemon juice to the pan and bring to a boil. Add remaining butter and olive oil. When the butter has melted, return the shrimp to the pan along with the parsley and cooked pasta. Add some of the reserved pasta water if additional moisture is needed. Stir well and season to taste with salt and pepper. Drizzle a bit more olive oil over the pasta and sprinkle with freshly grated Parmesan, if desired. Serve immediately.

8 servings

## Aunt B's Stuffed Shells

Note: Depending on how much cheese is filled in the shell, you may be able to use 2 baking dishes. If so, add additional marinara.

Note: See marinara sauce recipe on page 230.

1   (12 ounce) box of jumbo shell noodles
2   (15 ounce) containers of ricotta cheese
12   ounces shredded mozzarella cheese
1   cup grated Parmesan cheese

2   eggs
2   tablespoons parsley
    Salt to taste
    Pepper to taste
6 – 8   cups marinara sauce

Preheat oven to 350°. Grease or spray a 9 x 13 – inch baking dish. Cook pasta according to directions. Drain and cool on a paper towel. Mix ricotta, mozzarella, Parmesan, eggs, parsley, salt and pepper until well incorporated. Put a thin layer of marinara sauce in the bottom of the baking dish. Fill each shell with cheese mixture and place shells on top of the sauce, continuing until dish is full. Pour remainder of sauce over the shells. Bake for 50 – 60 minutes until sauce is bubbly.

6 – 8 servings

## Roasted Garlic Tomato Sauce with Meatballs

Note: When using plain olive oil for sautéing, add 2 teaspoons minced garlic.

1   medium onion, chopped finely
2   tablespoons roasted garlic olive oil
3   pounds tomatoes, peeled and mashed (about 4 cups)
1   teaspoon oregano
1   teaspoon Lawry's seasoned salt
1/4   teaspoon pepper
1   teaspoon sweet basil
1   tablespoon sugar
2   bay leaves

2   cups water
2   cans roasted garlic tomato paste

Meatballs:
1 1/2   pounds ground beef
1   teaspoon salt
1/2   onion, chopped
1/3   cup Parmesan cheese
2/3   cup Italian bread crumbs
1/4   teaspoon pepper
1   egg, beaten

Sauté onions in oil. Combine the garlic, tomatoes, oregano, seasoned salt, pepper, basil, sugar, bay leaves, water and tomato paste in a sauce pan. Bring to a boil, lower heat and simmer 2 hours or until desired consistency.

For meatballs, put the beef and onions in a skillet. Add salt and cook meat until browned. Remove from stove and drain the fat from the pan. Add the Parmesan, bread crumbs, pepper and egg to the meat. Mix well and form into balls. Place balls in the skillet and brown on all sides. Serve with pasta.

6 – 8 servings

# Besciamella Lasagna

*Tomato Sauce:*

| | |
|---|---|
| 1 | tablespoon olive oil |
| 3 | cloves garlic, chopped |
| 3 | (14 ounce) cans low sodium diced tomatoes |
| 1 | tablespoon dried parsley |
| 1/2 | tablespoon dried basil |
| 1 | teaspoon dried oregano |
| 1/2 | teaspoon pepper |

*Bechamel Sauce:*

| | |
|---|---|
| 1/4 | cup (1/2 stick) butter |
| 4 | tablespoons flour |
| 2 | cups milk |
| 1 | bay leaf |
| 1/2 | teaspoon freshly grated nutmeg |
| 1/2 | teaspoon salt |

*Filling:*

| | |
|---|---|
| 12 | ounces part skim ricotta cheese |
| 6 | ounces part skim shredded mozzarella |
| 6 | ounces grated Parmesan, divided |
| 6 | ounces grated Gruyère or similar cheese, divided |
| 2 | eggs |
| 1/2 | teaspoon dried parsley |
| 1/2 | teaspoon dried oregano |
| 13 | lasagna noodles, uncooked |

*Note: You can use your favorite jarred tomato sauce, but this is very tasty and so quick and easy to make. It can also be used for pasta or pizza.*

*Recommended wine – Lighter Italian whites, such as Pinot Grigio or Falanghing, won't overpower this full bodied dish.*

For the tomato sauce, heat saucepan until hot. Add the olive oil and heat 1 minute. Add the garlic and cook about 1 minute. Add tomatoes, parsley, basil, oregano and pepper. Simmer for 10 – 15 minutes. Puree using an immersion blender to the preferred consistency.

Prepare béchamel sauce while tomato sauce simmers. Turn stove to medium and heat a saucepan. Add butter and flour and whisk to combine. Stir constantly until it has a hint of brown color. Add the milk all at once and whisk until thoroughly blended. Add the bay leaf, nutmeg and salt. Simmer, stirring periodically, until it thickens (usually about 10 minutes). Set aside to cool.

Preheat oven to 350°. Grease or spray a 2 x 9 x 13 – inch pan. Mix ricotta, mozzarella, 4 1/2 ounces Parmesan, 4 1/2 ounces Gruyère, eggs, parsley and oregano in a bowl. Spoon 3/4 cup tomato sauce into prepared pan and spread to cover bottom of pan. Add a layer of lasagna noodles. Spoon 1/2 of the filling over the noodles. Remove bay leaf from the béchamel sauce and spoon 1/2 of it over the filling. Spoon 1/2 of the remaining tomato sauce over the béchamel sauce. Repeat lasagna, filling, béchamel and tomato sauce layers. Top with remaining shredded cheeses. Cover with foil and bake for 50 minutes or until golden brown and bubbly. Let stand for 20 minutes before serving.

8 – 10 servings

*The First Presbyterian Church, Lincoln's family church, has the pew used by the Lincoln's in the 1850's. This church is also home to seven beautiful Tiffany windows. While the church was established in 1828, this building was built in 1868. The bell in the tower today was the same one used in Lincoln's era.*

## Smoky Three Cheese White Pizza

*Recommended wine – Keep the wine light, fruity and simple, such as a Light Red Beaujolais or Cabernet Franc.*

8 slices bacon

1 tablespoon olive oil, divided

1 large onion, thinly sliced

1 (6 ounce) jar marinated artichoke hearts, drained and chopped

1 (12 – inch) prepared pizza crust

4 ounces smoked Swiss cheese, sliced

1/2 cup sour cream

1/2 cup crumbled feta cheese

1/4 teaspoon garlic powder

1/4 cup freshly grated Asiago or Parmesan cheese

1 tablespoon chopped fresh Italian parsley

Preheat oven to 450°. Cook bacon until crisp and drain on paper towels. Crumble and set aside.  In the same skillet, heat 1/2 tablespoon olive oil over medium heat. Add onion and sauté until tender and lightly browned. Stir in the bacon and chopped artichokes and sauté until heated through. Set aside.

Prepare the crust by brushing it with the remaining olive oil. Arrange Swiss cheese over the crust. Blend the sour cream, feta cheese and garlic powder and spread over the Swiss cheese. Top with the onion artichoke mixture and sprinkle with Asiago or Parmesan cheese. Place the pizza crust directly on the oven rack and reduce oven temperature to 425°. Bake for 10 to 12 minutes. Remove from oven and sprinkle with the chopped parsley. Cut into wedges.

4 servings

*This clean-shaven 30 foot tall statue of young Abraham Lincoln, named "The Rail Splitter", was created and built by Carl W. Rinnus in commemoration of the 150th Anniversary of Illinois' Statehood in 1968.*

## Spicy Asian Wraps

| | |
|---|---|
| 1 | cup freshly squeezed lime juice |
| 1 1/2 | tablespoons dark brown or palm sugar |
| 3 | tablespoons fish sauce |
| 1 | tablespoon roasted chili paste or Thai chili garlic paste |
| 1/2 | cup fresh cilantro leaves |
| 1 | jalapeño pepper |
| 3 | cloves garlic, peeled |

| | |
|---|---|
| 1 1/2 | pounds boned, skinned chicken breasts or flank steak |
| 10 | romaine or Boston bibb leaves |
| 1/4 | cup basil leaves, thinly sliced |
| 1/2 | red bell pepper, julienned |
| 1/2 | cucumber, julienned |
| 2 | scallions, julienned |
| 1 | avocado, diced |

*Variation: This can also be served salad style by tearing lettuce into bite size pieces and layering the other ingredients.*

*Recommended wine – Riesling pours well with the many flavors in Thai cuisine. You will need something slightly sweet after all that savory heat.*

*Note: Julienne, see page 82.*

Place lime juice, sugar, fish sauce, chili paste, cilantro, jalapeño (seeds removed for less heat) and garlic into blender or food processor and puree until smooth. Pour the marinade into a bowl with the chicken or flank steak and marinate in the refrigerator for 30 – 60 minutes. Heat a grill pan or outdoor grill to medium heat. Remove chicken or steak from marinade. Boil the remaining marinade for 10 minutes and use the reduced liquid as a sauce for the wraps.

Grill the chicken or steak 3 – 5 minutes on the first side or until well caramelized. Turn and continue to cook until done to your liking. Remove from grill and tent with foil. Let rest for 5 minutes. Cut against the grain into 1/4 – inch slices (or as thinly as you can). Divide slices evenly into the lettuce leaves and top with basil, red pepper, cucumber, scallions and avocado. Drizzle with the reduced marinade and serve immediately.

10 servings

*The Illinois State Fair, known for its agriculture theme, has over 1,000 stalls for livestock or horses.*

# Sidelines

*♛ The crown indicates a celebrity's recipe.*

# Roasted Artichoke Hearts

*Variation: If frozen artichoke hearts are not available, use 2 (9 ounce) jars of artichoke hearts in water. Less salt will be required.*

*Note: You can refrigerate the mixture overnight and let stand at room temperature for 30 minutes prior to serving.*

2   **(9 ounce) boxes frozen artichoke hearts, thawed**

3/4  **cup extra virgin olive oil, divided**

1 1/2  **teaspoons kosher salt, divided**
    **Freshly ground black pepper**

1   **shallot, minced**

3   **tablespoons freshly squeezed lemon juice**

2   **tablespoons white wine vinegar, divided**

1   **teaspoon Dijon mustard**

1/2  **cup chopped fresh basil leaves**

3   **tablespoons capers, drained**

1   **roasted red pepper from a jar, small diced**

1/4  **cup minced red onion**

1/4  **cup chopped parsley**
    **Pinch of hot red pepper flakes, (optional)**

Preheat oven to 350°. Place the artichoke hearts in a single layer on a jelly roll pan. Drizzle with 1/4 cup olive oil, sprinkle with 1/2 teaspoon kosher salt and freshly ground black pepper to taste. Toss to coat. Roast for 20 minutes.

Make the vinaigrette while the artichoke hearts are roasting. Place minced shallot, lemon juice, 1 tablespoon white wine vinegar, mustard, 1 teaspoon kosher salt and freshly ground black pepper to taste in a blender or in a food processor fitted with the steel blade. Blend for five seconds. Add the basil and blend to make a puree. With the blender or food processor running at low speed, slowly pour in 1/2 cup olive oil until it is incorporated and the vinaigrette is an emulsion.

Place the roasted artichokes in a large bowl and toss with enough vinaigrette to moisten. Add the capers, diced red pepper, red onion, parsley, 1 tablespoon white wine vinegar and red pepper flakes, if using. Toss gently. Sprinkle with additional kosher salt and freshly ground black pepper. Let stand at room temperature 30 minutes for flavors to blend. Serve at room temperature.

6 servings

# Asparagus with Bacon Bits

2   **teaspoons hazelnut oil or walnut oil**

1   **teaspoon fresh lemon juice**

3   **strips thick sliced bacon**

1/2  **small onion, finely chopped**

22  **asparagus stalks, preferably thick stalks, trimmed and peeled**
    **Salt to taste**
    **Freshly ground black pepper to taste**

Combine hazelnut oil and lemon juice; set aside. Cook bacon until lightly browned. Drain on paper towels, reserving 1 teaspoon of bacon grease. Dice the bacon strips and add to the onion. Bring a pot of salted water to a boil. Add the asparagus and cook until stalks are easily pierced with a knife, about 4 minutes. While asparagus is cooking, sauté the diced bacon and onions in the reserved bacon grease. When asparagus is done, drain and pat dry. Toss with the oil and lemon juice mixture. Season with salt and pepper to taste, adding more oil if needed. Drain bacon and onion and spoon over the asparagus.

6 servings

## Fresh Spring Asparagus and Parmesan Tart

| | | | | |
|---|---|---|---|---|
| 1 | pound asparagus (slender stalks are best) | 2/3 | cup grated Parmigiano-Reggiano cheese |
| 1 1/2 | tablespoons olive oil | 1/4 | teaspoon regular salt or 1/2 teaspoon sea salt |
| 1 | shallot, finely chopped | | Pepper to taste |
| 1 | sheet puff pastry | 1 | large egg yolk mixed with 1/2 teaspoon water |
| 2/3 | cup whole milk ricotta cheese at room temperature | | |

*Note: This makes an excellent appetizer when cut into smaller pieces.*

Preheat oven to 425°. Lightly flour a piece of parchment paper large enough to accommodate a 10 x 16 – inch pastry. Trim asparagus ends and cut each stalk into 3 sections with a diagonal cut. Heat olive oil in a large sauté pan. Add shallot and sauté about 2 minutes. Add asparagus and cook over medium-high heat about 5 minutes. Remove from heat.

Roll out pastry to a 10 x 16 – inch rectangle, and place onto the prepared parchment paper. Transfer the pastry and paper to a baking sheet. Spread ricotta in a thin even layer on pastry, leaving a 1 – inch border around the edge. Place asparagus mixture over the ricotta with the asparagus pieces running lengthwise with the pastry. Mix the salt with the grated cheese and sprinkle over all. Sprinkle with pepper to taste.

Brush the edge of the tart with the egg and water mixture. Bake until pastry is golden brown, 15 – 20 minutes. Let cool slightly and serve warm. Cut into 6 pieces for entree servings.

6 servings

## Brussels Sprouts with Balsamic Glaze

| | | | | |
|---|---|---|---|---|
| 3 | pounds Brussels sprouts | 1/3 | cup bread crumbs |
| 4 | slices bacon | 2 | tablespoons chives |
| 1/3 | cup white balsamic vinegar | 3/4 | teaspoon kosher salt, divided |
| 2 | tablespoons light brown sugar, packed | 1/2 | teaspoon pepper, divided |

Bring a large pot of salted water to a boil. Trim outer leaves and trim sprout ends. Cut a shallow X in the stem end of each sprout. Add sprouts to water and boil about 7 minutes. Drain and rinse sprouts. Fry bacon until crisp. Drain on a paper towel and set aside. Save bacon fat. Mix vinegar and brown sugar together and set aside. In a separate bowl, combine bread crumbs, chives, 1/4 teaspoon salt and 1/4 teaspoon pepper.

Place sprouts in the skillet with the bacon fat. Cook over medium high heat about 3 minutes coating the sprouts. Increase heat to high and add vinegar mixture. Stir to coat sprouts and cook until mixture reduces to a glaze, about 4 minutes. Add remaining salt and pepper. Place in a serving bowl and stir in the bread crumb mixture and crumbled bacon.

6 – 8 servings

## Apple and Raisin Stuffing

6   medium tart apples, peeled and chopped
1   medium onion, chopped
3   stalks celery, chopped
1/2   cup (1 stick) butter, melted
1 1/2   loaves bread, cubed

1/2   cup raisins
2   teaspoons cinnamon
3/4   teaspoon nutmeg
3/4   teaspoon allspice
2   eggs, slightly beaten
4 1/2   cups chicken broth

Preheat oven to 350°. Butter or spray a 9 x 13 baking pan. Sauté apples, onion and celery in butter. Combine bread, raisins, cinnamon, nutmeg and allspice and add to apple mixture. Combine eggs and chicken broth and add to apple mixture, mixing lightly. Spoon dressing into prepared pan. Bake 45 minutes or until puffed and brown.

12 servings

## Artichoke Prosciutto Gratin

6   ounces thinly sliced prosciutto
2   (14 ounce) cans artichoke hearts, drained and quartered
1   cup whipping cream
1 1/2   cups crumbled Gorgonzola cheese

1/2   cup pine nuts, toasted
1/4   cup grated Parmesan cheese
1   teaspoon chopped fresh sage

Preheat oven to 350°. Coat a 9 x 13 – inch baking dish with cooking spray. Cut each prosciutto slice crosswise in half. Wrap each artichoke quarter in a halved prosciutto slice. Place in a single layer in baking dish. Pour cream evenly over the artichoke bundles. Sprinkle with Gorgonzola, pine nuts, Parmesan and sage. Bake 25 minutes or until bubbling. Serve with crusty bread.

8 – 10 servings

## Asparagus Bundles

1   pound fresh asparagus spears, 5 – 6 inches long
8   slices prosciutto

6   tablespoons melted butter
Grated Parmesan cheese

Preheat oven to 350°. Wash and trim asparagus. Peel asparagus if it has thick stalks. Add to a pot of boiling water and cook for 2 minutes. Drain asparagus well and place into an ice water bath for about 3 minutes. Drain well. Divide the asparagus into 8 portions and wrap each portion with a slice of prosciutto. Lay bundles seam side down in a baking dish. Pour melted butter over the bundles and sprinkle with Parmesan cheese. Bake 15 minutes.

8 servings

## Maldaner's Restaurant
## Portobello Mushrooms and Asparagus

| | |
|---|---|
| 6 | ounces firm Portobello mushroom caps |
| 8 – 10 | thinly sliced asparagus spears |
| 12 | mint leaves |
| | Freshly ground salt |

| | |
|---|---|
| | Freshly ground pepper |
| 1/2 | cup extra virgin olive oil |
| 1 | lemon, halved |
| 3 – 4 | tablespoons crème fraiche |

Using a towel, brush or wipe the mushroom caps clean, checking the gills for hidden dirt (flick out dirt with end of a paring knife). Do not rinse the mushrooms. This can damage texture and flavor of the mushrooms. Using a Japanese mandoline, slice the mushrooms and asparagus as thinly as possible on the bias, alternating between mushrooms and asparagus, letting them fall into a loose, layered scatter on cold serving plates. Chop the mint and sprinkle over the mushrooms. Season evenly with salt and pepper, a generous drizzle of olive oil and squeeze fresh lemon juice in a trickle over the top. Thin the crème fraiche with additional cream if necessary to make it the consistency of thick paint. Finish with a drizzle of crème fraiche dipped with the tines of a fork.

Serves 4

*Note: When asparagus is in season, this is a very popular dish here at Maldaner's. We get our fresh asparagus from Jefferies Orchard and from local Farmers Markets.*

*Note: Crème fraiche is similar to sour cream, except a little softer. You can make your own by combining 1 tablespoon buttermilk with 1 cup heavy cream. Let sit at room temperature for 6 – 8 hours and then refrigerate for at least 24 hours before serving.*

## Asparagus Bake

| | |
|---|---|
| 1 | pound fresh asparagus spears |
| 1/4 | cup chopped onion |
| 6 | tablespoons butter, divided |
| 1 | (10 3/4 ounce) can cream of mushroom soup |
| 1/4 | cup milk (may use 2%) |

| | |
|---|---|
| 1 | (5 ounce) jar pimiento cheese spread |
| 1 | cup crushed butter flavored crackers |
| 3 – 4 | eggs, hard boiled and sliced |

Preheat oven to 350°. Grease or spray a 1 1/2 quart casserole. Trim tough ends from asparagus and cut or break into 1 – inch pieces. Partially cook spears in a small amount of water for 3 – 4 minutes. In a sauce pan, sauté onion in 2 tablespoons butter. Add undiluted soup, milk and pimento cheese to saucepan. Heat slowly until completely blended. Do not use a blender. Set aside. Melt the remaining butter and add to crackers mixing well. Set aside. Place half of the asparagus in a casserole. Cover with 1/2 of the sauce and 1/2 of the eggs. Make a second layer of asparagus spears, sauce and eggs, finishing with the prepared cracker crumbs. Bake 30 minutes or until bubbly.

6 servings

*Tip: Use more or less buttered cracker crumbs to suit. If doubling the recipe for a larger group, you may add crumbs in each layer.*

*Variation: If fresh asparagus is unavailable, substitute a 15 ounce can of asparagus spears or pieces.*

## Calico Beans

*Variation: Prepare the mixture as above and place in a crockpot. Cook on low for 6 – 8 hours.*

1   **pound bacon, partially cooked, drained**
1   **pound hamburger, browned well and drained**
1   **packet dry onion soup mix**
1   **cup barbeque sauce**

1/4   **cup brown sugar**
2   **(16 ounce) cans baked beans**
1   **(16 ounce) can pinto beans, drained and rinsed**
1   **(16 ounce) can dark red beans, drained and rinsed**

Preheat oven to 325°. Cut bacon into pieces. Combine bacon, hamburger, soup mix, barbeque sauce, sugar, baked beans, pinto beans and kidney beans in a large roasting pan. Place pan in the oven and cover with a lid or foil. Bake 1 1/2 hours. Serve with crisp bread.

12 – 18 servings

## Southwest Black Beans and Corn

*Note: Can be served hot, at room temperature or cold. If fresh corn is not available, use frozen corn, thawed.*

*Variation: This makes an excellent appetizer served with tortilla chips.*

1   **tablespoon canola oil**
1   **tablespoon extra virgin olive oil**
1   **small onion, diced**
2   **cloves garlic, finely diced**
6   **cups (large ears) fresh corn kernels**
1   **(15 ounce) can black beans, rinsed well and drained**
1   **(4 ounce) can diced green chiles**

1   **cup grape tomatoes, halved**
3   **green onions, thinly sliced**
3   **tablespoons chopped fresh cilantro**
    **Juice of 1 fresh lime**
    **Salt to taste**
    **Freshly ground black pepper to taste**

Heat canola oil and extra virgin olive oil in large Dutch oven over medium-high heat until oil begins to shimmer. Add diced onion and cook 4 minutes until softened. Add diced garlic and cook for 30 seconds longer. Reduce heat to low. Add corn. Cook for 5 minutes, stirring occasionally. Rinse and drain the black beans, then add them with the green chiles to Dutch oven. Cook 4 – 5 minutes until just heated through. Remove from heat. Stir in tomatoes, green onions, cilantro and lime juice. Season to taste with salt and freshly ground pepper.

6 – 8 servings

## Brussels Sprouts with Hazelnuts

1   (10 ounce) package frozen
Brussels sprouts
2   tablespoons butter

Salt
1/2   cup crushed hazelnuts

Cook the sprouts according to package directions, using 1 minute less time. Meanwhile, melt the butter in a skillet. Add salt to taste and crushed nuts. Carefully open the sprouts, avoiding the steam. Deposit the sprouts in the skillet and swirl around to cover with butter and nuts. Serve hot.

4 servings

## Hungarian Cabbage with Noodles

12   slices bacon
2   tablespoons sugar
1   tablespoon salt
1   large head cabbage (chopped)

8   ounces kluski noodles
1   cup sour cream
Paprika

*Note: Kluski pasta is a dense egg noodle pasta that is made to look like homemade pasta. The term often is used in labeling noodles.*

Preheat oven to 325°. Butter or spray a 9 x 13 – inch casserole. Cook bacon until crisp. Remove bacon from pan, cool and crumble. Add sugar and salt to the bacon drippings in the pan. Add cabbage and cook until tender. Meanwhile cook noodles according to package directions and drain. Stir cabbage, noodles and bacon together in pan. Spoon into casserole and bake covered for 45 minutes. Uncover and add sour cream in dollops. Sprinkle paprika over the top and return to oven for 5 minutes.

8 servings

## Augie's Front Burner Red Cabbage

1/2   cup duck fat (may substitute
other fat)
2   large onions, chopped
2   heads red cabbage, chopped
1/4   cup currant jelly
2   tablespoons honey
1/2   cup red wine vinegar
Ground cloves

Cinnamon
White pepper
Nutmeg
Garlic powder
Salt and pepper
2   tablespoons cornstarch
Water

Heat duck fat in large pot. Add onion and sauté for a few minutes. Add red cabbage and sauté for another 2 minutes. Add jelly, honey and red wine vinegar and stir. Add a pinch each of cloves, cinnamon, white pepper, nutmeg and garlic powder. Add salt and pepper to taste. Bring to a short boil and simmer for 10 minutes. Mix cornstarch with a small amount of cold water and stir into cabbage to thicken. Cook for another 5 minutes.

8 servings

# Roasted Cabbage Wedges

*Note: Char or blacken the cabbage a bit for even more flavor. After it is roasted, toast it under the broiler for about 5 minutes to attain a crispy golden brown. This makes a great side for pork or chicken.*

| | |
|---|---|
| 1 **medium head green cabbage (1 1/2 pounds)** | **Sea salt to taste** |
| 2 **tablespoons unsalted butter, melted** | **Freshly ground pepper to taste** |
| 3 **tablespoons olive oil** | 1/2 **cup water** |
| | 2 **tablespoons flat leaf parsley leaves** |

Preheat oven to 400°. Cut cabbage into 8 or more wedges and place on a baking sheet with sides. Drizzle with the melted butter and olive oil. Sprinkle with sea salt and pepper. Pour the water around the cabbage. Roast for a minimum of 30 – 40 minutes, turning several times. Wedges may fall apart as they cook. The cabbage should be tender and slightly crisp and golden brown all around. Remove from oven and season with more sea salt and pepper. Sprinkle with the parsley leaves and serve.

8 servings

# Illini Country Club
# Pickled Cabbage

*Note: See julienne on page 82.*

| | |
|---|---|
| 1 **cup sugar** | 1 **red onion, julienned** |
| 1 1/2 **cups apple cider vinegar** | 1 **jalapeño pepper, julienned** |
| 1 1/2 **cups chardonnay** | 1/2 **cup honey** |
| 1 **head purple cabbage, finely diced** | 1/4 **teaspoon salt** |
| 1 **head green cabbage, finely diced** | |

Combine sugar, vinegar and wine in a stock pot and heat until simmering. Combine purple and green cabbage, onions and pepper in a bowl and pour the simmering liquid over the vegetables. Stir in honey and salt. Cover with plastic wrap and refrigerate overnight before serving.

12 servings

# Amaretto Almond Carrots

*Note: Amaretto is an almond-flavored liqueur. Other similar liqueurs may be used.*

| | |
|---|---|
| 1/4 **cup slivered almonds** | 1/4 **cup amaretto liqueur** |
| 1 **pound fresh carrots (trimmed and peeled)** | 1/8 **teaspoon cinnamon** |
| 2 **tablespoons butter** | **Salt to taste** |
| | **Pepper to taste** |

Lightly toast slivered almonds in a dry skillet until fragrant. Set aside. Slice the carrots into 1/8 – inch thick coin shapes. Place carrots in a heavy sauce pan with the butter and gently simmer about 3 minutes, stirring occasionally. Add amaretto, cinnamon, salt and pepper. Continue to simmer until carrots are just tender, but not overcooked. Stir in toasted almonds and serve.

6 servings

## Butter Braised Carrots

| | | | |
|---|---|---|---|
| 12 | slender carrots | 1/4 | cup dry or semi-dry white wine |
| 1 | medium onion, chopped | 1/4 | cup minced fresh parsley |
| 4 | tablespoons (1/2 stick) butter | | Salt and pepper |
| 2 | teaspoons sugar | | |

Peel carrots and cut into 3 – inch lengths. Place carrots in a skillet and add water to barely cover. Cover and bring to a boil. Reduce heat and simmer for 10 – 12 minutes until tender. Drain water from carrots. Add onion, butter, sugar and wine to skillet. Cook over medium high heat, shaking pan or stirring gently, until the wine evaporates and the onions are lightly browned. Mix in parsley and season to taste with salt and pepper.

6 servings

*Note: If slender carrots are not available, use 8 – 10 carrots and cut them into halves or quarters vertically. Dried parsley (2 tablespoons) may be substituted for fresh parsley.*

## Illini Country Club
## Pickled Cucumbers

| | | | |
|---|---|---|---|
| 1 1/2 | cups rice wine vinegar | 1 | red onion, sliced and rings separated |
| 1 1/2 | cups water | | Chopped mint for garnish |
| 1 | cup sugar | | |
| 3 | English cucumbers, sliced | | |

Combine vinegar and water. Add sugar and stir until it dissolves. Add cucumbers and onion rings. Cover and refrigerate overnight. Serve garnished with mint.

16 – 24 servings

## Gloria Schwartz
## Carrot Tzimmes

| | | | |
|---|---|---|---|
| 8 | carrots, sliced 3/4 – inch thick | 1 | tablespoon flour |
| 1/2 | cup water (or more, if needed) | 1/2 | cup raisins |
| 1/3 | cup honey | 1 | (8.25 ounce) can crushed pineapple, drained |
| 1 | tablespoon fresh lemon juice | 1/2 | cup coarsely chopped pared apple |
| 1/2 | teaspoon salt | | |
| 1 | tablespoon margarine, melted | | |

In a heavy saucepan, cook carrots, covered, in the water for 5 minutes. Do not drain. Stir in the honey, lemon juice and salt and mix well. Cover and simmer 20 minutes. Prepare a beurre manié with the margarine and flour together. Stir the beurre manié into the carrots along with the raisins, pineapple and apple and mix well. Cover and simmer for 10 more minutes before serving.

6 servings

*Note: Beurre manié is a paste made from flour and butter that is used to thicken sauces. It is similar to a roux.*

## Glazed Carrots with Grapes and Walnuts

6  cups (1 1/2 pounds) carrots,
   peeled and sliced about
   1/4 – inch thick
1/4  cup (1/2 stick) unsalted butter
1  cup chicken stock
3  tablespoons sugar

1  cup seedless red grapes,
   halved
1/2  cup chopped walnuts
   Salt to taste
   Pepper to taste

Combine carrots, butter, stock and sugar in a wide sauté pan over high heat. Bring to a boil and then reduce the heat to medium low. Simmer uncovered until the carrots are tender and the pan juices are reduced to a syrupy glaze, 8 – 10 minutes. Stir in grapes and walnuts and season to taste with salt and pepper.

6 – 8 servings

## Greek Style Carrots

1  pound carrots, peeled and
   sliced
2  tablespoons olive oil
1  clove garlic, minced
4  large green onions, sliced

1/2  teaspoon oregano leaves
1/2  teaspoon salt
1  tablespoon fresh lemon juice
   Fresh parsley for garnish

Parboil carrots for 5 minutes. Drain. Heat the oil in a medium pan. Add garlic and sauté for 2 minutes. Add carrots, green onions, oregano and salt. Cook covered over low heat for 15 minutes. Sprinkle with lemon juice. Garnish with fresh parsley.

4 servings

*Vachel Lindsay was born in this home near the Executive Mansion and lived here all his life. An early 1900's poet, he was an advocate of "singing poetry", the ancient Greek style emphasizing sounds in recitation. He is known best in Springfield for his poem,* Abraham Lincoln Walks at Midnight, *with Abe's spirit walking in his old environs recalling his many friends and neighbors.*

## Glazed Green Bean Bundles

8 slices bacon
1 pound fresh green beans, stemmed
1/4 cup (1/2 stick) margarine or butter

1/4 cup brown sugar
1 clove garlic, minced

*Variation: Use a 16 ounce bag of frozen whole green beans cooked according to package directions.*

Preheat oven to 350°. Grease or spray a shallow 9 x 13 – inch baking pan. Pre-cook the bacon until just beginning to brown. Remove excess grease. Pre-cook the green beans in boiling water or steam them for 6 minutes, just until crisp tender. Drain green beans and arrange in 8 bundles. Wrap each bundle with bacon and secure with toothpick. Place in shallow baking dish. Melt margarine or butter and stir in brown sugar and garlic. Pour over bundles and bake until glaze is shiny, about 30 minutes.

8 servings

## Hot Marinated Green Beans

16 ounces fresh green beans
1/2 large or 1 small red onion, thinly sliced
2 tablespoons olive oil
1/2 teaspoon sugar, or to taste
1 tablespoon balsamic vinegar (optional)

1 teaspoon thyme
Salt to taste
Pepper to taste
2 slices bacon, cut into pieces and cooked

*Variation: Use frozen green beans if fresh are not available. Add 2 tablespoons of dried cherries for color and a different taste.*

Boil beans 4 minutes. Drain, rinse and set aside. In a large skillet, sauté onions in olive oil until limp and brown. Sprinkle with a little sugar and, if desired, balsamic vinegar. Add thyme, salt and pepper to taste and cook another 3 minutes. Return beans to skillet and heat until warm, about 2 minutes. Add bacon pieces and stir well.

4 – 6 servings

## Garlic and Rosemary Roasted Red Potatoes

2 pounds new red potatoes, sliced
2 tablespoons olive oil
Rosemary, to taste

1 garlic clove, finely chopped
Salt to taste
Pepper to taste

*Note: If potatoes are large, halve or quarter them.*

*Variation: Add small Vidalia or sweet onions to the potatoes.*

Preheat oven to 400°. Layer potatoes in a single layer on a sheet pan. Drizzle with olive oil and sprinkle with rosemary, garlic, salt and pepper. Toss to cover potatoes thoroughly with oil and seasoning. Bake until well browned, for about 40 – 60 minutes. Stir occasionally while baking.

4 servings

### Julianne Glatz
# Nana's German Spinach

1-1/2  pounds fresh spinach

  3  slices good quality bacon, diced

2 – 3  slices homemade type white bread

4 – 6  small green onions green and white parts, thinly sliced

1/4  cup unbleached flour

Kosher or sea salt

Freshly ground pepper

Freshly ground nutmeg to taste

Remove any large and tough stems from the spinach. (If you are using "baby" spinach that does not have large stems, you may want to decrease the weight to around a pound.) Wash the spinach well to remove any grit and dirt, but do not drain. Cook the spinach in a large pot just until wilted. Do not overcook. Remove from the heat and transfer to a large bowl to cool. Do not drain. When the spinach has cooled, squeeze by handfuls, reserving the liquid. Measure the liquid and add enough water (if necessary) to measure 1 cup. Place the squeezed spinach on a chopping board. Top with the bread and onions. With a large knife, chop the spinach, bread and onions. Some prefer the mixture more finely chopped and some with more texture.

Meanwhile, sauté the bacon in a large pan until crisp. Remove from the pan and reserve. Add the flour and cook for a couple of minutes. Whisk in the reserved spinach liquid, bring to a simmer, and cook for about 2 – 3 minutes or until thickened. Add the chopped spinach/bread/scallion mixture and cook for a couple of minutes to heat through. Season to taste with the salt, pepper, and nutmeg.

6 – 8 servings

# Deluxe Green Peas

1  (16 ounce) package frozen peas

4  tablespoons (1/2 stick) butter, divided

1/2  teaspoon salt

Dash pepper

1  teaspoon sugar

1  tablespoon chopped pimiento (optional)

1/4  cup onion (optional)

Dash Fleur de Sel or sea salt (optional)

Combine peas and 1 1/2 tablespoons butter. Cook covered in a small amount of water over medium heat, about 10 – 12 minutes. Drain. Add salt and pepper. Stir in sugar. If using, sauté pimiento and onion in 1 tablespoon butter until soft. Add to peas. Cover and heat through. Top with remaining butter. Sprinkle with Fleur de Sel, if desired.

4 – 6 servings

## Creamy Garlic Mashed Potatoes

| | | | |
|---|---|---|---|
| 6 | medium russet potatoes | 1 | teaspoon salt, or to taste |
| 1 | cup milk | 1 | teaspoon pepper, or to taste |
| 1 1/2 | teaspoons finely minced garlic | | |
| 1/2 | cup (1 stick) butter, cut into pieces | | |

*Variation: Use half and half in place of milk for creamier potatoes.*

Peel and dice potatoes into 1/2 – inch cubes. Place the cubed potatoes in a medium saucepan and cover with water. Bring water to a boil. Reduce heat and cook until potatoes are tender (about 20 minutes). Meanwhile, heat the milk and the garlic until simmering in separate saucepan. Remove from heat and set aside. Drain cooked potatoes and return to pan. Add butter, salt and pepper. Add the milk and garlic mixture gradually until potatoes reach the proper consistency, mashing until smooth and creamy.

4 – 6 servings

## Grilled Potatoes and Onions

| | | | |
|---|---|---|---|
| 3 | pounds new potatoes, washed and quartered | 2 | tablespoons olive oil |
| 2 | medium onions cut in 1 – inch pieces | 2 | cloves garlic, minced |
| 1/2 | cup chopped parsley | 1 | teaspoon salt |
| | | 1 | teaspoon freshly ground pepper |

*Note: These may be prepared as individual servings also.*

Cut 2 pieces of aluminum foil, each 24 – inches long. Toss the potatoes, onions, parsley, oil, garlic, salt and pepper in a large bowl. Place half of the mixture in the center of one of the pieces of foil. Fold the foil sides to the center, seal and then seal the top and bottom tightly. Repeat with the second half of the potatoes and remaining foil strip. Place the foil pouches on the grill over a high heat. Cook for about 30 minutes or until the potatoes are tender. Remove from the grill. Let sit for 5 minutes. Carefully unwrap foil to permit the steam to escape. Remove food from foil and serve.

8 servings

## American Harvest Potato Dumplings

| | | |
|---|---|---|
| 5 | pounds russet potatoes | Drizzle olive oil |
| 5 | cups flour | Salt and pepper |
| 8 | egg yolks | Nutmeg |

*Note: Also known as gnocchi. They are nice and light and go well with most sautéed vegetables.*

Peel the potatoes, boil in water until done then put through a ricer. Let cool to room temperature. Make a well in the potatoes. Put the flour, eggs, oil, salt, pepper and nutmeg in the center. Incorporate with a fork until it forms a dough. Knead for twenty minutes. Roll into logs on a floured surface and cut into dumplings. Poach in a large pot of salted water until they float. Shock in ice water.

*Tip: Other oils will cause the flavor to vary.*

---

# Parmesan Potato Cakes

| | |
|---|---|
| 1 **pound potatoes** | 1 **clove garlic, minced** |
| 1/4 **cup Parmesan cheese** | **Salt to taste** |
| 1 **egg, lightly beaten** | **Pepper to taste** |
| 2 **tablespoons onion, minced** | 2 **cups bread crumbs, divided** |
| 1 **tablespoon parsley, minced** | **Olive oil for frying** |

Peel potatoes and cut into 2 – inch cubes. Add to large pot of salted water. Cover, bring to a boil and cook until very tender. Drain and mash until smooth. Set aside to cool.

Whisk together Parmesan, egg, onion, parsley, garlic, salt and pepper. Combine with the mashed potatoes. Add 1 cup bread crumbs and stir only until blended. Form mixture into large walnut-sized balls and flatten into cakes with your hands. Coat the cakes on each side with the remaining bread crumbs. Heat 1/8 – inch olive oil in a skillet over medium high heat. Add pancakes, reduce heat to medium and fry until golden brown on one side; turn and fry on the other side. Drain on paper towels.

4 servings

---

 # Sangamo Club
# Potato Gratin Dauphinoise

| | |
|---|---|
| 1 **garlic clove** | **Salt to taste** |
| 3 **tablespoons butter, divided** | **Pepper to taste** |
| 3 **pounds russet potatoes, peeled, thinly sliced (not rinsed)** | 2 **cups shredded Gruyère cheese** |
| | 3 **cups heavy cream** |

Preheat oven to 350°. Rub the inside of a shallow medium casserole with garlic, then rub with 1 tablespoon butter. Make a layer of the potatoes, overlapping. Sprinkle them with salt and pepper and some cheese. Repeat layering until potatoes are all used, ending with cheese. Pour cream over potatoes. Dot the top with remaining butter. Bake for 40 minutes or until golden and tender.

10 – 12 servings

*The Grill Room of the Sangamo Club is a casual, yet intimate dining room with the bar featuring an arched mirror which echos the arched window of the main dining room. Its contemporary art deco design with the large recessed lighting and receding arches lends a feeling of casual elegance to any meal.*

## Potatoes au Gratin

| | | | | |
|---|---|---|---|---|
| 6 | medium potatoes | 1 | teaspoon black pepper |
| 1/4 | cup (1/2 stick) butter | 3 | cups milk |
| 3 | tablespoons flour | 3 | cups grated cheddar cheese |
| 1/4 | cup minced onions | | Paprika for sprinkling |
| 1 | teaspoon salt | | |

*Variation: Add 1 pound of diced ham to create an entrée.*

Preheat oven to 350°. Grease a 3 quart casserole. Cook potatoes in jackets in water over medium heat until it boils. Drain, cool, peel and thickly slice the potatoes. Melt butter, whisk in flour and stir over low heat until bubbly. Add onion, salt and pepper. Add milk slowly in thin stream whisking constantly. Remove from heat and stir in cheese until it melts. Layer potatoes and cheese sauce in the casserole, ending with cheese sauce. Sprinkle with paprika. Bake for about 45 minutes or until bubbly and lightly browned.

8 – 10 servings

## Potatoes Romanoff

| | | | | |
|---|---|---|---|---|
| 4 | medium russet potatoes | 1 | teaspoon salt |
| 1 | cup dairy sour cream | 1/8 | teaspoon pepper |
| 4 | green onions, sliced | | Paprika |
| 1 1/4 | cups shredded sharp cheddar cheese, divided | | |

*Tip: May be prepared in advance, refrigerated and baked before serving. Allow a few minutes extra baking time.*

Preheat oven to 350°. Butter a 1 1/2 quart casserole. Cook potatoes in jackets until tender. Peel and shred. Combine potatoes, sour cream, onions, 3/4 cup cheese, salt and pepper and mix well.

Pour potato mixture into casserole. Sprinkle with remaining cheese and paprika. Bake 30 – 40 minutes.

6 servings

## Easy Baked Sauerkraut

| | | | | |
|---|---|---|---|---|
| 1 | (30 ounce) can sauerkraut, drained and rinsed | 1/3 | cup white sugar |
| 1 | (14 1/2 ounce) can diced tomatoes | 1/3 | cup brown sugar, packed |
| 1 | small onion, chopped | 6 | slices bacon, cooked and crumbled |

Preheat oven to 325°. Butter or spray a 3 quart casserole or baking pan. In a large bowl, combine the sauerkraut, tomatoes, onion, white sugar, brown sugar and bacon. Pour ingredients into prepared pan and bake for 30 – 40 minutes.

8 servings

## Roasted Potatoes with Garlic and Lemon

| | | | | |
|---|---|---|---|---|
| 5 – 6 | potatoes, peeled and cut into evenly sized wedges | | 2 | lemons, juiced, more is desired |
| 1/2 | cup olive oil | | 1/2 | cup chicken broth |
| 1 1/2 | teaspoons dried oregano | | | Salt and freshly ground black pepper to taste |
| 1 | teaspoon garlic powder | | | |

Preheat oven to 400°. In a large mixing bowl, add the potatoes and toss them with the olive oil, oregano, garlic powder, lemon juice, chicken broth, salt and pepper until they are well coated. Line a sheet pan or a roasting pan with lightly greased or sprayed aluminum foil. Place the potatoes in the pan in a single layer and drizzle with any remaining marinade. Bake for approximately 60 minutes. Carefully turn the potatoes halfway through cooking to prevent them from sticking and to brown them evenly. Re-season with salt and pepper and squeeze a bit more lemon juice over them (if desired) when they are fresh out of the oven.

8 servings

## Lemon Rice Pilaf

| | | | | |
|---|---|---|---|---|
| 2 | tablespoons olive oil | | 3 | tablespoons, finely grated lemon zest |
| 1 | small onion, finely chopped | | 8 | mint leaves, finely chopped |
| 1 | cup basmati white rice | | | Salt to taste |
| 3 | cups chicken broth, divided | | | White pepper to taste |
| 2 – 4 | tablespoons butter, melted (optional) | | | Parmesan cheese for garnish |
| 2 | tablespoons whipping cream (optional) | | | Mint leaves for garnish (optional) |
| 3 | tablespoons Parmesan cheese, grated | | | |

Place saucepan over low heat and pour in the olive oil. Stir in the onion when oil is warm. Cook gently, stirring occasionally, for about 3 minutes until the onion is soft and translucent. Increase heat to medium and add rice, stirring it until it is coated with oil, about 2 minutes. Add 2 cups chicken broth and stir well. Bring to boil. Reduce heat to low, cover and cook until rice has absorbed the liquid, adding additional chicken broth as needed until the rice is cooked and broth absorbed, about 12 minutes. Stir in the butter and whipping cream (if using), Parmesan and lemon zest. Gently add mint leaves and season with salt and pepper. Serve with a sprinkle of Parmesan cheese and mint leaves for garnish if you wish.

6 servings

# Spinach Casserole

3 (10 ounce) packages chopped spinach, thawed, drained and patted dry

2 cups (8 ounce) shredded Swiss cheese, divided

1 cup Parmesan cheese, divided

1/2 cup chopped onions

1 cup fresh mushrooms, sliced

1 (10 3/4 ounce) can cream of mushroom soup

1 cup mayonnaise

3 eggs, lightly beaten

Salt to taste

Pepper to taste

Garlic salt to taste

Preheat oven to 375°. Spray a 2 1/2 or 3 quart casserole. Set aside. In a large bowl, combine spinach, 1 cup Swiss cheese, 1/2 cup Parmesan cheese, onions and mushrooms. Combine mushroom soup, mayonnaise, eggs, salt, pepper and garlic salt and whisk. Pour soup mixture over vegetables and mix well. Pour the entire mixture into the casserole and top with remaining Swiss cheese and Parmesan. Bake covered for 20 minutes. Uncover and bake an additional 20 minutes or until top is lightly browned.

16 servings

# Grilled Squash and Zucchini with Honey Lime Dressing

*Dressing:*

1/2 cup olive oil

1/3 cup fresh lime juice (about 2 large limes)

3 tablespoons honey

1/4 cup chopped fresh cilantro

Salt and freshly ground pepper to taste

*Vegetables:*

1/4 cup olive oil

2 garlic cloves, minced

1/4 cup seeded canned chipotle pepper, (or to taste)

2 teaspoons ground cumin

Salt and pepper to taste

2 medium zucchini, cut lengthwise into 1/2 – inch planks

2 medium summer squash, cut lengthwise into 1/2 – inch planks

In a small bowl, whisk together the olive oil, lime juice, honey, cilantro and salt and pepper to taste. Reserve dressing for serving. In a medium bowl, combine the olive oil, garlic, chipotle pepper, cumin, salt and pepper to taste. Mix well. Add the squash and zucchini planks and toss so they are completely covered with the mixture. Place the squash on the grill over a medium-hot fire and cook for about 3 minutes on each side or until browned. Remove from the grill, place on a platter and drizzle with the dressing and serve.

4 – 6 servings

## Three Ingredient Butternut Squash

Variation: Substitute
maple syrup for sugar.

| | | | |
|---|---|---|---|
| 1 | large butternut squash | 1/2 | cup sugar (brown or white) |
| 6 | tablespoons butter | | |

Preheat oven to 350°. Grease or spray a 9 x 13 – inch baking pan. Peel and seed squash. Slice into 1/2 – inch slices. Place in baking dish in a single layer. Dot squash with butter and sprinkle with sugar. Bake 45 – 60 minutes until tender.

6 servings

## Zucchini Casserole

*Variation: Use a
mixture of red, orange,
yellow and green
peppers.*

*Note: For even more
flavor, this can be
prepared a day ahead
and refrigerated until
ready to bake and
serve.*

| | | | |
|---|---|---|---|
| 4 | cups sliced zucchini | 1 | cup grated Parmesan cheese |
| 2 | cups boiling water | | Salt to taste |
| 2 | eggs | | Pepper to taste |
| 1 | cup mayonnaise | 1 | tablespoon butter |
| 1 | medium onion chopped | 1/2 | cup bread crumbs |
| 1/4 | cup chopped green pepper | | |

Preheat oven to 350°. Butter or spray a 1 1/2 quart baking dish. Cook zucchini in boiling water until tender and drain. In large mixing bowl, beat the eggs and then add mayonnaise, onion, green peppers, cheese, salt and pepper. Stir in cooked zucchini. Turn into baking dish. Dot with butter and cover with bread crumbs. Bake for 30 minutes or until casserole is bubbly and top is nicely browned.

6 – 8 servings

## Stewed Rhubarb

*Variation: Cook
uncovered on top
of stove, stirring
occasionally, until
rhubarb is very soft.*

| | | | |
|---|---|---|---|
| 6 | stalks rhubarb, cut into 1 – inch pieces | 4 | cups water, using what is needed |
| 1 | cup sugar, more for sprinkling | 1 | cup ricotta cheese (optional) |
| | Zest of one orange (less if preferred) | | |

Preheat oven to 325°. Put rhubarb into a medium baking dish. Sprinkle with sugar and orange zest. Add enough water to cover. Bake, uncovered, until very soft, about 1 hour. Transfer rhubarb with slotted spoon to a bowl and set aside. Boil remaining liquid over medium high heat until thick and syrupy, about 20 minutes. Pour syrup over rhubarb. Serve at room temperature with a spoonful of ricotta cheese (if using) with sugar sprinkled on top.

6 – 8 servings

## Bourbon Street Sweet Potato Casserole

**Sweet Potato Mixture:**

| | |
|---|---|
| 3 | **cups mashed sweet potatoes (about 4 – 5 medium size)** |
| 1/2 | **cup sugar** |
| 2 | **eggs** |
| 1/2 | **cup (1 stick) butter, softened** |
| 1 | **tablespoon vanilla extract** |
| 2 | **tablespoons bourbon** |

**Topping:**

| | |
|---|---|
| 1/2 | **cup brown sugar, packed** |
| 1/3 | **cup flour** |
| 1 | **cup chopped pecans** |
| 1/3 | **cup butter, softened** |

*Tip: Wrap sweet potatoes individually in foil and bake for approximately one hour or until soft when squeezed. Scoop the flesh from the skins and mash.*

*Note: Casserole may be prepared up to one day in advance. Allow extra baking time when casserole has been refrigerated.*

Preheat oven to 350°. Butter a 2 quart casserole. Combine potatoes, sugar, eggs, butter, vanilla and bourbon. Beat with electric mixer for two minutes and pour into prepared casserole.

For the topping, combine brown sugar, flour, pecans and butter with a fork and sprinkle on top of potatoes. Bake for 30 minutes.

8 servings

## Chipotle Mashed Sweet Potatoes

| | |
|---|---|
| 4 | **medium sweet potatoes, peel and cut into large pieces** |
| 1 – 2 | **tablespoons canned chipotle peppers** |
| 1 | **cup cream** |

| | |
|---|---|
| 2 | **tablespoons unsalted butter** |
| | **Salt to taste** |
| | **Freshly cracked black pepper to taste** |

In a medium sized sauce pan bring 2 quarts of water to a boil over high heat. Add the sweet potatoes and cook for about 10 minutes or until they are easily pierced by a fork. While the potatoes are cooking, blend the chipotle peppers in a food processor. Combine peppers with the cream and butter in a small saucepan. Cook over medium heat until the butter is melted, about 5 minutes. Drain the potatoes and place them in a medium bowl. Add the cream mixture and mash the potatoes with a fork until the cream is mixed in and the potatoes are fairly smooth. Add salt and pepper to taste and serve.

4 – 6 servings

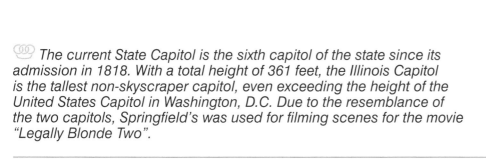

*The current State Capitol is the sixth capitol of the state since its admission in 1818. With a total height of 361 feet, the Illinois Capitol is the tallest non-skyscraper capitol, even exceeding the height of the United States Capitol in Washington, D.C. Due to the resemblance of the two capitols, Springfield's was used for filming scenes for the movie "Legally Blonde Two".*

### Augie's Front Burner
# Couscous

2 cups chicken broth
Salt
1 tablespoon olive oil
1 (10 ounce) package couscous
1/2 tomato, diced
1/2 cucumber, diced

2 scallions, diced
Cumin Lime Vinaigrette, available locally at specialty shops
Mixed baby greens, for garnish

Combine broth, salt to taste and olive oil in a medium sauce pan and bring to a boil. Stir in couscous and cover. Remove from heat and let stand 5 minutes. Fluff couscous lightly. Combine tomato, cucumber and scallions. Add couscous and vinaigrette to vegetables. Spoon into individual molds until cold so they congeal. To serve, invert mold onto a plate and garnish with mixed baby greens.

4 servings

## Gorgonzola Polenta

*Note: This is awesome and well worth the effort. It is wonderful with a roasted or grilled chicken or pork entrée.*

3 cups milk, (whole or 2%)
3 tablespoons unsalted butter
3/4 cup polenta (cornmeal)
3 tablespoons sour cream
2 1/2 tablespoons grated Gruyère cheese
2 1/2 tablespoons grated Parmesan cheese

1/3 cup crumbled Gorgonzola cheese, plus 6 thin 1 – inch square slices
1/3 cup golden raisins
Freshly grated nutmeg
Salt to taste
Freshly ground pepper to taste
Fine bread crumbs

Preheat oven to 450°. Spray six 1/2 cup ramekins or custard cups with cooking spray. Spray or generously butter a 9 x 13 – inch baking dish. In a medium size sauce pan, bring the milk and butter to a boil. Add the cornmeal in a thin stream, stirring constantly with a wooden spoon until very thick and smooth, about 5 minutes. Stir in the sour cream, Gruyère, Parmesan, crumbled Gorgonzola, raisins and a couple pinches of nutmeg. Beat until smooth. Remove from heat and add salt and pepper to taste. Spoon the mixture into the prepared ramekins. Smooth the top and cool for at least 15 minutes until set. Use a knife to loosen polenta from ramekins and unmold into the baking dish. Place a slice of Gorgonzola on top of each and sprinkle with a fine layer of bread crumbs. Bake for 10 – 12 minutes then broil until lightly golden. Serve immediately.

6 servings

## Illini Country Club
## Parmesan Grits

| | | | |
|---|---|---|---|
| 6 | cups chicken stock | 4 | ears of fresh corn cut off the cob |
| 2 | cups heavy cream | | |
| 2 | cups of dry stone-ground grits | 1/2 | cup (1 stick) butter |
| 1/4 | cup sugar | 1 | cup grated Parmesan |

Add chicken stock and cream to a sauce pot and bring to a simmer. Whisk in grits and sugar; simmer for 20 minutes on low heat. Add corn and continue cooking 10 more minutes. Add butter and cheese; let dissolve and remove from heat.

## American Harvest
## Spicy Pickled Vegetables (Giardiniera)

| | | | |
|---|---|---|---|
| 3/4 | cup cider vinegar | 6 | heads cauliflower, cut into mini florettes |
| 1 | quart water | | |
| 1 | cup salt | 10 | red bell peppers, diced |
| 1 | cup sugar | 2 | red onions, diced |
| 1 | cup crushed red chili peppers | 8 | carrots, diced |
| 1 | cup Aleppo | 1 | bunch celery, diced |
| 2 | cups pickle spice | 12 | cloves garlic, sliced |
| 2 | cups olive oil | | |

Combine vinegar, water, salt, sugar, crushed chili peppers, Aleppo, pickle spice and olive oil and bring to a boil. Let simmer for one hour. Strain over the vegetables into a plastic container. Add a scoop of ice and chill.

Serves a large group

*Note: We use these as a nice addition for our salads and our sandwiches. It keeps its crunch as long as you ice it down right after pouring the hot pickling brine over it. It will last up to two weeks if it is stored properly. This is a really fun way to dress up a cheese plate.*

*Note: Aleppo is a Syrian chile. Crushed red pepper may be substituted and the recipe would still be great. The recipe may be halved, but the vegetables will hold for a long time jarred since it's pickled.*

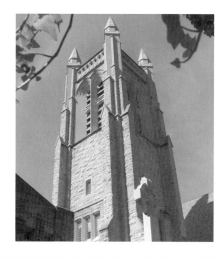

*The tower at Westminster Church was completed in 1956 following the plans of the pre-eminent architectural firm of Cram, Goodhue and Ferguson of Boston who designed the Neo-Gothic church building. It houses an iron bell that has for generations called worshipers to three of the four church locations over the years. This bell was dedicated in 1840 and, for some time served as the fire bell for the young town of Springfield. The King's Daughters Organization is happy to call Westminster Presbyterian Church home for our annual meeting as well as many member activities.*

## Orange Nut Sweet Potatoes

| | |
|---|---|
| 6 medium sweet potatoes, peeled | 1 cup orange juice concentrate |
| 1/3 cup packed brown sugar | 2 teaspoons grated lemon peel |
| 1 tablespoon cornstarch | 1/2 cup chopped pecans (optional) |

Butter or spray a 9 x 13 – inch baking pan. Place sweet potatoes in a large sauce pan and cover with water. Bring to a boil. Reduce heat. Cover and cook for 30 – 40 minutes or until tender. Drain and cool, then cut into 1/2 – inch slices. Arrange slices in the prepared baking pan.

Preheat oven to 325°. Combine brown sugar and cornstarch in a small saucepan. Whisk in orange juice concentrate and lemon peel. Bring to a boil. Cook and stir for 1 – 2 minutes or until thickened. Pour over sweet potatoes. Sprinkle with pecans, if desired. Bake uncovered for 30 – 35 minutes or until sweet potatoes are heated through and the sauce is bubbly.

12 servings

## Sangamo Club
## Ratatouille Niçoise

| | |
|---|---|
| 2 large eggplants cut in 1 – inch cubes | 4 zucchinis, cut in 1 – inch cubes |
| Salt | 4 large tomatoes, cut in 1 – inch cubes |
| 1/2 cup olive oil, more as needed | 2 tablespoons chopped fresh parsley |
| 2 large yellow onions, peeled and cut in 1 – inch cubes | 2 tablespoons chopped fresh basil |
| 7 cloves garlic, peeled and minced | 1 teaspoon fresh thyme leaves |
| 1 green bell pepper, cut in 1 – inch cubes | Juice of 1 lemon |
| 1 red bell pepper, cut in 1 – inch cubes | Salt and pepper to taste |

Toss eggplant with salt, place in a colander to drain for 20 minutes. Rinse eggplant and pat dry. While eggplant is draining, pour oil into skillet and sauté onions until golden. Add garlic and continue to cook for one minute. Place the onion and garlic mixture in a large pot and set aside. Repeat the cooking process with the green and red peppers, then zucchini, then eggplant, then tomatoes. Add each batch of cooked vegetables to the pot as they are cooked. Simmer the vegetable mixture for five to ten minutes, adding parsley, basil, thyme and lemon juice. Add salt and pepper to taste. Serve hot, warm or at room temperature.

Serves approximately 8

## Spanikopita

6  tablespoons flour

3  eggs, beaten

2  cups cottage cheese

2  cups cheddar cheese shredded

1  teaspoon salt

2  (10 ounce) boxes frozen spinach, thawed and drained

Pepper to taste

Preheat oven to 350°. Grease or spray a 1 quart casserole dish. Measure flour into a bowl and add beaten eggs, mixing thoroughly. Add the cottage cheese, cheddar cheese and salt, mixing well. Add the spinach. Add pepper to taste. Pour into a casserole dish and bake, uncovered, for 1 hour. Let stand a few minutes before serving.

12 servings

The George W. Bunn House, located in a neighborhood known as "Aristocracy Hill", was built in the Queen Anne style in 1883 for Sara Bunn Jones and her husband, attorney Frank Hatch Jones. In 1948 John Edward Sankey and his wife Kate Chatterton Sankey bought the house, living there until his death in 1982. The house was completely renovated in 2010.

# Tempting Treats

— *continued on next page*

*The crown indicates a celebrity's recipe.*

# Tempting Treats

👑 *The crown indicates a celebrity's recipe.*

## Melt In Your Mouth Cookies

**Cookies:**
- 1 1/4 cups flour
- 1/2 cup cornstarch
- 1/3 cup confectioners' sugar
- 3/4 cup (1 1/2 sticks) butter, softened
- 1 teaspoon grated lemon peel
- 1 tablespoon lemon juice

**Frosting:**
- 3/4 cup confectioners' sugar
- 4 tablespoons (1/2 stick) butter, softened
- 1 teaspoon grated lemon peel
- 1 teaspoon lemon juice

Note: Refrigerate until serving. The logs can be frozen for up to two months, slightly thawed, sliced and baked, but it will be hard to keep this cookie around for that long.

Grease or lightly spray cookie sheet or line with parchment paper. Combine flour, cornstarch, sugar, butter, grated lemon peel and lemon juice in large mixing bowl. If using a mixer, beat at low speed, scraping bowl often, until well mixed (2 – 3 minutes). Divide dough in half. Shape each half into an 8 x 1 – inch roll. Wrap in plastic wrap and refrigerate until firm (1 – 2 hours) and up to two days. Preheat oven to 350°. With a sharp knife, cut each roll into 1/4 – inch slices. Place 2 – inches apart on cookie sheet. Bake for 8 – 12 minutes or until set. Cookies will not brown. Cool completely before frosting.

Combine confectioners' sugar, butter, lemon peel and lemon juice in a small bowl. Beat at medium speed, scraping bowl often, until fluffy (1 – 2 minutes). Frost cooled cookies.

4 dozen

## Pistachio Butter Cookies

- 1 cup (2 sticks) butter
- 1 cup sugar
- 3 tablespoons milk
- 1 1/2 teaspoons lemon extract or flavoring
- 1 1/2 cups flour
- 1/4 teaspoon salt
- 3/4 cup coarsely chopped pistachio nuts

Cream the butter and sugar. Add the milk and lemon extract. Combine the flour and salt and add to the butter mixture. Fold in the nuts. Roll dough into a 2 – inch roll. Wrap in plastic wrap and chill several hours or overnight.

When ready to bake, preheat oven to 375°. Remove plastic from dough and slice the dough into 1/4 – inch slices. Place on an ungreased cookie sheet and bake 10 – 12 minutes or until lightly browned.

4 – 5 dozen cookies

## Spectacular Chocolate Chippers

Notes: *Try 1 1/4 cups semisweet chocolate chips and 1/2 cup milk chocolate chips in this recipe. Kosher salt seems to add the element of surprise in each bite.*

1/2   **cup (1 stick) unsalted butter, softened**
3/4   **cup light brown sugar, packed**
1   **egg**
2   **tablespoons vanilla extract**
3/4   **cup coarsely chopped dates**
1   **cup flour**

1/2   **teaspoon baking soda**
1/2   **teaspoon Kosher salt**
1/4   **teaspoon baking powder**
1/2   **cup grated coconut**
1/2   **cup granola**
3/4   **cup coarsely chopped walnuts**
1 3/4   **cups chocolate chips**

Preheat oven to 350°. Cover a cookie sheet with parchment paper or use a silicone baking mat. In the large bowl of an electric mixer, cream the butter and brown sugar until smooth. Add the egg and vanilla and beat well. Stir in the dates and let the mixture sit 5 minutes to soften the dates. Beat at high speed for 3 minutes or until mixture is very light brown and creamy. Combine the flour, baking soda, salt and baking powder in a small bowl whisk to eliminate any lumps. Add to creamed mixture. Stir in coconut, granola, walnuts and chocolate chips thoroughly. Drop the batter by tablespoonfuls onto prepared cookie sheet, about 1 1/2 – inches apart. Bake until lightly browned, about 10 – 15 minutes. With a spatula, immediately remove cookies from cookie sheet and cool on a wire rack. Store cookies in an airtight container.

48 cookies

## Sugar Baby Cookies

1   **cup brown sugar, firmly packed**
1/2   **cup butter, softened**
1   **egg**
1   **teaspoon vanilla**
2   **cups flour**
3/4   **teaspoon baking powder**
3/4   **teaspoon baking soda**
1/3   **cup sour cream**
1 3/4   **cups cashew halves (optional)**

**Frosting:**
1/2   **cup butter**
2   **cups powdered sugar**
3   **tablespoons milk**
1   **teaspoon vanilla**

Preheat oven to 350°. Combine brown sugar and butter in large mixer bowl. Beat at medium speed, scraping bowl often, until creamy (1 – 2 minutes). Add egg and vanilla and beat until well mixed (1 – 2 minutes). Combine flour, baking powder and soda and whisk lightly. Add flour mixture to butter mixture alternating with sour cream until well mixed. Stir in cashews by hand. Drop dough by level tablespoonfuls 2 – inches apart onto ungreased cookie sheets. Bake for 10 – 12 minutes or until golden brown. Cool completely.

Melt butter in heavy 1 quart saucepan over medium heat. Cooking, stirring occasionally, until butter foams and begins to turn golden (4 – 6 minutes). Watch closely. Immediately remove from heat. Pour butter into a bowl and cool 5 minutes. Add powdered sugar, milk and vanilla and beat until smooth. Frost cooled cookies. Top with cashew half, if desired.

## American Harvest
## Lemon Basil Shortbread Cookies

| | | | |
|---|---|---|---|
| 1 | cup flour | 1 | tablespoon fresh lemon juice |
| 1/2 | cup confectioners' sugar, more for pressing cookies | 1/2 | teaspoon finely grated lime zest |
| 1/2 | cup (1 stick) chilled unsalted butter, cut into 1/2 – inch cubes | 1/4 | teaspoon kosher salt |
| 2 | tablespoons sliced fresh basil leaves | | Sanding or coarse sugar (optional) |
| 1 | teaspoon finely grated lemon zest | | |

*Note: We use these as a garnish on our strawberry lemon curd tarts. See page 219 for Lemon Curd recipe.*

Preheat oven to 375°. Place flour, confectioners' sugar, butter, basil, lemon zest, lemon juice, lime zest and salt in a food processor. Pulse mixture until large, moist clumps form. Measure level tablespoonfuls of dough; roll between your palms to form balls. Place on a large baking sheet. They do not spread much after they are pressed. Lightly dust the bottom of a flat measuring cup with powdered sugar and press cookies into 2 – inch rounds, dusting cup bottom with powdered sugar as needed to prevent sticking. Sprinkle tops of cookies with sanding or course sugar, if using. (If you refrigerate the dough until chilled it helps them to keep their shape and not melt.)

24 cookies

## Chewy Chocolate Cookies

| | | | |
|---|---|---|---|
| 2 | cups flour | 2 | cups sugar |
| 3/4 | cup cocoa powder | 2 | eggs |
| 1 | teaspoon baking soda | 2 | teaspoons vanilla extract |
| 1/2 | teaspoon salt | | Sugar for coating cookies |
| 1 1/4 | cups (2 1/2 sticks) butter, softened | | |

Preheat oven to 350°. Line a baking sheet with parchment paper or use a silicone sheet. Sift or whisk flour, cocoa powder, baking soda and salt together in a small bowl. In another bowl, cream the butter and sugar until well mixed. Add eggs and vanilla and beat until well mixed. Add flour mixture and stir just until incorporated. Chill 1 hour. Form into 1 – inch balls and roll in granulated sugar. Place 2 – inches apart on prepared baking sheet. Bake for 9 – 12 minutes or until set around edges. Let cool on baking sheet for 5 minutes before removing to a rack.

36 cookies

## Chocolate Nut Surprise Cookies

| | | | | |
|---|---|---|---|---|
| 2 1/2 | cups rolled oats | | 1 | teaspoon baking soda |
| 1 | cup unsalted butter, softened | | 1/2 | teaspoon salt |
| 1 | cup granulated sugar | | 1 | (12 ounce) package chocolate chips |
| 1 | cup light brown sugar, packed | | 1 | (8 ounce) milk chocolate bar, finely chopped |
| 2 | large eggs | | | |
| 1 | teaspoon vanilla extract | | 1 1/2 | cups chopped nuts of choice |
| 2 | cups flour | | | |
| 1 | teaspoon baking powder | | | |

Preheat oven to 375°. Line a cookie sheet with parchment paper. Process the oats to a powdery mixture in a blender or food processor. Cream the butter and the sugars until light, then stir in eggs and vanilla. Combine oatmeal, flour, baking powder, baking soda and salt and add to butter mixture, mixing thoroughly. Stir in chocolate chips, chopped chocolate and nuts. The dough mixture is heavy and becomes difficult to stir near the end. Roll into balls and place 2 – inches apart on a cookie sheet. Bake 10 minutes or until lightly browned. Do not over bake. Let rest at least 5 minutes before removing from pan.

56 cookies

## Français Fudge Cookies

| | | | | |
|---|---|---|---|---|
| 1/2 | cup butter | | 1/2 | teaspoon salt |
| 2 | squares unsweetened chocolate | | 1/2 | teaspoon baking soda |
| | | | 1/2 | cup finely chopped walnuts |
| 1 | cup sugar | | 1/2 | cup flaked coconut |
| 1 | egg | | 1 | cup rolled oats (not instant or quick cooking) |
| 1 | teaspoon vanilla | | | |
| 1 | cup flour | | | |

Preheat oven to 350°. Melt butter and chocolate in a medium glass mixing bowl at 50 percent in the microwave. Stir occasionally until the chocolate is completely dissolved. Remove from microwave and cool slightly. Stir in sugar, egg and vanilla. Lightly whisk flour, salt, baking soda, walnuts, coconut, and oatmeal in another small bowl. Add flour mixture to the chocolate mixture and mix thoroughly. Form into small balls, flatten slightly and place on ungreased cookie sheet. Bake for 10 minutes until set. Do not overcook.

36 cookies

## Black Bottom Mini Cupcakes

*Topping:*
- 1  egg
- 1  (8 ounce) cream cheese, softened
- 2/3  cup sugar
- 1  (6 ounce) mini chocolate chips

*Bottom:*
- 1 1/2  cups of flour
- 1/4  cup cocoa
- 1  teaspoon baking soda
- 1  cup sugar
- 1/2  cup oil
- 1  cup water
- 1  teaspoon vanilla extract
- 1  tablespoon vinegar

*Tip: This is a good recipe to freeze. Put baked cupcakes on cookie sheet until frozen, then pop off and put in a freezer bag until needed. Take out about 1 hour before serving.*

Topping: put egg in bowl and mix lightly, add cream cheese and combine. Add sugar and combine, then add mini chocolate chips and mix thoroughly. Set aside – it will get slightly stiff.

Bottom: mix all flour cocoa and baking soda then set aside. Mix sugar and oil, add water, vanilla and vinegar. Slowly incorporate the dry ingredients until mixed thoroughly.

Fill cupcake papers 1/2 full, add a tablespoon of topping to each cupcake (to cover top) leaving 1/8 to top. Bake at 350° for 20 minutes. Do not over bake – top doesn't brown. This recipe makes a lot, but they go fast. If you make regular-sized cupcakes the baking time needs to be adjusted accordingly.

## Strawberry Ice Cream Pie

- 1 1/2  cups finely ground graham cracker crumbs
- 1/4  cup sugar
- 6  tablespoons (3/4 stick) butter, melted
- 1  10 ounce package frozen sliced strawberries, defrosted
- 1  3 ounce package strawberry gelatin
- 1  pint vanilla ice cream

*Tip: Sugar free gelatin does not change the taste and is easily substituted. The frozen berries can be replaced with a similar amount of fresh berries and the recipe can be adapted by substituting raspberries and raspberry gelatin.*

Preheat oven to 375°. Combine crumbs, sugar and butter and pat into a 9 – inch pie pan. Bake until edges are browned, about 7 – 8 minutes. Remove from oven and cool.

Drain strawberries using a strainer over a large measuring cup. Add water to the juice to make 1 1/4 cups of liquid and heat this to boiling. Remove from heat and dissolve gelatin in the hot liquid. Add ice cream by the spoonful and stir until melted. Chill until thickened but not set. Fold the drained berries into this mixture and pour into the cooled shell. Refrigerate until solid.

8 servings

# State Journal-Register
# Chocolate Almond Lace Cookies

*\*Published with permission of the State Journal-Register Cookie Contest*

| | |
|---|---|
| 2/3 | **cup unbleached flour** |
| 2 | **tablespoons Dutch process cocoa powder** |
| 3/4 | **cup butter, softened** |
| 1 | **cup sugar** |
| 3/4 | **teaspoon vanilla extract** |
| 1 1/2 | **cups finely ground blanched almonds** |

**Ganache:**

| | |
|---|---|
| 1/3 | **cup whipping cream** |
| 3 | **raspberry tea bags** |
| 4 | **ounces chopped, good quality milk chocolate** |

Stir flour and cocoa powder together in a small bowl. In a large bowl beat butter, sugar and vanilla until light and fluffy. Beat in ground almonds; add the flour mixture just until combined. Cover the bowl and chill for at least an hour, until the dough is easy to handle.

Preheat oven to 350°. Line a cookie sheet with parchment paper. Shape the dough into 1 – inch balls and place them on a cookie sheet. Press each ball to flatten slightly. Bake for 12 – 15 minutes or until firm. Cool completely on the cookie sheet placed on a wire rack.

While cookies cool, make ganache. Heat the cream in a small saucepan just to the boiling point. Drop in the tea bags and allow them to soak for 15 minutes. Remove tea bags from cream, pressing them with the back of a spoon to release as much liquid as possible. Bring cream to a boil. Pour hot cream over chocolate in a small bowl. Stir until chocolate is melted and the mixture is smooth and glossy. Spread about 1 teaspoon of ganache on the flat side of a cookie and sandwich it with the flat side of another cookie. Press very lightly. Chill until the filling firms. Keep the cookies in the refrigerator for up to 3 days. They taste best when allowed to come to room temperature before serving.

2 dozen cookies

*The Abraham Lincoln Presidential Library is a reference library. It houses many work places related to the preservation and storage of Lincoln artifacts as well as archives of the Illinois State Library. The circular room pictured is a popular venue for receptions, while other large rooms in the building are used for meetings and training. There are regular exhibits on the walls of the first two floors.*

## State Journal-Register
## Iced Crackle Citrus Cookies

*Published with permission of the State Journal-Register Cookie Contest*

### Dough:

- 3/4   cup (1 1/2 sticks) unsalted butter, softened
- 1 1/4   cups sugar
- 1   tablespoon finely grated citrus zest (Meyer or regular lemon, tangerine or lime)
- 2   large egg yolks, at room temperature
- 3/4   teaspoon lemon extract
- 1/4   teaspoon orange extract (for tangerine cookies, use 1 teaspoon orange extract and omit lemon extract)
- 2   cups flour
- 1/4   teaspoon baking soda
- 1/4   teaspoon fine salt

### Icing:

- 1   cup confectioners' sugar, sifted
- 2   tablespoons colored sanding sugar (yellow, orange or green, depending on flavor of cookie)
- 1   tablespoon finely grated citrus zest (same flavor as cookie)
- 2 - 3   tablespoons freshly squeezed citrus juice (same flavor as cookie)

Preheat oven to 375°. Lightly grease cookie sheets. Beat butter in medium bowl with electric mixer on medium high until smooth. Add sugar and citrus zest and continue to beat until light and fluffy, about 2 minutes. (The creaming is important to get a great texture, so don't skimp here.) Add yolks, 1 at a time, beating well after each addition. Beat in extracts. Whisk flour, baking soda and salt together in a bowl. Stir dry ingredients into the wet mixture, mixing at low speed to make a soft dough. Use a tablespoon or cookie scoop to dip rounded spoonfuls of the dough. Place about 2 – inches apart on cookie sheets. Freeze on pans at least 30 minutes before baking. Bake cookies straight from the freezer until edges are firm and bottoms are lightly browned, 15 – 17 minutes. Transfer to rack to cool.

To prepare icing, mix confectioners' sugar, colored sugar and appropriate flavored zest in medium bowl. Add citrus juice and mix with electric mixer to make a firm but pourable icing. (If needed, add up to 1 teaspoon more juice, but keep in mind that if the icing is too thin, it won't set.) Dip rounded side of cooled cookies into icing, then let excess fall back into the bowl. Place cookies icing side up on a rack until the icing sets.

3 dozen cookies

*The Pasfield Building at 6th and Monroe in Springfield's historic downtown was built in 1888 and is on the National Register of Historic Places. The Pasfield family were early settlers of Springfield, arriving in 1831. Dr. George Pasfield was recognized as one of the wealthiest men in central Illinois, as well as a personal friend of Abraham Lincoln.*

*Published with permission of the State Journal-Register Cookie Contest

## State Journal-Register
## Italian Lemon Ricotta Cookies

**Cookies:**

| | |
|---|---|
| 2 1/2 | cups flour |
| 1 | teaspoon baking powder |
| 1 | teaspoon kosher salt |
| 1/2 | cup (1 stick) unsalted butter, softened |
| 2 | cups sugar |
| 2 | eggs |
| 1 | (15 ounce) container whole-milk ricotta cheese |

| | |
|---|---|
| 3 | tablespoons freshly squeezed lemon juice |
| | Finely grated zest of 1 lemon |

**Glaze:**

| | |
|---|---|
| 1 1/2 | cups confectioners' sugar, sifted |
| 3 | tablespoons freshly squeezed lemon juice |
| | Finely grated zest of 1 lemon |

Combine the flour, baking powder and salt in medium bowl. Set aside. In a large bowl, beat the butter and sugar with an electric mixer until light and fluffy, about 3 minutes. Add the eggs one at a time, beating well after each. Add the ricotta cheese, lemon juice and lemon zest, stirring well. Stir in the dry ingredients just until combined. Cover the bowl with plastic wrap and chill the dough at least 2 hours, until the dough will hold its rounded shape when dropped onto the baking sheets.

Before baking the cookies prepare the glaze by combining the sugar, lemon juice and zest in a small bowl and stirring until smooth. Set the glaze aside and stir again between each batch of cookies.

Preheat oven to 375°. Line the cookie sheets with parchment paper. Using a small ice cream scoop or cookie scoop, drop the dough in rounded mounds onto baking sheets, about 2 tablespoons of dough per cookie. Bake 15 minutes, just until set and slightly golden around the edges. Remove cookies from the oven and spread each hot cookie with 1/2 teaspoon of the glaze. The glaze will melt slightly and set up into a translucent, somewhat crackly coating as the cookies cool. Let glazed cookies rest on baking sheet 20 minutes before removing to wire racks to finish cooling. Line the cool baking sheet with a fresh sheet of parchment between each batch of cookies.

42 cookies

## Amaretto Almond Cookies

| | |
|---|---|
| 1/2 | cup (1 stick) butter, softened |
| 1/2 | cup granulated sugar |
| 1 | egg |

| | |
|---|---|
| 1/2 | cup ground almonds or almond meal |
| 2 | teaspoons amaretto liqueur |
| 1 1/4 | cups flour |

Preheat oven to 400°. Cream butter and sugar, then beat in the egg. Add almonds and amaretto, mixing well. Add the flour in several small portions and mix well after each addition. Drop by teaspoonfuls, 1 1/2 – inches apart on ungreased cookie sheets. Bake 5 – 8 minutes or until lightly browned.

24 cookies

## State Journal-Register
# Raspberry Orange Sandwich Cookies

**Cookies:**

| | |
|---|---|
| 1 | (8 ounce) package cream cheese, softened |
| 1 1/2 | cups butter, softened |
| 1 | cup sugar |
| 2 | teaspoons orange extract |
| 2 1/4 | cups flour |
| 1/2 | teaspoon baking soda |

**Filling:**

Small jar of your favorite raspberry jam (seedless is best)

**Coating:**

| | |
|---|---|
| 1 | orange |
| | Sugar for coating |
| | Semisweet chocolate chips, melted |

*Published with permission of the State Journal-Register Cookie Contest*

*Note: Julienne see page 82.*

Beat cream cheese, butter, sugar and orange extract until blended. Mix in flour and baking soda. Wrap dough in plastic wrap and chill in refrigerator for 2 hours or overnight.

Preheat oven to 350°. Lightly grease cookie sheet. Roll cookie dough on floured surface about 1/4 – inch thick and cut into desired shapes. Bake 10 – 12 minutes. Cool on a wire rack.

For filling, place jam in small pan over medium heat and cook until slightly reduced. Set aside and let it cool. For coating, peel and julienne only the orange part of an orange peel and coat it in sugar. (Add some orange zest to reduced jam also, if you wish.) Sandwich two cookies with the raspberry jam. Dip half of each cookie into melted chocolate and garnish with julienned sugared orange zest before chocolate hardens. Place on rack until chocolate hardens.

18 – 24 sandwich cookies

# Old Fashioned Sugar Cookies

| | | | |
|---|---|---|---|
| 1 | cup Crisco or lard | 1 | teaspoon baking soda |
| 2 | cups sugar | 1/2 | teaspoon salt |
| 2 | eggs | 1/4 | teaspoon baking powder |
| 2 | teaspoons lemon juice | | Zest of 1 lemon |
| 1 | teaspoon vanilla extract | 1/2 | teaspoon nutmeg |
| 3 | cups flour | 1 | cup buttermilk |

Preheat oven to 350°. Spray or lightly grease a cookie sheet. Cream the shortening and sugar together until light and fluffy. Add eggs, lemon juice, and vanilla and mix well. In a separate bowl, combine the flour, baking soda, salt, baking powder, lemon zest and nutmeg. Alternately, add the dry ingredients and buttermilk into the shortening and sugar mixture. Mix just until combined. Drop by tablespoonfuls onto cookie sheet. Sprinkle with sugar and bake 10 minutes or until lightly browned. Cool 5 minutes on cookie sheet before transferring to wire rack.

36 cookies

## Outer Park Pinwheels

*Tip: The rolls can be frozen for up to two months. Thaw these colorful cookies until able to slice and bake.*

**Filling:**

1 1/2  cups dried cranberries
    1  (10 ounce) jar cherry jam or preserves
    1/4  cup water
    1/2  teaspoon ground cinnamon

**Dough:**

    1/4  cup (1/2 stick) butter, softened
1 1/2  cups sugar

    3  egg whites
    3  tablespoons oil
    2  tablespoons fat free milk
    2  teaspoons vanilla extract
1 1/2  teaspoons grated orange peel
3 1/3  cups flour
    3/4  teaspoon baking powder
    1/2  teaspoon ground cinnamon
    1/8  teaspoon baking soda

For the filling, combine cranberries, preserves, water and cinnamon in a small saucepan. Cook at medium heat, stirring occasionally, until liquid is absorbed and cranberries are softened. Remove from heat and cool slightly. Transfer to a blender or food processor and blend until smooth. Transfer to a bowl and cool to room temperature or refrigerate. This can be made up to two days ahead.

For the dough, cream the butter and sugar in a large mixing bowl. Stir in egg whites, oil, milk, vanilla, and orange peel. In a small bowl combine the flour, baking powder, cinnamon and baking soda and whisk lightly. Add to creamed mixture and mix just until combined.

Divide dough in half. On a floured surface, roll one portion of dough into a 9 x 14 – inch rectangle. Spread with half of the filling. Roll up jelly roll style, starting with a long side. Repeat with remaining dough and filling. Wrap each roll in plastic wrap and refrigerate for at least 4 hours or up to two days.

When ready to bake cookies, preheat oven to 375°. Coat a baking sheet with cooking spray or use a silicone mat. Unwrap dough and cut into 1/2 – inch slices. Place 2 – inches apart on baking sheet. Bake for 10 – 12 minutes or until bottoms are lightly browned. Do not over bake. Remove to wire racks to cool.

60 cookies

## Betty's Bingo Cookies

    1  cup (2 sticks) unsalted butter
    1  cup sugar
    1  teaspoon vanilla extract
    1/2  cup finely chopped pecans
1 1/2  cups flour

    1  teaspoon cream of tartar
    1  teaspoon baking soda
        Pinch of salt
    2  cups cornflakes, crushed

Preheat oven to 350°. Lightly grease or spray a cookie sheet. Cream butter, sugar and vanilla. Combine pecans, flour, cream of tartar, baking soda and salt and add to butter mixture just until mixed. Fold in cornflakes. Drop by heaping teaspoonfuls 2 – inches apart onto the baking sheet. Bake 10 – 12 minutes or until lightly browned.

24 – 36 cookies

## Sugar Cookie Cutouts

**Cookies:**

| | |
|---|---|
| 1 | cup (2 sticks) butter, softened |
| 2/3 | cup sugar |
| 1/2 | teaspoon salt |
| 1 | egg |
| 2 | teaspoons vanilla extract |
| 2 1/2 | cups flour, plus flour for rolling |

**Frosting:**

| | |
|---|---|
| 4 | cups confectioners' sugar |
| 1/4 | teaspoon salt |
| 1/4 | cup whipping cream or half and half |
| 1 | teaspoon clear vanilla extract |
| | Food coloring or colored sprinkles |

*Hint: Baking cookies on a silicone mat saves cleanup time, cookies will never stick, and you can use these mats for many years of baking.*

Cream the butter, sugar and salt together. Beat in the egg and vanilla. Add flour, mixing just until well blended. Lay two large pieces of plastic wrap (approximately 20 – inches apiece) overlapping by 2 – inches on the long side. Place the dough on this wrap and gently press the dough into a large disk (a thin disk makes it easier to roll). The dough will be sticky, but will firm up in the refrigerator. Refrigerate at least 3 – 4 hours or up to three days.

Preheat oven to 350°. Use a silicone baking mat, or lightly spray a regular baking sheet. Let the dough sit out about 15 minutes to come to nearly room temperature before rolling. Use a generous amount of flour on the rolling surface as well as both the top and the bottom of the dough disk to prevent sticking. Roll out the dough to 1/4 – inch thickness. Cut out cookies using a well-floured cookie cutter. Gather scraps into a ball and re-roll. Place 2 – inches apart on the prepared cookie sheet and bake 8 – 10 minutes or until barely colored. Cool completely before frosting.

Frosting: Mix confectioners' sugar, salt, cream and vanilla in a medium mixing bowl. Beat well, scraping sides of bowl occasionally while beating. Add additional cream if needed to reach the proper spreading consistency. Test spreading consistency on one cookie before finishing. Stir in food coloring if desired, or sprinkle cookies with colored sugar or other decorations after frosting.

70 small cookies

## Oatmeal Cinnamon Cookies

| | | | |
|---|---|---|---|
| 1 | cup (2 sticks) butter | 2 | teaspoons cinnamon |
| 2 | cups sugar | 1 1/2 | teaspoons baking soda |
| 2 | eggs | | Dash of salt |
| 2 | tablespoons molasses | 2 | cups quick oats |
| 2 | teaspoons vanilla | 1 | cup raisins |
| 2 | cups flour | 1 | cup pecans (optional) |

Preheat oven to 350°. Grease and flour a cookie sheet. Cream the butter and sugar until light and fluffy. Beat in eggs, molasses and vanilla, mixing well. Combine flour, cinnamon, baking soda and salt. Add to creamed mixture just until combined. Stir in oats, raisins and pecans. Drop by tablespoonfuls 2 – inches apart onto cookie sheet. Bake for 10 – 11 minutes until lightly browned. Let rest on cookie sheet until set, about 5 minutes. Transfer to wire rack to cool.

4 dozen cookies

## Date Nut Pinwheels

*Tip: These rolls can be made ahead and frozen for up to two months. Thaw slightly and bake as directed.*

**Filling:**
- 1/2 cup water
- 1/2 cup sugar
- 1 pound pitted dates, chopped
- 1 cup chopped nuts

**Dough:**
- 1/2 cup butter
- 1/2 cup brown sugar, packed
- 1/2 cup sugar
- 1 egg
- 1/2 teaspoon vanilla extract
- 2 cups flour
- 1/2 teaspoon soda
- 1/2 teaspoon salt

Combine water, sugar, dates and nuts and cook over medium-low heat until thickened. Cool. This can be made up to one day ahead and refrigerated until ready to use.

Cream the butter, brown sugar and sugar in a large mixing bowl. Add egg and vanilla. Place flour, soda and salt into a small bowl and whisk lightly. Add this to the creamed mixture and mix to blend in the flour. Divide dough into two parts. Roll each half into a 1/2 – inch thick rectangle on a well-floured piece of parchment paper. Spread each rectangle with 1/2 of the date mixture. Roll each rectangle as a jelly roll beginning with a long end. Wrap each roll in plastic wrap and chill 4 hours or up to two days.

When ready to bake cookies, preheat oven to 375°. Lightly grease or spray a baking sheet. Remove from refrigerator and slice each roll into 1/4 – inch thick pieces. Place 2 – inches apart on prepared cookie sheet and bake for 10 minutes or until lightly browned. Remove to a rack to cool.

42 cookies

## Berry Berry Yummy Bars

- 1 pound (4 sticks) butter, softened
- 4 egg yolks
- 2 cups sugar
- 4 cups flour
- 1 (18 ounce) jar raspberry, cherry, or apricot preserves
- 1 cup nuts, chopped (optional)
- Confectioners' sugar for sprinkling

Preheat oven to 325°. Grease a jelly roll pan. Combine butter and egg yolks. Add sugar. Add flour, one cup at a time. Pat 1/2 of batter into the bottom of the pan and a little up the sides. Spread preserves on batter. Drop remaining batter by teaspoonfuls over the preserves and pat down lightly. Top with nuts. Bake for 40 – 60 minutes or until light, golden brown. Sprinkle with confectioners' sugar. Cool and cut into bars.

36 – 48 bars

## Apricot Almond Bars

**Crust:**

| | | |
|---|---|---|
| 1 | cup (2 sticks) butter, melted |
| 1/2 | teaspoon vanilla extract |
| 1/2 | cup sugar |
| 2 | cups flour |

**Filling:**

2/3   cup apricot preserves

**Topping:**

| | |
|---|---|
| 2 | egg whites |
| 1/2 | teaspoon almond extract |
| 1 | cup confectioners' sugar, sifted |
| 1/3 | cup thinly sliced almonds (optional) |

*Tip: Use your favorite jam as an alternative flavor.*

Preheat oven to 350°. Line a 9 x 13 – inch pan with metal foil or parchment paper, bringing the edges up and over the edges of the pan. Set aside. Combine butter, vanilla, sugar and flour. Spread butter mixture over bottom of the pan. Bake for 25 minutes. Do not over bake. Set aside to cool. When cool, spread preserves over the crust. Raise oven temperature to 400°.

Combine egg whites and almond extract, then add confectioners' sugar and mix well. Spread topping over the preserves. Sprinkle with almonds, if using. Bake for 20 minutes. Cut immediately before the filling begins to harden. Cut into 1 1/2 – inch squares.

About 3 1/2 dozen bars

## Cheesecake Brownies

**Chocolate Mixture:**

| | |
|---|---|
| 1/2 | cup (1 stick) butter |
| 4 | squares (4 ounces) unsweetened chocolate |
| 4 | eggs, room temperature |
| 1/4 | teaspoon salt |
| 2 | cups sugar |
| 1 | teaspoon vanilla extract |
| 1 | cup flour |

**Cheese Mixture:**

| | |
|---|---|
| 2 | (8 ounce) packages cream cheese, softened |
| 2 | eggs |
| 1/2 | cup sugar |
| 1 | teaspoon vanilla extract |

Preheat oven to 350°. Grease or spray a 9 x 13 – inch baking pan. Melt butter and chocolate in microwave at 50 percent power, mixing occasionally until smooth. Cool chocolate mixture. Beat eggs and salt until light in color and foamy. Gradually add the sugar until well mixed. Add vanilla with the last sugar addition. Fold in the cooled chocolate and the flour as quickly as possible, until barely mixed. Spread into the prepared pan.

For the cheese mix, beat the cream cheese, eggs, sugar and vanilla until well mixed. Drop by the spoonfuls on top of the chocolate layer and smooth, completely covering the layer. Bake 30 – 35 minutes just until sides are firm and center barely jiggles. They will continue to firm up after removing from the oven. Cool completely and then refrigerate.

24 – 32 brownies

## Chocolate Peanut Butter Bars

| | | | | |
|---|---|---|---|---|
| 1 | cup sifted flour | | 1 | cup sugar |
| 2 | teaspoons baking powder | | 1 | egg, well beaten |
| 1/4 | teaspoon salt | | 2 | squares (1 ounce each) chocolate, melted |
| 1/2 | cup chopped peanuts | | | |
| 2 | tablespoons shortening | | 1/2 | cup milk |
| 1/2 | cup peanut butter | | | |

Preheat oven to 350°. Grease or spray a 9 – inch square shallow baking pan. Mix flour, baking powder and salt; stir in peanuts. Set aside. Cream together shortening, peanut butter and sugar. Beat in egg and chocolate. Add flour-nut mixture alternately with milk. Turn into prepared pan and bake for 25 – 30 minutes, until the batter pulls away from the sides of the pan and the center is set. Cool before cutting into squares.

20 bars

## Lemon Coconut Squares

**Base:**

| | | | | |
|---|---|---|---|---|
| 1 1/2 | cups flour | | 2 | tablespoons flour |
| 1/2 | cup brown sugar, packed | | 1/2 | teaspoon baking powder |
| 1 | cup (2 sticks) butter, softened | | 1/4 | teaspoon salt |
| | | | 1/2 | teaspoon vanilla extract |

**Filling:**

| | | | | |
|---|---|---|---|---|
| 2 | eggs, beaten | | | **Frosting:** |
| 1 | cup brown sugar, packed | | 2 | cups confectioners' sugar, sifted |
| 1 | cup coconut | | 4 | tablespoons lemon juice |
| 3/4 | cup chopped pecans | | 2 | tablespoons melted butter |

Preheat oven to 275°. For the base, mix flour, brown sugar and butter. Pat down into an ungreased 9 x 13 – inch baking pan and bake for 10 minutes.

Adjust oven temperature to 350°. For the filling, thoroughly mix eggs, brown sugar, coconut, pecans, flour, baking powder, salt and vanilla. Spread on the hot base and bake for 20 minutes. Remove from oven and place on a rack to cool.

For the frosting, thoroughly mix confectioners' sugar, lemon juice and butter. Spread less than half of the frosting on the filling while it is still warm. Cool completely. Spread remaining frosting. Cut into squares.

24 servings

## Limo Lemon Bars

**Crust:**

2 cups flour
1/2 cup confectioners' sugar
1 cup butter (melted)

**Filling:**

4 tablespoons flour
1/2 teaspoon baking powder

4 large eggs slightly beaten
6 tablespoons lemon juice
2 cups sugar
4 tablespoons flour
1/2 teaspoon baking powder

**Topping:**

Confectioners' sugar, sifted

*Note: Add 1 – 2 teaspoons of grated lemon rind to the filling for a more intense lemon flavor. You can replace lemon with lime juice adding a couple of drops of green food color for lime flavored bars.*

Preheat oven to 350°. For the crust, combine the flour and confectioners' sugar. Add the melted butter and mix until dry ingredients are damp. Press crust into an ungreased 9 x 13 – inch baking pan. Bake 20 – 25 minutes until light brown. Do not over bake.

Combine the flour and baking powder. Set aside. Combine eggs and lemon juice; then add the sugar and stir until well blended. Fold the egg mixture into the flour mixture. Pour over baked crust and bake another 25 minutes. Cool and then sprinkle with confectioners' sugar. Cool before cutting. Cut into 1 1/2 – inch squares.

3 1/2 dozen bars

## Nana's Almond Bars

**Crust:**

1 cup (2 sticks) unsalted butter, softened
2 cups flour
1/2 cup confectioners' sugar

**Filling:**

8 ounces cream cheese, softened
1/2 cup sugar
2 eggs
1 teaspoon almond extract

**Frosting:**

1 1/2 cups confectioners' sugar, sifted
1 1/2 tablespoons milk
1/4 cup (1/2 stick) unsalted butter, softened
1 teaspoon almond extract

Preheat oven to 350°. Grease or spray a 9 x 13 – inch pan. For the crust, mix butter, flour and confectioners' sugar together until well blended and pat into prepared pan. Bake 20 – 25 minutes. While the crust is baking, beat the cream cheese, sugar, eggs and almond extract together for the filling. Pour over the cooked crust and bake an additional 15 – 20 minutes or until set. Cool. For the frosting, thoroughly cream confectioners' sugar, milk, butter and almond extract. Spread on cooled bars. Refrigerate to "firm up" the frosting. Return to room temperature for serving.

24 bars

## Go Nuts for These Bars

**Bottom Layer:**
- 4 **cups pecan pieces, finely chopped**
- 1/2 **cup butter, melted**
- 6 **tablespoons sugar**

**Second Layer:**
- 28 **ounces caramels, unwrapped**
- 1 1/3 **cups heavy cream, divided**
- 2 **cups pecans, coarsely chopped**

**Top Layer:**
- 16 **ounces semi sweet chocolate chips**
- 1/4 **cup confectioners' sugar (optional)**

Preheat oven to 350°. Combine the pecan pieces with butter and sugar. Press evenly into a 9 x 13 baking pan. Bake 12 – 15 minutes until lightly browned. Set aside to cool.

Melt the caramels with 2/3 cup cream in a microwave in 1 minute intervals stirring until smooth after each addition. Cool to lukewarm. Pour over the crust. Sprinkle coarsely chopped nuts over caramel mixture. Melt chocolate with 2/3 cup of cream and powdered sugar if using. Pour over pecans. Smooth with a spreading knife. Refrigerate to set and cut into small squares.

18 – 24 bars

## Apple Cake with Amaretto Caramel Sauce

**Cake:**
- 1/4 **cup (1/2 stick) butter**
- 1 **cup sugar**
- 1 **egg**
- 1 **cup flour**
- 1/4 **teaspoon salt**
- 1 **teaspoon baking soda**
- 1 **teaspoon cinnamon**
- 1/4 **teaspoon nutmeg**

**Caramel Amaretto Sauce:**
- 1/2 **cup (1 stick) butter**
- 1 **tablespoon flour**
- 1/4 **cup brown sugar, packed**
- 1/2 **cup sugar**
- 1/2 **cup evaporated milk**
- 1 **teaspoon vanilla extract**
- 1 **tablespoon amaretto**

Preheat oven to 350°. Grease a 9 x 13 – inch baking pan. Cream the butter and sugar in a large bowl. Add the egg and blend thoroughly. In another bowl, combine flour, salt, baking soda, cinnamon and nutmeg, whisking gently or sifting to combine. Stir into the creamed mixture. Spread mixture into prepared pan and bake for approximately 40 minutes or until the cake draws away from the sides of pan slightly and springs back to the touch.

Sauce: Combine butter, flour, brown sugar, white sugar and milk. Place over medium heat and bring mixture to a boil, stirring constantly. Remove from heat and stir in vanilla and amaretto. Serve warm or cool.

18 servings (sauce yields 3/4 cup)

## American Harvest
## Sour Cream Orange Cake with Burnt Sugar Frosting

**Cake:**

| | |
|---|---|
| 1/2 | cup (1 stick) butter, softened |
| 1 | cup sugar |
| 3 | eggs |
| 1 | teaspoon vanilla extract |
| 3 | cups flour |
| 1 | teaspoon salt |
| 1 | teaspoon baking powder |
| 1 | teaspoon baking soda |

| | |
|---|---|
| 8 | ounces sour cream |
| 6 | ounces frozen orange juice concentrate, thawed |

**Frosting:**

| | |
|---|---|
| 1/2 | cup sugar |
| 6 | tablespoons water |
| 4 | egg yolks |
| 1 | cup (2 sticks) butter, softened |
| 1/2 | cup caramel sauce |

*Variation: Bake the cake as two 9 – inch layers or three 8 – inch layers. Turn the layers onto racks to cool before frosting.*

Preheat oven to 350°. Grease a 9 x 13 – inch baking pan and lightly flour the bottom. In a large mixing bowl, cream butter and sugar until light. Beat in eggs one at a time, beating well after each addition. Beat in vanilla.

In another bowl, combine the flour, salt, baking powder and baking soda; sift once. With mixer on low, add dry ingredients to the creamed mixture, about 1 cup at a time, alternating with sour cream and orange juice and ending with the flour. Mix until well blended. Spoon the batter into the prepared pan. Bake for 45 - 50 minutes or until a cake tester or wooden pick comes out clean when inserted in center of cake. Cool for 10 minutes in the pan on a rack.

Frosting: Cook the sugar and water in a saucepan over high heat. Bring the mixture to a boil and cook until the mixture reaches 240°, soft ball stage. Beat the egg yolks using a mixer fitted with paddle. With the mixer running, slowly add the hot syrup. Beat until the mixture is thick and cool, about 5 minutes. In a mixing bowl, beat the butter well. Add the butter to the syrup mixture, a tablespoon at a time and beat well. Add the caramel sauce and beat well. Frost the cooled cake.

20 – 24 servings

## Island Bay Yacht Club
## Sin Chocolate Cake

| | |
|---|---|
| 6 | eggs |
| 2 | tablespoons cornstarch |
| 1/4 | cup of water |
| 24 | ounces (1 1/2 pounds) semisweet chocolate, divided |

| | |
|---|---|
| 2 | cups (4 sticks) plus 2 tablespoons lightly salted butter, divided |
| 1 | cup sugar |
| 1 | cup heavy cream |

Preheat oven to 350°. Line a 9 – inch round cake pan with foil. Mix eggs, cornstarch and water together in a stainless steel bowl. Set aside.

In a double boiler, melt 16 ounces semisweet chocolate, 2 cups of butter and sugar. Into this hot mixture, slowly pour the egg mixture, stirring continuously. Pour into prepared cake pan. Bake for 90 minutes. Remove from oven and allow cake to cool while preparing topping. Melt the remaining semi sweet chocolate, cream and remaining 2 tablespoons of butter together in a double boiler. Turn cake out onto a cookie sheet and remove foil. Pour chocolate mixture over the top and sides of the cake and cool for two hours before serving.

12 servings

## Brandy Walnut Cake

Hint: Cake can be
frozen without the
sauce for up to
3 months.

Superfine Sugar –
See page 206 (Orange
Chiffon Cake)

**Cake:**

| | |
|---|---|
| 1 | cup pitted dates, chopped |
| 1 | cup boiling water |
| 1 | teaspoon baking soda |
| 2 1/2 | tablespoons unsalted butter, softened |
| 1 | cup superfine sugar |
| 1 | large egg |
| 1 1/2 | cups flour |
| | Pinch of salt |
| 3 | teaspoons baking powder |
| 1/2 | cup chopped walnuts or pecans |

**Brandy Sauce:**

| | |
|---|---|
| 1/2 | cup sugar |
| 1/4 | cup cold water |
| 1/2 | teaspoon unsalted butter |
| 1/2 | teaspoon vanilla extract |
| 1/4 | cup brandy or rum |

Preheat oven to 350°. Lightly butter a 9 – inch pie pan or line it with parchment paper. Place dates in a small bowl, cover with boiling water and add baking soda. Let soak until they are soft. While dates are swelling, combine butter and sugar and beat until light. Add the egg, incorporating it thoroughly. Sift or whisk flour, salt and baking powder together. Add flour mixture to butter mixture. Stir in the date and water mixture and nuts. Pour batter into prepared pan and bake 45 minutes or until a toothpick inserted in center comes out dry. Allow to cool in pan while preparing sauce.

Combine sugar and water in a saucepan over medium-high heat. Bring to a boil and stir frequently until sugar is dissolved, about 5 minutes. Remove from heat and stir in butter and vanilla and then the brandy. Remove the cake from the pan to a rack and cool slightly. To serve, cut into wedges and top with brandy sauce.

Serves 6 – 8

## Almond Cake

| | |
|---|---|
| 1 | (18 1/4 ounces) box yellow cake mix (without pudding) |
| 1 | (5.3 ounce) package instant vanilla pudding |
| 4 | eggs |
| 1/2 | cup vegetable oil |

| | |
|---|---|
| 1 | cup cold water |
| 1 | (12 1/2 ounce) can Solo Almond Filling (not paste) |
| | Glaze or raspberry syrup (optional) |

Preheat oven to 350°. Combine cake mix, pudding mix, eggs, vegetable oil, water and almond filling in electric mixer bowl. Beat at medium low speed until batter is smooth. Pour batter into ungreased angel food cake pan. Place cookie sheet under cake pan. Bake 1 hour or longer. Cake is done when inserted knife blade comes out clean. Check with the knife a couple of minutes before you think it is done. It can fool you. Cool. Remove from pan. Serve as is or drizzle a light glaze over the top and let it drip down the edges, or drizzle raspberry syrup on a plate and top with the cake. This freezes well.

16 servings

## Orange Carrot Cake

**Cake:**

| | |
|---|---|
| 1/2 | cup vegetable oil |
| 1 | cup applesauce |
| 1 1/2 | cups brown sugar, packed |
| 4 | eggs |
| 2 | tablespoons orange juice concentrate |
| 1 | tablespoon grated orange peel |
| 1 | cup flour |
| 1 | cup whole wheat flour |
| 3/4 | teaspoon salt |
| 2 | teaspoons baking powder |
| 2 | teaspoons baking soda |
| 2 1/2 | teaspoons cinnamon |
| 1 | teaspoon powdered ginger |

| | |
|---|---|
| 3 | cups grated carrot |
| 1 | (8 ounce) can crushed pineapple, drained |
| 3/4 | cup toasted walnuts, optional |
| 1/2 | cup white raisins, optional |
| 1 | cup coconut, optional |

**Orange Icing:**

| | |
|---|---|
| 2 | (8 ounce) packages light cream cheese, room temperature |
| 1/2 | cup (1 stick) butter, room temperature |
| 2 | teaspoons vanilla extract |
| 2 | tablespoons orange juice concentrate |
| 4 | cups confectioners' sugar |

*Variation: Bake in three 8 or 9 – inch layer pans for 20 – 25 minutes.*

Preheat oven to 325°. Grease a 9 x 13 – inch pan. Cream vegetable oil, applesauce, and brown sugar; add eggs. Add orange juice concentrate and orange peel. In another bowl, combine flour, wheat flour, salt, baking powder, baking soda, cinnamon, and ginger; whisk gently or sift to combine. Add to the creamed sugar mixture until just barely mixed. Fold or stir in carrot, pineapple, walnuts, raisins and coconut.

Spread batter into the prepared pan and bake approximately 45 minutes or until the cake draws away from the sides of pan slightly and springs back to the touch. Cool before frosting.

Icing: Beat the cream cheese, butter, vanilla and orange juice concentrate until well blended. Stir in the confectioners' sugar until frosting is the proper consistency for spreading.

18 servings

*In the early 1900's, "Broadwell's Corner", as it was known, at the northwest corner of Fifth and Washington, was touted as "one of the busiest spots in the city." Stuart Broadwell was a well liked druggist that operated Broadwell's Drugstore for over 40 years.*

## True Blue Pudding Cake

**Fruit:**
- 3 cups blueberries, fresh or frozen
- 1 teaspoon cinnamon
- 1 tablespoon lemon juice

**Batter:**
- 1 cup flour
- 1/2 cup sugar
- 1 teaspoon baking powder
- 1/2 cup milk
- 3 tablespoons butter, melted
- 1/4 teaspoon vanilla extract

**Topping:**
- 1/2 cup sugar
- 1 tablespoon cornstarch
- 1 cup boiling water

Preheat oven to 350°. Grease an 8 x 8 – inch baking dish.

Toss blueberries, cinnamon and lemon juice together. Place in baking dish. Combine flour, sugar, baking powder, milk, butter and vanilla and spoon over berries. Mix together sugar and cornstarch. Sprinkle over batter. Pour boiling water over the entire cake. Bake for 50 minutes or until lightly golden brown on top. Serve warm with ice cream.

12 – 16 servings

## Bourbon Pecan Fudge Cake

**Cake:**
- 2 cups sugar
- 2 cups flour
- 1/3 cup cocoa powder
- 1/3 teaspoon baking soda
- 1/2 teaspoon salt
- 1 cup (2 sticks) margarine or butter
- 1/2 cup water
- 1/2 cup bourbon
- 1/2 cup buttermilk
- 2 eggs
- 1 teaspoon vanilla extract
- 1/2 cup pecans, chopped

**Buttercream Frosting:**
- 4 teaspoons butter
- 4 teaspoons vegetable shortening (or use all butter)
- 1 cup confectioners' sugar
- 4 teaspoons unsweetened cocoa
- 1 teaspoon half and half

Preheat oven to 350°. Lightly grease a 9 x 13 – inch pan. Combine sugar, flour, cocoa powder, baking soda and salt in a large mixer bowl. Heat margarine or butter and water until it reaches the boiling point; lower heat and add bourbon. Slowly add the liquid to the dry ingredients, mixing constantly as liquid is added. Beat in buttermilk. Mix in eggs and vanilla. Add pecans. Pour batter into prepared pan. Bake 30 minutes or until a toothpick inserted in the center has moist crumbs on it. Do not over bake. Cool completely before frosting.

Frosting: Combine butter and shortening and beat until softened. Sift the confectioners' sugar and cocoa together. Slowly mix the sugar mixture into the butter mixture. Add half and half as needed to obtain the correct spreading consistency. Spread buttercream on top of cake.

18 servings

# Vanilla Pound Cake

| | |
|---|---|
| 1 | cup (2 sticks) unsalted butter, room temperature |
| 2 3/4 | cups extra fine granulated sugar (granulated sugar in blender or food processor for a minute will work) |
| 1 | vanilla bean |
| 5 | large eggs |
| 1 | egg yolk |
| 2 1/2 | cups plus 3 tablespoons, sifted flour |
| 1 | tablespoon potato starch or corn starch |
| 1/2 | teaspoon salt |
| 1/4 | teaspoon baking soda |
| 8 | ounces sour cream |
| 2 | tablespoons heavy cream |
| 1 | tablespoon pure vanilla extract |
| 1/4 | cup brandy |
| 1 | tablespoon amaretto |
| 1 | tablespoon rum |
| 1 1/2 | teaspoon whiskey |
| | Confectioners' sugar, for sprinkling |
| | Whipped cream and berries (optional) |

Heat oven to 350°. Spray an 11 1/2 cup Bundt pan with oil spray.

Combine butter and sugar in the bowl of a standing mixer fitted with the paddle. Slice open vanilla pod and scrape seeds into the mixture. Blend on low speed for 2 – 3 minutes. Add eggs and egg yolk, one at a time, fully incorporating each egg as it is added. Combine flour, potato starch, salt and baking soda. Set aside. Combine sour cream, cream, vanilla, brandy, amaretto, rum and whisky. Turn mixer to low speed and quickly add the flour mixture alternately with the sour cream mixture, a bit at a time. (No more than one minute). Scrape the sides and bottom of the mixing bowl and mix on medium about 20 seconds. Pour batter into Bundt pan until it is 3/4 full. Level with spatula. Bake 45 minutes and test for doneness, when a few crumbs cling to the testing tool. Cool 5 – 10 minutes. Remove cake from pan and cool completely. Slice and sprinkle with confectioners' sugar. Serve with whipped cream and berries.

Sugar can be reduced by 1/4 cup for less sweet flavor.

*Abraham Lincoln owned only one home. He and Mary lived in Springfield from 1844 to 1861, enlarging the smaller original with a second story to accommodate their growing family of three active boys. Several homes of his neighbors have been restored to recreate the atmosphere of his time. Son Robert donated the Home in perpetuity as a public site.*

*Variation: Make a warm raspberry sauce using 1/2 cup seedless raspberry preserves, 1/4 cup brandy, 1/4 cup water with 1 tablespoon sugar dissolved in it. Heat the preserves, brandy and sugar water until smooth. Serve warm.*

**Custard:**

10 ounces bittersweet chocolate chips

1 cup (2 sticks) butter, cut into pieces

1/4 cup seedless raspberry preserves

5 eggs

1/3 cup sugar

1 teaspoon vanilla extract

**Fresh raspberries for garnish**

**Sweetened whipped cream for garnish**

**Fresh Raspberry Sauce:**

2 (12 ounce) packages frozen unsweetened raspberries, thawed

**Sugar to taste**

**Rum to taste**

Preheat oven to 325°. Butter 8 ramekins and line bottoms with greased parchment rounds, greased side up. Mix chocolate, butter and preserves in a saucepan. Stir over low heat until chocolate melts. Remove from heat and cool mixture to lukewarm, stirring often. Beat eggs, sugar and vanilla until thick. Gradually whisk in chocolate mixture. Divide batter among prepared ramekins. Bake for about 30 minutes or until set. Serve immediately.

For the fresh raspberry sauce, puree raspberries in a food processor and add sugar and rum to taste. Strain mixture into a bowl, pressing pulp to extract juices.

Serve the cakes warm or at room temperature. Garnish with the raspberry sauce, fresh raspberries and whipped cream.

8 servings

## Apple Sheet Cake

**Cake:**

2 cups sugar

1 1/2 cups canola oil

1 teaspoon vanilla extract

2 eggs

3 cups flour

2 teaspoons baking powder

1 teaspoon salt

Dash of nutmeg

1/2 teaspoon cinnamon

3 cups chopped Granny Smith apple or other apple that maintains shape in cooking

**Topping:**

1/4 cup sugar

1 teaspoon cinnamon

Chopped nuts, optional

Preheat oven to 350°. Grease jellyroll pan. Cream sugar, oil and vanilla then add eggs and beat until fluffy. Combine flour, baking powder, salt, nutmeg and cinnamon and whisk together. Add apples to flour mixture. Add creamed mixture to apple mixture and fold until thoroughly mixed. It becomes a very stiff mixture. Spread or pat into the prepared pan. For topping, combine sugar and cinnamon, sprinkle over top. Sprinkle with nuts, if using. Bake for 25 – 30 minutes until it springs back to touch and a toothpick tests done. Cool and serve with a dollop of whipped cream, ice cream or just by itself.

24 – 36 servings

## Chocolate Sauerkraut Cake

**Cake:**

| | |
|---|---|
| 1/2 | cup (1 stick) butter |
| 1 1/2 | cups sugar |
| 3 | eggs |
| 1 | teaspoon vanilla extract |
| 2 | cups flour |
| 1 1/2 | teaspoon baking soda |
| 3/4 | teaspoon cream of tartar |
| 1/4 | teaspoon salt |
| 1/2 | cup cocoa powder |
| 1 | cup water |
| 2 | cups sauerkraut (16 ounce can) drained, rinsed and drained, finely chopped |

**Frosting:**

| | |
|---|---|
| 6 | squares (6 ounces) semi-sweet chocolate |
| 4 | tablespoons (1/2 stick) butter |
| 1/2 | cup sour cream |
| 1 | teaspoon vanilla extract |
| 1/4 | teaspoon salt |
| 2 | cups confectioners' sugar, sifted |
| | Coconut for sprinkling (optional) |

*Tip: Use good sauerkraut. Some less expensive brands do not cook up well.*

Preheat oven to 350°. Grease and flour a 9 x 13 – inch pan. Cream butter and sugar. Beat in eggs one at a time. Stir in vanilla. Sift together flour, baking soda, cream of tartar, salt, and cocoa powder. Add flour mixture to creamed mixture alternately with water. Stir in sauerkraut, mixing well. Pour into the prepared pan. Bake 35 – 40 minutes.

Prepare frosting while cake is cooling. Melt chocolate and butter in a double boiler or over low heat. Remove from heat and blend in sour cream, vanilla and salt. Add confectioners' sugar and beat until smooth. Spread frosting over cooled cake.

16 – 24 servings

## Coconut Flan

| | |
|---|---|
| 1/2 | cup sugar |
| 6 | eggs |
| 1 | (14 ounce) can condensed sweet milk |
| 1 | (12 ounce) can evaporated whole milk |

| | |
|---|---|
| 1 | (15 ounce) can Coco Lopez© (cream of coconut) |
| 1/3 | cup coconut |

Preheat oven to 375°. Brown the sugar over low heat and pour into a 9 – inch round cake pan. Set aside. In a blender, combine eggs, condensed milk, evaporated milk, cream of coconut and coconut; blend thoroughly. Pour mixture into cake pan with sugar. Place this in a larger pan containing 1/2 – inch water. Bake for 1 hour. Remove from oven and let cool. When cool, refrigerate 8 hours or overnight. To unmold, run knife around edge of pan. Dip bottom of pan quickly in hot water and invert onto serving plate.

8 – 10 servings

# Apple Amaretto Cupcakes

*Cake:*

1 1/2  cups flour
  1/2  teaspoon baking powder
  1/4  teaspoon baking soda
  1/4  teaspoon salt
  3/4  teaspoon sugar
  1/4  cup cream cheese, softened (regular or low fat)
  1/4  cup (1/2 stick) butter, softened
    2  tablespoons amaretto
    1  teaspoon vanilla extract
    1  egg
  1/2  cup sour cream (regular or low-fat)
  1/4  cup milk
  3/4  cup tart apple, peeled and finely chopped or grated
    1  tablespoon flour

*Streusel:*

    2  tablespoons flour
    2  tablespoons brown sugar or 1 tablespoon Brown Splenda Blend
  1/4  teaspoon cinnamon
    2  tablespoons butter, chilled
    2  tablespoons sliced almonds

*Glaze:*

    1  cup confectioners' sugar
    4  teaspoons milk (regular or 2%)

Preheat oven to 350°. Coat a 12 cup muffin tin with spray or put cupcake papers in the cups and coat with cooking spray. Combine flour, baking powder, baking soda and salt and whisk lightly. Set aside. Combine sugar, cream cheese and butter; beat until well blended. Add amaretto, vanilla, and egg and beat together. Set aside. Combine sour cream and milk and whisk lightly. Set aside. Combine apple and flour and toss to coat apples. Add flour mixture and sour cream mixture alternately to sugar mixture, beginning and ending with flour mixture. Fold apple into batter. Pour batter into cups, filling each 2/3 full.

Streusel: Combine the flour, sugar and cinnamon. Add butter and cut in with knives until mixture becomes a coarse meal; add almonds. Sprinkle mixture over cupcakes. Bake 25 – 30 minutes or until toothpick inserted in center of a cupcake comes out clean. Cool 15 minutes before removing cupcakes from pan.

Glaze: Combine confectioners' sugar and milk with a whisk. Drizzle over cupcakes.

12 servings

*The interior of the Illinois State Capitol makes extravagant use of beautiful woodwork, stonework of various types and colors, intricate tile patterns on the floors many portraits and statuary in niches.*

## Apple Scotch Cake

**Cake:**
- 1/2 cup (1 stick) butter, softened
- 3/4 cup sugar
- 2 eggs
- 1 tablespoon vanilla extract
- 1 cup applesauce
- 2 cups flour
- 1 teaspoon baking soda
- 1 teaspoon salt
- 1 teaspoon cinnamon
- 1/2 teaspoon ground cloves
- 2/3 cup butterscotch morsels

**Scotch (Broiled) Icing:**
- 1/2 cup milk
- 3 tablespoons butter, softened
- 1/2 cup brown sugar, packed
- 2/3 cup butterscotch morsels
- 1 cup coconut, packed
- 1 cup finely chopped pecans

*Note: The leftovers of this moist cake are as good as the original cake!*

Preheat oven to 350°. Grease a 9 x 13 – inch baking pan. Cream butter and sugar in a large bowl; stir in eggs, vanilla and applesauce. Combine flour, baking soda, salt, cinnamon and cloves in another bowl, whisking gently or sifting to combine. Stir into the creamed mixture. When these are barely mixed, fold or mix in butterscotch morsels. Spread mixture into prepared pan and bake for approximately 30 minutes or until the cake draws away from the sides of pan slightly and springs back to the touch. Remove from oven; then turn oven to broil.

Prepare icing while the cake bakes. Mix milk, butter, brown sugar, butterscotch morsels, coconut and pecans in a heavy pan over medium heat. Carefully spread the icing over the cake as soon as it is removed from the oven. Broil 1 – 3 minutes until icing bubbles and is lightly browned.

18 – 24 servings

## Maldaner's Restaurant
## Tres Leches Cake

- 1 cup milk
- 1/2 cup butter
- 6 eggs
- 2 cups sugar
- 2 cups flour, sifted
- Pinch of salt
- 2 teaspoons baking powder
- 1 teaspoon vanilla extract
- 1 (12 ounce) can evaporated milk
- 1 (14 ounce) can sweetened condensed milk
- 1 cup cream
- Whipping cream, as needed
- Fresh berries, washed and prepared for serving

*Note: This classic cake is a favorite at Maldaner's. We always have fun at the local Farmers Market picking out fresh blackberries and raspberries for this delectable cake.*

Preheat oven to 350°. Grease and flour a 2 x 5 x 9 – inch pan. Heat the milk and butter until it is warm enough to melt butter. Beat eggs until light and fluffy; add sugar and beat until mixture is smooth. Sift flour, salt and baking powder together and mix into the eggs until barely wet. Add the hot milk and butter mixture. Add the vanilla, mixing thoroughly. Pour into prepared pan, and bake for 35 minutes. Remove from oven and cool. When cool, poke several holes in the top of the cake. Mix evaporated milk, sweetened condensed milk and cream and pour 1/2 of the mixture over the cake; add more as needed. Top with whipped cream and fresh berries.

8 servings

## Italian Cream Cake

Cake:
- 1/2 cup (1 stick) margarine
- 1/2 cup shortening
- 2 cups sugar
- 5 eggs, separated
- 2 cups flour
- 1 teaspoon baking soda
- 1 cup buttermilk
- 1 teaspoon vanilla extract
- 1 (8 ounce) can coconut, divided
- 1 cup pecans, divided

Creamed Frosting:
- 1 (8 ounce) package cream cheese, softened
- 1/2 cup (1 stick) margarine
- 1 pound confectioners' sugar
- 1 teaspoon vanilla extract

Preheat oven to 350°. Grease three 9 – inch round baking pans. Cream the margarine and shortening in large mixer bowl. Add sugar and mix until smooth. Add egg yolks and beat well. Combine flour and baking soda; add to creamed mixture alternating with buttermilk. Stir in vanilla, 1/2 cup coconut and 1/2 cup nuts. Beat egg whites to a stiff peak; fold egg whites into cake mixture. Pour cake mixture into the prepared pans. Bake about 25 minutes, or until top springs back when lightly touched. Cool on wire racks.

Frosting: Combine cream cheese and margarine and beat until smooth. Add confectioners' sugar and vanilla and mix thoroughly. Add remaining coconut and pecans. Spread frosting between layers of cake and on top.

12 servings

## Banana Split Cake

- 1 (18 1/4 ounce) box yellow cake mix, plus required ingredients
- 1 (20 ounce) can crushed pineapple
- 1/2 cup sugar
- 1 (0.9 ounce) box instant vanilla pudding
- 1 (8 ounce) package cream cheese, softened
- 1 cup flaked coconut, more for sprinkling
- 2 – 3 bananas
- 1 (16 ounce) container nondairy whipped topping
- 1/2 cup chopped pecans
- 1/2 cup chopped maraschino cherries

Preheat the oven to 350°. Coat a 9 x 13 – inch baking dish with shortening or no-stick cooking spray. Prepare cake mix according to package instructions. Remove from oven to cool on a rack. While cake is baking, place pineapple and sugar in a small pan and bring to a boil over medium heat; remove from heat. As soon as the cake is removed from the oven punch holes in it with a large fork. Pour pineapple mixture over cake. Let cake cool. Mix pudding according to package directions and whip in cream cheese. Stir in the coconut. Spread cream cheese mixture over the cake. Slice bananas in a layer over the pudding mixture. Spread whipped topping over the bananas. Sprinkle pecans, cherries and coconut over the cake. Refrigerate until ready to serve.

16 – 24 servings

# Inverted Cranberry Cake

**Topping:**

| | |
|---|---|
| 6 | **tablespoons unsalted butter** |
| 1 1/2 | **cups sugar** |
| 2 | **tablespoons water** |
| 1 | **teaspoon ground cinnamon** |
| 4 | **cups cranberries at room temperature, rinsed and picked over** |
| 1 | **teaspoon orange zest (optional)** |

**Cake:**

| | |
|---|---|
| 1 1/4 | **cups flour** |
| 1/2 | **teaspoon baking soda** |
| 1/2 | **teaspoon salt** |
| 6 | **tablespoons (3/4 stick) unsalted butter, softened** |
| 1/2 | **cup sugar** |
| 1/2 | **cup light brown sugar, packed** |
| 2 | **large eggs** |
| 3/4 | **cup sour cream** |
| 1 | **teaspoon vanilla extract** |

*Note: Cake can be topped with ice cream or lightly sweetened whipped cream.*

Preheat oven to 350°. Generously grease a 9 – inch springform pan and wrap the outside with foil to avoid leakage. Set the pan aside on a baking sheet. Melt the butter in a medium saucepan. Add the sugar, water and cinnamon. Cook over medium heat, stirring until the sugar dissolves, about 3 minutes. Stir in the cranberries and cook for another 2 minutes until the cranberries start to pop. Fold in orange zest if using. Pour into the pan and spread evenly. Set aside.

Mix flour, baking soda and salt in a bowl and lightly whisk. Beat the butter, sugar and brown sugar on medium speed until smooth and fluffy, about 1 minute. Add eggs, 1 at a time, mixing well after each addition. Mix in sour cream and vanilla until combined. Add the flour mixture and mix until smooth. Transfer the batter to the springform pan, spreading it evenly over the cranberries. Bake 40 – 50 minutes or until the top is golden brown and the edges just begin to pull away from the sides. A toothpick inserted in the center should come out clean. Set the cake on a rack for 10 minutes to cool. Run a knife around the edges to loosen cake and invert onto a plate. Remove foil ring from bottom of pan. Replace any cranberries that have escaped. Cut into wedges and serve.

14 servings

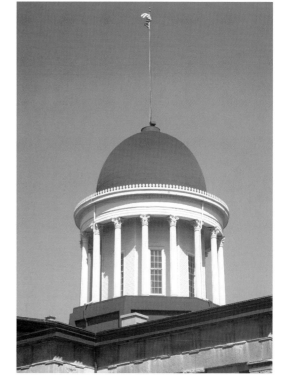

Lincoln and the "Long Nine" voted to move the Capitol to Springfield. When he was a legislator, there were no paved streets, only board sidewalks, and pigs wandered in the dirt. The Old State Capitol has been beautifully restored, with tours and events sponsored by the Illinois Historic Preservation Agency. The flag flying so proudly is lowered to half staff when a member of the US Military Forces is killed in action. The grounds are used for many activities, including an annual juried art fair, historic re-enactments, speeches and concerts.

# Orange Chiffon Cake

*Note: To make superfine sugar, process 1 1/2 cups granulated sugar in a food processor for 30 – 60 seconds.*

6   large eggs, separated while cold, plus one egg white

2 1/4   cups sifted cake flour

1 1/2   cups superfine sugar, divided (see note)

1   tablespoon baking powder

1/2   teaspoon salt

2   tablespoons grated orange zest

1/2   cup vegetable, corn, canola or safflower oil

3/4   cup freshly squeezed orange juice

1   teaspoon vanilla extract (optional)

1/2   teaspoon cream of tartar

Preheat oven to 325°. Let the egg whites and yolks come to room temperature. Put the flour, 1 1/4 cups sugar, baking powder, salt and orange zest in the mixing bowl. Using the paddle attachment, beat until combined. Make a well in the center and add the egg yolks, oil, orange juice and vanilla (if using) and mix. Set aside. In another bowl, using the whisk attachment, beat the egg whites until foamy. Add the cream of tartar and beat until egg whites reach soft peaks. Slowly add remaining 1/4 cup sugar and beat until egg whites become stiff peaks. Using a rubber spatula, fold the egg whites into the batter in three additions, until barely blended. Work gently to prevent deflating the batter. Pour the batter into a 10 – inch, ungreased tube pan, preferably a two piece pan. Bake 55 – 60 minutes or until a toothpick inserted in the center of the cake comes out clean, and the cake springs back when lightly pressed. Remove cake from the oven and immediately invert over a bottle or paper towel holder to suspend it over the counter. Let cake cool completely before removing from the pan, about 1 1/2 – 2 hours. To remove the cake from the pan, loosen the cake from the sides and bottom of the pan. Place right side up onto a greased wire rack. Dust the top with confectioners' sugar or drizzle with a glaze. Serve with whipped cream or ice cream and fresh fruit. Store in an airtight container

8 – 10 servings

This historic city block across from the Old State Capitol begins at the left of the block with the Lincoln-Herndon Law Office. The other storefronts were frequestly visited by Abe. The present-day Prairie Archives is a delightful used-book store with a wondrous inventory and knowledgeable owners. There are three popular restaurants for visitors to the many nearby Lincoln sites.

# Red Velvet Cake with Cream Icing

1/2 **cup shortening**

1 1/2 **cups sugar**

2 **eggs**

2 **ounces red food coloring**

3 **tablespoons cocoa**

2 1/4 **cups cake flour**

1 **teaspoon salt**

1 **cup buttermilk**

1 **teaspoon vanilla extract**

1 **teaspoon baking soda**

1 **teaspoon white vinegar**

**Frosting:**

1/2 **cup shortening**

1 **cup (2 sticks) butter, softened**

3 **cups confectioners' sugar, sifted**

1 **teaspoon vanilla extract**

1 **teaspoon almond extract**

Note: *If you choose not to flatten the tops of the bottom layer, be sure to place the rounded side of the layer down when putting on the cake plate.*

Preheat oven to 350°. Butter and lightly flour two 9 – inch cake pans. Cream shortening, sugar and eggs until well blended. Combine the food coloring and cocoa together making a paste; add to the creamed mixture. Sift together flour and salt. Add to the creamed mixture alternately with buttermilk. Stir in vanilla. Combine baking soda and vinegar and blend into the batter. Divide batter into the prepared cake pans. Bake for 35 minutes or until toothpick inserted in center comes out clean. Let cake cool about 5 minutes then turn out onto racks to cool completely before frosting.

Frosting: Cream shortening and butter together. Add confectioners' sugar, one cup at a time, until frosting reaches the correct spreading consistency. Stir in vanilla and almond extract until well blended. Brush the crumbs away on the top, bottom and sides of each layer. Using a very sharp serrated knife, level the top of one layer by carefully slicing away the rounded part on the top. Place one cake layer on a cake plate. Cover top and sides of layer with frosting. Place second cake layer, bottom (flat) side down on top. Spread remaining frosting over the top and sides of cake.

12 servings

*The Rees Memorial Carillon, located in Washington Park, is the 5th largest Carillion in the world, towering at 132 feet high. The dedication and first International Carillon Festival were held at the same time in 1962. The 51st Carillon Festival, the longest running in the world, was held in 2012.*

# Sunny Circle Lemon Cake

*Variation: To make a Bavarian style cake, bake the cake in two layers rather than three. Place the bottom layer of the cake on the cake plate; spread a layer of butter cream frosting on the cake; Place the second layer on the bottom layer, fastening it with toothpicks to prevent sliding. Add the outside edge of frosting and ice the sides of the cake. Fill the center of the top with the lemon cream filling. Half of a recipe of the lemon cream filling is enough.*

**Cake:**
- 1 cup (2 sticks) butter
- 2 cups sugar
- 2 eggs, yolks and whites separated
- Juice and grated zest of 1 lemon
- 1 1/2 teaspoons baking soda
- 2 1/2 cups cake flour
- 1 cup milk

**Lemon Cream Filling:**
- 1 cup granulated sugar
- 1/4 cup cornstarch
- 1/8 teaspoon salt
- 1 cup boiling water
- 5 eggs, beaten and strained
- Juice of 2 lemons (6 tablespoons)
- Grated zest of 1 lemon
- 4 tablespoons (1/2 stick) butter, melted

**Buttercream Frosting:**
- 3/4 cup (1 1/2 sticks) butter, softened
- 3 1/2 cups confectioners' sugar
- 2 tablespoons cream
- 1/4 teaspoon vanilla extract
- 2 tablespoons lemon juice
- 1 teaspoon lemon zest, grated

Preheat oven to 350°. Grease and flour three 9 – inch cake pans. Cream butter and sugar. Beat egg yolks and add to butter mixture. Add lemon juice and zest. Combine baking soda with flour and add alternating with milk. Beat egg whites to a stiff froth and fold into the batter. Pour evenly into prepared pans and bake 25 minutes or until the top springs back when lightly touched. Check regularly the last few minutes.

Filling: Combine sugar, cornstarch and salt. Add boiling water. Cook for about 5 minutes over medium high heat. Beat eggs well and strain if strings remain. Remove a small amount of the sugar water and add eggs to this gradually. Add eggs to boiling mixture 1/3 at a time, stirring after each addition. Mix well and whisk in the juice, zest and butter. Simmer, stirring constantly until thickened. Remove from heat and strain if necessary for any curdled eggs. Place in a bowl and cover with waxed paper or plastic wrap to cool until ready to use. Whisk before using.

Frosting: Whip butter until light and creamy. Gradually add confectioners' sugar. Add cream, vanilla, lemon juice and lemon zest. Add additional cream if necessary to reach frosting consistency. Beat 3 – 4 minutes.

Remove cakes from pans and brush off crumbs. Place one layer of cake on a serving dish. Place a row of frosting along the outside edge (to keep the filling from oozing out). Place half of the filling onto the center of the cake. Top with second cake layer. Place a row of frosting around this layer and spread the lemon cream filling over the rest of the layer. Place top layer on the filling. Ice the top and sides with buttercream frosting.

12 servings

## Boulevard Blueberry Pie

*Pie:*
- 4 heaping cups fresh blueberries (or frozen berries slightly thawed), divided
- 1/2 cup water
- 1/2 cup sugar
- 2 rounded tablespoons cornstarch, dissolved in 2 tablespoons water
- 1 tablespoon butter
- 1 1/2 tablespoons Grand Marnier (orange flavored liqueur)
- 1/4 cup slivered almonds, toasted
- 1 (9 – inch) baked pie shell

*Almond Crème:*
- 1 cup cold heavy cream
- 2 tablespoons sugar
- 3/4 teaspoon almond extract

*Hint: This is best made the day you serve it. You can bake the pie crust the day before but serve within 4 hours of spreading the cream.*

Combine 1 cup blueberries and water in a blender and puree until smooth. Pour into a medium saucepan. Add the sugar and dissolved cornstarch. Cook over medium heat, stirring constantly, until thickened. Remove from the heat and stir in the butter and liqueur. Gently fold in almonds and remaining blueberries. Spoon into pie shell and chill.

Combine the cream, sugar and extract in a small chilled bowl. Whip with chilled beaters until stiff peaks form and dollop onto the pie just before serving.

8 servings

## A Little Different Pumpkin Pie

- 1/2 teaspoon salt
- 1 teaspoon cinnamon
- 1/2 teaspoon ginger
- 3/4 cup sugar
- 2 eggs
- 1 cup heavy cream
- 1/2 cup milk
- 1 3/4 cups fresh pumpkin puree or pure pumpkin puree
- 1 chilled 9 – inch pie shell

*Variation: For more flavor, reduce ginger to 1/4 teaspoon and add 1/4 teaspoon each of mace, allspice and nutmeg with a pinch of cloves.*

Preheat oven to 400°. Combine salt, cinnamon, ginger and sugar and set aside. Beat eggs and add the cream and milk. When the sugar and egg mixtures are prepped, begin making the filling. Put the pumpkin in an uncoated stainless or aluminum sauce pan. Cook over direct heat for 10 minutes, stirring regularly, until it is caramelized. Stir hot pumpkin into sugar mixture. Do not let the pumpkin cool! Add egg mixture and beat until filling is smooth. Pour immediately into pie shell and bake for 40 minutes until pastry is golden brown. The pie should have no cracks on top. The filling in the center may jiggle a little.

6 servings

# Blackberry Patch Cobbler

*Note: Use different mixes of berries. However, this may require an adjustment the sugar depending on how tart the berries are.*

8   cups of blackberries (fresh or frozen, slightly thawed)
1 1/4   cups sugar, divided
1/4   cup instant tapioca
  Juice of 1/2 lime
1/2   teaspoon salt, more if needed
1   cup flour

1/2   teaspoon baking powder
1/2   cup (1 stick) cold unsalted butter, cubed
1/2   cup pecans, coarsely chopped
1   cup packed coconut
1   egg
2   tablespoons water

Preheat oven to 375°. Place berries into a lightly greased 2 quart baking dish or 9 x 13 – inch pan. Add 1/2 cup sugar, tapioca, lime juice and 1/4 teaspoon of salt. Let rest for 15 minutes. Combine flour, 3/4 cup sugar, baking powder and 1/4 teaspoon salt. Cut butter into flour mixture; add the pecans and coconut until the butter is well incorporated. Lightly beat the egg with the water and blend into the flour mixture. Arrange the topping over the berries in clumps, covering evenly. Bake for 45 – 50 minutes or until topping is golden and the filling is thick and bubbly. Cool for at least 1 hour to allow the berries to thicken. This is great served with vanilla ice cream.

12 servings

# Blueberry Lane Cobbler

4   cups fresh or frozen blueberries
1/2   cup plus 1 tablespoon sugar, divided
1   tablespoon cornstarch
1/2   teaspoon grated lemon peel
1   teaspoon lemon juice
1/4   teaspoon cinnamon

1   cup flour
1 1/2   teaspoons baking powder
2   teaspoons grated orange peel
1/4   teaspoon salt
3   tablespoons shortening
1/3   cup milk
1   egg

Preheat oven to 400°. Grease or spray a 2 quart baking dish. Combine blueberries, 1/2 cup sugar, cornstarch, lemon peel, lemon juice and cinnamon in a medium saucepan. Cook over medium heat until it bubbles. Lower heat and cook five minutes, stirring frequently until thickened. Transfer filling to the baking dish. Combine flour, 1 tablespoon sugar, baking powder, orange peel and salt. Cut in shortening. Mix milk with beaten egg and then stir into flour mixture just until flour is moistened. Drop heaping tablespoons of the topping onto the fruit. Bake 20 – 25 minutes or until browned and bubbly. Serve with ice cream or whipped cream.

6 – 8 servings

## French Raspberry Custard

| | |
|---|---|
| 3 **cups fresh raspberries** | 1/2 **cup heavy cream** |
| 3 **eggs** | 1 **cup whole milk** |
| 1/2 **cup sugar** | 1 **tablespoon kirsch** |
| 1/3 **cup flour** | |

*Variation: Vanilla or any berry liqueur may be substituted for kirsch.*

Preheat oven to 375°. Butter a deep 9 – inch quiche dish or pie plate. Place berries in dish, no more than 2 layers deep. Beat eggs, sugar, flour, cream, milk and kirsch together thoroughly. Pour mixture over berries and bake for 50 – 60 minutes, until a knife inserted in the center comes out clean.

8 servings

## Macadamia Key Lime Pie

| | |
|---|---|
| 1 1/2 **cups graham cracker crumbs** | 4 **large egg yolks** |
| 1/4 **cup granulated sugar** | 1 1/2 **teaspoons grated lime zest** |
| 1/2 **teaspoon cinnamon** | 1/2 **cup key lime juice** |
| 1/2 **cup macadamia nuts, ground** | 1 1/2 **cups whipping cream** |
| 1/2 **cup (1 stick) unsalted butter, melted** | 1/2 **cup confectioners' sugar** |
| 21 **ounces sweetened condensed milk** | **Key lime, to garnish** |

*Note: If made in advance, refrigerate without the whipped cream and add just before serving.*

Preheat oven to 350°. Combine graham cracker crumbs, sugar, cinnamon, macadamia nuts and butter. Pat into a 10 – inch pie plate or 10 – inch spring form pan. Bake 6 – 8 minutes or until slightly browned. Remove from oven and cool on a rack. Whisk together milk, egg yolks, lime zest and key lime juice. Pour mixture into the crust. Bake for 25 – 30 minutes or until set.  Refrigerate to cool, about 30 minutes. Place whipping cream into mixer bowl. Sift sugar into the cream. Beat with wire attachment until it forms soft peaks. Spread whipped cream over the crust. Refrigerate at least 1 hour before serving. Garnish with slivers of key lime.

12 servings

Abraham Lincoln, seated near the Union Station Visitors Center, perhaps contemplates his chief concern, how to keep the United States united. As a legislator, he recognized the importance of "internal improvements", even lawyering for railroad interests. The Civil War occupied his entire presidency, so he had much to consider. His Presidential Library and Museum across the street tell the story in ways that would have mystified, but delighted him.

## Oak Ridge Peach Pie

*Note: Canned or frozen peaches may be substituted.*

2   **pie crusts, homemade or refrigerated**

1/3   **cup granulated sugar**

4   **cups peaches, peeled and sliced**

1   **teaspoon lemon juice**

1/3   **cup brown, packed or raw sugar**

3/4   **teaspoon ground cinnamon**

1/4   **cup instant tapioca**

2   **teaspoons butter**

Preheat oven to 375°. Line a 9 – inch pie pan with a pastry round and sprinkle it with the granulated sugar. Arrange peaches in the crust and drizzle with lemon juice. Combine brown sugar, cinnamon and tapioca and let sit 15 minutes. Sprinkle sugar mixture over peaches. Dot peaches with butter. Cover with top pastry. Seal and flute edge and make several slits in the top crust. Bake for 20 minutes. Reduce heat to 350° and bake 35 – 40 minutes or until crust is nicely browned. Use a circle of foil or a pie shield to prevent the outer edges from over-browning.

8 servings

## Spanish Cream Pie

*Note: This pie has the consistency of a very light angel food cake and is wonderful with fresh raspberry or strawberry sauce and berries, or top with 1/2 cup black walnuts, pecans or shaved chocolate.*

3   **egg whites**

1/2   **cup sugar, divided**

1 1/2   **teaspoon vanilla**

1 1/2   **cup milk**

4 1/2   **tablespoons cornstarch**

1/2   **teaspoon salt**

1   **baked pie shell**

1 1/2   **cups whipping cream**

1/4   **cup confectioners' sugar**

Beat egg whites until stiff, add 1/4 cup of sugar and vanilla; continue beating until creamy. Set aside. Combine milk, cornstarch, salt and 1/4 cup sugar in a medium saucepan. Cook over medium heat, stirring constantly, until clear and thick for approximately 10 – 12 minutes. Pour the boiling mixture into the egg whites, while beating continuously. Pour into baked pie shell. Chill.

Whip the cream and confectioners' sugar in a chilled bowl until soft peaks form. Spread the whipped cream onto the chilled pie.

8 servings

## Spaulding Apple Crisp

**Pie:**

- 8 cups (1 – inch chunks from peeled, cored tart apples)
- 1 teaspoon lemon zest
  Juice of 1 lemon
- 1 teaspoon cinnamon

**Topping:**

- 1/2 cup flour
- 3/4 cup brown sugar, packed
- 1/4 cup granulated sugar
- 1 teaspoon cinnamon
- 1/8 teaspoon salt
- 1/2 cup (1 stick) cold unsalted butter, cut into small pieces
- 1/2 cup oatmeal (not instant)
- 1/2 cup slivered almonds (optional)

*Note: 8 large apples yield about 8 cups.*

Preheat oven to 375°. Toss the apples with lemon zest, juice and cinnamon and put into a deep, unbuttered 2 quart baking dish. Combine flour, brown sugar, granulated sugar, cinnamon and salt in a large bowl. Using a pastry blender, cut the cold butter into the mixture until it resembles coarse bread crumbs. Add oatmeal, mixing it in with a spoon or fork. Do not over blend. Scatter the topping evenly over the apples. Sprinkle with almonds. Bake until topping is golden brown, the juices are bubbling and the apples are tender, about 50 – 55 minutes.

8 servings

## Try It You'll Like It Rhubarb Pie

- 3 1/2 cups rhubarb, fresh or frozen, thawed and drained
- 2 1/2 cups plus 1 tablespoon flour, divided
- 1/2 cup white sugar

- 1 9 – inch pie shell
- 1/4 cup butter, melted
- 1/2 cup brown sugar, packed
- 1 cup plain cornflake cereal
- 1/2 cup flour

*Note: We almost tossed this recipe, but after tasting, realized it had to be included. It was unanimously agreed it is simply wonderful.*

Preheat oven to 350°. Combine rhubarb, 1 tablespoon flour and white sugar. Place in pie shell. Combine butter, brown sugar, cornflakes and flour. Pat cornflake mixture on top of pie filling. Bake 40 minutes. Turn off oven and leave pie in oven another hour. Serve warm.

# Tipsy Two Crust Pie Dough

*Tip: You can keep this in the freezer for 2 months before baking.*

2 1/2   **cups flour**
  2   **tablespoons sugar**
  1   **teaspoon salt**
  4   **tablespoons shortening, chilled**
 12   **tablespoons unsalted butter, cut into1/4 – inch pieces and chilled**

4   **tablespoons ice cold water**
4   **tablespoons vodka, very cold or stored in freezer**

Place the flour, sugar and salt in a food processer and pulse until combined. Scatter shortening and butter pieces over the flour mixture and process until mixture has the texture of small crumbs. Combine the water and vodka. Sprinkle water mixture over the dough mixture and pulse a few times until the dough just starts to come together. Divide dough into 2 pieces, pat into a disk covered in plastic wrap and refrigerate for at least 1 hour. Remove 1 disk from refrigerator and let sit for 5 minutes. On a lightly floured surface, with a rolling pin roll from the center out and rotating around the dough until the round is a few – inches larger in area than the pie pan. Place in the pie pan.

For a double crust pie: Pour in filling of choice. Roll out the second disk and place the crust over the filling. Flute the edges of the crust and make slits in the top crust to permit steam to escape. Bake according to pie instructions, covering the edge of the crust with foil or a baking crust guard to prevent over-browning if needed.

For two single crust pre-baked pies: Flute the edges and place in freezer for at least 1/2 hour before baking. Preheat the oven to 425° for a convection oven or 450° for a conventional oven. Remove the pie shell from the freezer and with the tip of a knife put tiny pin pricks all over the pie shell. Cook on convection heat if possible for the first 5 minutes as this helps keep the shell from shrinking. Take off convection heat and cook for an additional 5 – 6 minutes or until golden brown. Cool on a rack.

Yield: Two pie crusts

# Wonderful Pecan Pie

*Note: Yes. The oven temperature is 275°.*

6   **tablespoons unsalted butter**
1   **cup dark brown sugar, packed**
1/2   **teaspoon salt**
3   **large eggs**
3/4   **cup light corn syrup**

1   **tablespoon vanilla extract**
2   **cups (8 ounces) pecans, toasted and chopped into small pieces**
1   **(9 – inch) pre-baked pie shell**

Preheat oven to 275°. Melt butter in a medium sized saucepan. Mix in sugar and salt until the butter is absorbed. Beat in eggs, corn syrup and vanilla. Heat this mixture until it is shiny and warm to the touch. Remove from heat and stir in pecans. Pour mixture into the warm shell (reheat shell for 5 minutes if it has cooled since baking) and bake for 50 – 60 minutes until the center feels set, yet soft like gelatin when gently pressed.

8 servings

## U-Pick Cream Pie

**Pie:**

| | |
|---|---|
| 2 | cups milk |
| 1/3 | cup sugar |
| 1/4 | teaspoon salt |
| 3 | egg yolks |
| 1 | cup half and half |
| 1/4 | cup cornstarch |
| 1 | tablespoon butter |
| 1 | tablespoon vanilla |

| | |
|---|---|
| 2 | medium bananas, very thinly sliced |
| 1 | baked deep dish 9 – inch pie crust |

**Topping:**

| | |
|---|---|
| 1 | cup cold heavy cream |
| 1 | tablespoon sugar |
| 1 | teaspoon vanilla |

Combine milk, sugar and salt in a medium saucepan and heat over medium low heat until almost boiling. Whisk the egg yolks, half-and-half and cornstarch together and carefully add 1/2 – 1 cup of the hot milk mixture to this and mix. Next, whisk this cornstarch mixture into the hot milk. Whisk constantly until the mixture boils and thickens to a pudding like consistency. Remove from heat; add butter and vanilla and mix.

Spread 1/3 of the custard mixture into the baked pie shell. Layer half of the banana slices over the custard mixture, slightly overlapping them. Cover with second 1/3 of the custard mixture and layer with remaining banana slices. Top the bananas with the final 1/3 of the custard mixture. Cool and refrigerate until quite cool.

For the topping, chill bowl and beaters. Beat cream with the sugar and vanilla until soft peaks form.

8 servings

*Variations: Base cream may be used to make Chocolate or Coconut Cream Pie.*

*For chocolate cream pie: increase the sugar to 1 cup and add 3 – 4 squares (depending on how much chocolate you prefer) of chopped unsweetened chocolate to the hot milk mixture. Stir until melted and then proceed as above.*

*To make coconut cream pie: add 1 packed cup of coconut to the milk and cornstarch base during thickening. If desired, add lightly browned coconut to the pie topping immediately before serving.*

*Tip: This pie is best eaten the day it is made, but you can cook the shell the day before.*

*Lincoln's final resting place dominates a 12 1/2 acre plot in Oak Ridge Cemetery. Designed by Larkin G. Mead, built of granite and completed in 1874, the exterior gallery has a bronze statue at each corner, representing the Army, Navy, Artillery and Cavalry. Accessed from corridors exquisitely wrought of marble from five states and four countries, the sarcophagus is buried deep below the burial chamber where Mary and their sons are in crypts.*

# Zucchini Pie

Note: It is fun substituting this for an apple pie. Great when zucchini is in season and in overabundance.

**Filling:**
- 5 cups zucchini, peeled, cubed
- 2 tablespoons lemon juice
- Dash of salt
- 1 1/4 cups white sugar
- 1 1/4 teaspoons cinnamon
- 1 1/2 teaspoons cream of tartar
- Dash of nutmeg
- 3 tablespoons flour
- 2 pie shells
- 1 tablespoon butter, sliced thinly for dotting pie filling
- 1 egg, beaten
- 2 tablespoons white sugar

Preheat oven to 400°. Peel zucchini and cut into quarters lengthwise, then remove seeds and cut crosswise (as you would cut apples for pie). Toss with lemon juice to prevent from turning brown. Place zucchini in a pan with the salt. Sauté until just tender, when a knife easily pierces the slices. Stir together the sugar, cinnamon, cream of tartar, nutmeg and flour. Remove zucchini from pan with a slotted spoon. Add zucchini to flour mixture. Toss the zucchini until it is coated. This mixture will be thin. Pour filling into a 9 – inch pie shell, dot with butter and cover with second pie crust. Slit decorative holes in top to vent. Brush with the egg wash and sprinkle with sugar. Bake for 40 minutes or until golden brown.

8 servings

# Mimi's Mango Custard

Tip: Frozen fruit may be used. Two 12 ounce packages, thawed, yield approximately 3 1/2 cups. Ramekins can be made up to 3 days ahead and garnished at serving time.

- 3 1/2 cups peeled mangos or peaches cut into large chunks
- 1 cup skim or regular evaporated milk
- 1 cup very hot water (not boiling)
- 2 envelopes clear gelatin
- 1/2 cup sugar
- Raspberry puree and/or Kiwi and/or mixed berries for garnish
- 1 lime

Put half the mango chunks and the evaporated milk into a blender and puree. Add enough remaining mango to blender to yield 4 1/2 cups. Heat the water in microwave bowl until almost boiling. Add gelatin and sugar and stir until both are totally dissolved. This will take 2 – 3 minutes. Pour gelatin mixture into the blender and blend at a low speed until thoroughly mixed with fruit. Pour mixture into 1/2 cup ramekins and chill for at least 3 hours. Serve in the ramekins or unmold onto a plate. To unmold, dip into a bowl of hot water, being careful that the water does not touch the pudding. Use a knife to loosen sides and invert custard onto a plate. Garnish with fruit, diced mango (if there is extra) and a squeeze of lime juice.

12 servings

# Ice Cream Layered Cake

**Cake:**
- 1/2   **cup dried tart cherries**
- 1/2   **cup orange juice, or Grand Marnier or other orange flavored liqueur**
- 1   **(5.5 ounce) package amaretto cookies (Italian macaroons) or almond biscotti**
- 1/4   **cup almonds, toasted**
- 5   **tablespoons unsalted butter, melted**
- 1 1/2   **pints chocolate ice cream, softened**
- 1   **(3 ounce) bar imported milk chocolate, chopped**
- 1 1/2   **pints raspberry sorbet, softened**
- 1 1/2   **pints pistachio ice cream, softened**
- 1   **tablespoon grated orange peel**

**Hot Fudge Sauce:**
- 1   **cup whipping cream**
- 1/2   **cup light corn syrup**
- 6   **ounces bittersweet chocolate, chopped**
- 6   **ounces semi-sweet chocolate, chopped**

*Note: Hot fudge sauce can be prepared in advance and refrigerated. Warm the sauce in the microwave to serve. Dessert can be made several days ahead. If you have a small ice cream freezer this can be used to mix the layers easily.*

Boil the dried tart cherries and orange juice or liqueur until all the liquid is absorbed. Cool completely.

Line a 9 x 9 – inch baking pan with foil, extending over sides of pan. Finely grind cookies and almonds in a food processor; add butter and pulse several times until crumbly. Press crumbs onto bottom of the pan and place in the freezer.

Mix chocolate ice cream, chopped chocolate and cooked cherries in a medium bowl. Spoon mixture over the crust and smooth the top. Freeze 30 minutes. (Rinse bowl when done to use later.) Top with raspberry sorbet, smoothing top. Mix pistachio ice cream and orange peel in the medium bowl and spoon over the raspberry sorbet layer, smoothing top. Cover and freeze at least 4 hours or overnight.

Prepare the hot fudge sauce just prior to serving. Bring the whipping cream and corn syrup to a boil; remove from heat and add the bittersweet and semi-sweet chocolate. Stir until incorporated.

Using foil as an aid, lift cake from pan. Remove foil and use a sharp knife to smooth the sides and show off the beautiful color. Cut into squares and serve plated on a small pool of hot fudge sauce.

8 – 10 servings

# Lemon Glazed Cheesecake

*Tip: Cheesecakes set from the outside in. To test for doneness, shake the pan gently. The very center of the cake should jiggle just slightly.*

*Tip: To avoid the cracks that often form in cheesecake, run a knife between the pan and the cake when you take it out of the oven. This will loosen the cake from the edges so that it can shrink slightly without cracking as it cools.*

**Cheesecake:**

- 6 **tablespoons unsalted butter, melted**
- 2 **cups finely ground graham cracker crumbs**
- 1 **cup plus 2 tablespoons sugar, divided**
- 3 **(8 ounce) packages any cream cheese, softened**
- 1/4 **cup lemon juice**
- 1 **tablespoon vanilla, divided**
- 3 **large eggs, at room temperature**

- 2 **teaspoons grated lemon rind**
- 2 **cups sour cream**

**Lemon Glaze:**

- 1/2 **cup sugar**
- 1 1/2 **tablespoons cornstarch**
- 1/4 **teaspoon salt**
- 3/4 **cup water**
- 1/3 **cup lemon juice**
- 1 **egg yolk**

Preheat oven to 350°. Mix butter, graham crumbs and 2 tablespoons sugar together. Press mixture on sides and bottom of an ungreased 10 – inch spring-form pan. Combine cream cheese and 3/4 cup sugar and beat for 2 minutes until soft. Add lemon juice and 2 teaspoons vanilla. With mixer on lowest speed, add eggs, one at a time, mixing only until each egg is incorporated into the batter. Fold in the lemon rind. Pour into crust and bake 35 minutes or until done. Remove from oven. Combine sour cream, 1/4 cup sugar and 1 teaspoon vanilla and spread over top of cake. Return to oven for an additional 10 minutes. Cool 30 minutes.

Prepare the glaze while the cheesecake cools. In a saucepan, combine sugar, cornstarch and salt. Whisk water, lemon juice and egg yolk together and add to sugar mixture. Cook over low heat, stirring constantly until it comes to a slow boil. Spread the glaze over the cheesecake. Chill several hours or overnight.

16 servings

*Edwards Place was the home of Benjamin and Helen Edwards who were involved in the social and political life of Springfield in Lincoln's era. There are a number of period artifacts still in the house today. It is currently maintained by the Springfield Art Association.*

## Amaretto Bread Pudding

**Sauce:**

| | |
|---|---|
| 1/2 | cup cream |
| 1/2 | cup milk |
| 3 | tablespoons sugar |
| 1/4 | cup amaretto |
| 2 | teaspoons cornstarch |

**Bread Pudding:**

1   pound Challah or Hawaiian sweet bread, cubed

| | |
|---|---|
| 4 | cups (1 quart) half and half |
| 2 | tablespoons unsalted butter, softened |
| 1 1/2 | cups sugar |
| 3 | eggs at room temperature |
| 2 | tablespoons almond extract |
| 3/4 | cup golden raisins |
| 3/4 | cup sliced almonds |
| | Whipped cream (optional) |

*Note: If you wish to make your own Challah Bread see recipe on page 77.*

For the sauce, bring the cream, milk and sugar to a boil in a small saucepan. In a small bowl mix the amaretto and cornstarch and whisk into cream mixture. Stir constantly until the sauce thickens. This sauce can be made up to three days ahead. Re-warm to serve.

Combine bread with the half and half in a large bowl. Cover and let sit for 1 hour, stirring occasionally.

Preheat oven to 325°. Place the rack in the center of the oven. Grease a 9 x 13 – inch pan with the butter. Whisk together the sugar, eggs and almond extract in a medium size bowl. Stir this mixture into the bread mixture. Fold in the raisins and sliced almonds. Spoon the mixture into the prepared pan. Bake 50 minutes, or until firm. Top individual servings with sauce and whipped cream if desired.

8 – 10 servings

## Incredibly Delicious
## Lemon Curd

| | |
|---|---|
| 4 | large egg yolks |
| 1/2 | cup plus 2 teaspoons sugar |
| 3 | ounces lemon juice (use liquid measuring cup) |

| | |
|---|---|
| 4 | tablespoons butter |
| 1/8 | teaspoon vanilla paste |

*Variation: Vanilla extract can be used in place of vanilla paste using the same measure.*

Mix eggs yolks and sugar together and let sit for five minutes. Add the lemon juice and mix well. In a heavy nonreactive pan, stirring continually especially the edges, bring the mixture to a slight simmer. This should take about seven minutes over medium heat. It should reach 180°. Once the curd is very thick, strain it with a nonreactive strainer into a small bowl. When it cools to 140°, stir in the butter and the vanilla paste. The lemon curd can now be used for tarts, cake filling or mixed with whipped cream and fresh blueberries.

1 cup

## Barbie Blonde Bread Pudding

Note: Miniature bottles of the two kinds of rum needed can be found at most liquor stores. They are enough for the recipe.

**Pudding:**

| | |
|---|---|
| 3 | large eggs, whipped lightly |
| 1/2 | cup whipping cream |
| 1 | cup sugar |
| 1 | cup brown sugar |
| 1 | tablespoon banana extract |
| 1/4 | cup gold rum |
| 4 | cups milk |
| 1/4 | cup (1/2 stick) butter |
| 1 | (16 ounce) loaf French bread, cut into 1 – inch cubes |

**Sauce:**

| | |
|---|---|
| 1/2 | cup butter |
| 1/2 | cup brown sugar |
| 1/4 | cup dark rum |
| 1/2 | teaspoon banana extract |
| 2 | bananas, sliced |

Preheat oven to 325°. Grease a 9 x 13 baking dish. Combine eggs, whipping cream, sugar, brown sugar, banana extract and gold rum in a large bowl. Heat milk and butter in a large saucepan over medium high heat until butter melts, stirring constantly. Do not boil. Add a small amount of the milk mixture gradually into the egg mixture. When it is warmed, add remaining milk mixture, stirring constantly. Spread bread cubes in baking dish. Pour egg mixture evenly over the bread, pressing it down to absorb the liquid. Let sit for at least 1 hour or overnight. Bake 45 – 55 minutes. Cool on a wire rack for 30 minutes before serving.

Prepare the sauce while the pudding cools. Combine butter, sugar, rum and extract in a saucepan. Cook over medium high heat, stirring occasionally, for 5 minutes. Do not boil. Remove from heat. To serve, distribute sliced bananas evenly over each serving and top with the sauce.

10 – 12 servings

## Lemon Tart

| | | | |
|---|---|---|---|
| 1 | cup sugar | 1/2 | cup (1 stick) butter, melted |
| 2 | tablespoons flour | 1/2 | teaspoon vanilla |
| 4 | eggs | 1/4 | teaspoon almond extract |
| 1 | tablespoon grated lemon rind | 1 | frozen 9 – inch deep dish pie shell |
| 6 | tablespoons lemon juice (about 3 lemons) | 1/4 | cup slivered almonds (optional) |

Preheat oven to 350°. Position oven rack in lower third of the oven. Stir sugar and flour together in a bowl. Put eggs in large mixer bowl. Add sugar and flour mixture and beat until light in color and slightly thickened, about 3 minutes. Stir in lemon rind, lemon juice, butter, vanilla and almond extract. Pour into pie shell and place on a baking sheet. Bake 20 – 25 minutes or until filling is set and lightly browned.

If using almonds, while the tart is baking, toast the slivered almonds in a skillet over medium heat, stirring until just lightly browned, about 4 – 5 minutes. Sprinkle toasted almonds over top of tart when it is removed from the oven. Cool on wire rack.

8 servings

## Grilled Nectarines and Plums

2  **cups of water**

1/3  **cup honey, plus 2 tablespoons divided**

1  **(3 – inch) vanilla bean split lengthwise**

1/4  **cup frozen fat free whipped topping, thawed**

2  **tablespoons mascarpone cheese**

4  **nectarines, halved and pitted**

4  **plums, halved and pitted Cooking spray**

2  **cups cherries, halved and pitted**

2  **tablespoons sliced almonds, toasted and chopped**

*Tip: Slightly firm fruit will stand up to the heat better than very ripe fruit. Grilling intensifies the fruit's sweetness and flavor. Fresh mint as a garnish is nice.*

Combine water and honey in a small saucepan over a medium high heat. Scrape the vanilla bean seeds into the honey mixture and discard the bean. Bring to a boil and cook until reduced to 1 1/4 cups, which should take about 15 minutes. Combine the whipped topping, cheese and 2 tablespoons honey and stir until smooth. Set aside. Lightly spray both sides of nectarines and plums with cooking spray. Place nectarines and plums cut side down and grill 2 minutes on each side or until soft. To serve, place a nectarine and plum half in each of 8 shallow bowls. Top each serving with 1/4 cup cherries; then drizzle each with 2 tablespoons of the honey-vanilla bean mixture. Spoon 2 teaspoons of the whipped topping-cheese mixture on each and sprinkle with 3/4 teaspoon nuts.

8 servings

## Strawberry Shortcake Southern Style

**Toppings:**

2  **quarts fresh or frozen strawberries**

3/4  **cup sugar or as needed Whipped topping**

**Shortcake:**

2  **cups flour plus 2 tablespoons, divided**

2/3  **cup shortening**

1/2  **cup milk**

1/3  **cup sugar, divided**

4  **tablespoons melted butter, divided**

*Note: This is an old family recipe. Not your ordinary shortcake recipe.*

Wash and stem strawberries. Slice strawberries and place in a large bowl. Blend together strawberries and sugar. Set aside.

Preheat oven to 400°. Sift 2 cups of flour into a large bowl and cut in shortening until particles are the size of rice. Add milk all at once. Mix quickly with a fork. Divide shortcake in half. Sprinkle 1 tablespoon of flour on a flat surface and roll shortcake in the flour. Gently knead. Roll out until it is as thin as pie crust, not worrying about shape and adding additional flour if needed. Transfer to a cookie sheet. Brush surface with half of the melted butter and sugar. Place in oven and bake until golden brown, about 10 – 12 minutes. Remove from oven and cool. Repeat with other half of shortcake.

To serve, break shortcake in small pieces, place in a bowl and spoon strawberries over the top. Garnish with whipped topping or ice cream.

6 – 8 servings

## Mixed Berry Trifle

4 cups (1 quart) fresh or unsweetened frozen red raspberries

1/3 cup sugar

1/4 cup cornstarch

1/2 cup water

1 2/3 cups milk

1 cup sour cream

1 (5.1 ounce) package instant French vanilla pudding

Grated rind from 1 orange

1 (8 ounce) container Cool Whip

Juice of 1/2 orange

1 (16 ounce) pre-packaged pound cake

6 tablespoons Grand Marnier or orange juice

4 cups (1 quart) fresh strawberries, quartered

4 cups (1 quart) fresh blueberries

4 cups (1 quart) fresh raspberries or blackberries

Mint leaves (optional)

Combine raspberries and sugar in a saucepan and cook until bubbly. Mix cornstarch with water and add to raspberries. Cook until thickened. Press thru sieve to remove seeds. This can be done up to 3 days ahead.

Combine milk, sour cream and pudding mix in a bowl and stir until thick. Let this set up in the refrigerator, then fold in orange rind, Cool Whip and orange juice. Cut cake into bite sized pieces and layer 1/2 of the pieces in a large glass bowl. Sprinkle with 1/2 of the Grand Marnier. Layer with 1/2 of the raspberry sauce, 1/2 of the strawberries, 1/2 half of the blueberries, 1/2 of the fresh raspberries or blackberries and 1/2 of the vanilla pudding mixture. Repeat these layers, reserving some berries for garnish. Garnish with mint leaves if desired.

16 servings

## Sweet Cravings

1 (8 ounce) package any cream cheese, softened

1/2 cup (1 stick) butter, softened (no substitutes)

1/4 teaspoon vanilla extract

3/4 cup confectioners' sugar

2 tablespoons brown sugar, packed

3/4 cup miniature semi-sweet chocolate chips

3/4 cup finely chopped pecans, crushed Oreo cookies, or mini M & M's

Crackers or pretzels for serving

In a mixing bowl beat cream cheese, butter and vanilla until fluffy. Gradually add the confectioners' sugar and brown sugar. Beat just until combined. Stir in chocolate chips. Cover and refrigerate for 2 hours. Place cream cheese mixture on a large piece of plastic wrap; shape into a ball. Refrigerate for at least 1 hour. Roll cheese ball in pecans, crushed cookies or M & M's before serving.

12 servings

## Pumpkin Cheesecake

**Crust:**

1 1/2   cups gingersnap cookie
        crumbs (about 28, 2 – inch
        cookies)

1/4     cup granulated sugar

3       tablespoons butter or
        margarine, melted

**Cheesecake:**

3       (8 ounce) packages cream
        cheese, softened

3/4     cup granulated sugar

1/4     cup packed light brown sugar

1       (15 ounce) can pure pumpkin
        puree

2/3     cup gingerbread flavored liquid
        latte coffee creamer

2       eggs

2       tablespoons cornstarch

1/4     teaspoon ground cloves

**Topping:**

1       (16 ounce) carton sour cream,
        at room temperature

1/2     cup granulated sugar

1       teaspoon vanilla

*Variation: Substitute cinnamon vanilla crème latte creamer and 1/2 teaspoon ginger or 1/2 cup whipping cream mixed with 1/2 teaspoon ground ginger and 1/2 teaspoon cinnamon*

Preheat oven to 350°. Lightly grease a 9 – inch springform pan. Combine cookie crumbs, granulated sugar and butter in medium bowl for the crust. Press into the bottom and 1 – inch up the side of prepared pan. Freeze for 5 minutes.

For the cheesecake, thoroughly cream the cream cheese, granulated sugar and brown sugar in large mixer bowl. Beat in pumpkin, coffee creamer and eggs. Add cornstarch and cloves and beat well. Pour into crust. Bake for 65 – 75 minutes or until edge is set but center still moves slightly. Remove from oven.

While cake is baking prepare the topping. Mix sour cream, sugar and vanilla in a small bowl. Spread sour cream mixture over surface of hot cheesecake and bake for an additional 5 minutes. Run knife around edge of cheesecake. Cool completely on a rack. Remove from pan and refrigerate for several hours or overnight.

16 servings

## Quick Fudge Fix

1       (1 pound) box confectioners'
        sugar

1/2     cup cocoa

1/4     teaspoon salt

1/4     cup milk

1       tablespoon vanilla extract

1/2     cup (1 stick) butter, cut into
        pieces

1       cup chopped nuts

Grease or spray a 9 x 13 – inch baking sheet. Stir sugar, cocoa, salt, milk and vanilla together in a 1 1/2 quart microwaveable bowl until partially blended. The mixture will be too stiff to thoroughly blend. Drop butter pieces over the top of the batter. Place in microwave and cook about 2 minutes. Stir vigorously until smooth. If butter has not completely melted in cooking, it will as mixture is stirred. Blend in nuts. Let cool completely before cutting.

3 – 4 dozen pieces

# Riverside Ricotta Tart

*Note: The crust can be made up to one day ahead and stored covered with plastic wrap at room temperature.*

**Crust:**

- **1 cup finely ground vanilla or chocolate wafers (about 35)**
- **2 tablespoons granulated sugar**
- **3 tablespoons unsalted butter, melted**

**Filling:**

- **1 (15 ounce) container of whole-milk ricotta (about 1 1/2 cups)**
- **3 ounces cream cheese, softened**
- **2/3 cup granulated sugar**
- **2 tablespoons flour**
- **1/4 teaspoon salt**
- **3 egg yolks**
- **1 tablespoon finely grated orange zest**
- **1 tablespoon orange flavored liqueur or orange juice**
- **Fresh berries and/or fresh raspberry puree for serving**
- **Strips of orange zest or segments of orange for garnish**
- **Mint sprigs for garnish**

Preheat oven to 350°. Position rack in center of oven. Mix the cookie crumbs and sugar with a fork until well blended. Drizzle the melted butter over the crumbs and mix with the fork or your fingers until the crumbs are evenly moistened. Put the crumbs in an ungreased 9 1/2 – inch fluted tart pan with a removable bottom. Spread crust crumbs over the bottom of the pan and around the inside edge of the pan. Bake the crust until it is lightly browned, about 10 minutes. Remove from oven and cool on a wire rack while preparing filling.

Beat the ricotta and cream cheese using an electric mixer at medium speed until well blended and no lumps remain, about 3 minutes. Add the sugar, flour and salt, beating until well blended, about 1 minute. Add the egg yolks, orange zest and orange liqueur or juice and beat until just incorporated. Spread filling evenly into the crust. Bake until the filling just barely jiggles when the pan is gently shaken, about 30 – 35 minutes. Cool on wire rack and refrigerate until well chilled before serving. Serve with fresh berries and/or a fresh raspberry puree and garnish with orange zest or segments and a sprig of mint.

16 servings

*Famed Arts and Crafts period artist George Mann Niedecken was commissioned to create this fountain for the main entrance hall of Susan Lawrence Dana's home designed by Frank Lloyd Wright. Titled* The Moon Children, *it depicts them pouring water to replenish Earth. The art glass window behind the fountain uses one of Wright's many variations on the sumac theme.*

## White Chocolate Cheesecake with Raspberry Sauce

**Cheesecake:**

- 1/4 cup (1/2 stick) unsalted butter
- 2 cups finely ground vanilla wafers or butter cookies
- 1 ounce grated white chocolate
- 1/4 cup sugar
- 4 (8 ounce) packages any cream cheese, room temperature
- 1 cup sugar
- 4 tablespoons crème de cassis
- 1/4 teaspoon salt
- 4 large eggs, room temperature
- 3 ounces white chocolate, shaved
- 2 cups sour cream
- 1/4 cup sugar
- 1 teaspoon almond extract

**Raspberry Sauce:**

- 1 bag (12 ounce) frozen red raspberries
- 3 tablespoons crème de cassis
- 1/3 cup sugar or to taste
- 1/4 cup cornstarch mixed with 1/4 cup water

*Hint: To avoid the cracks that often form in cheesecake, run a knife between the pan and the cake when you take it out of the oven. This will loosen the cake from the edges so that it can shrink slightly as it cools without cracking.*

*Note: The raspberry sauce can be prepared up to 3 days ahead. Refrigerate until ready to use.*

Preheat oven to 350°. Melt butter and combine with cookie crumbs, grated white chocolate and sugar until blended. Press mixture on sides and bottom of an ungreased 10 – inch spring form pan.

Combine cream cheese and sugar and beat for 2 minutes until soft. Add crème de cassis and salt. With mixer on lowest speed, add eggs, one at a time, mixing only until each egg is incorporated into batter. Fold in the shaved chocolate. Pour into crust and bake 40 – 50 minutes. Cheesecakes set from the outside in. To test for doneness, shake the pan gently. The very center of the cake should jiggle just slightly. Combine sour cream, sugar and almond extract and spread over top of cake. Return to oven for an additional 10 minutes.

Sauce: Combine frozen raspberries, crème de cassis and sugar in a saucepan and cook until bubbly. Add cornstarch and water mixture and cook until thickened. Press through a sieve to remove seeds. Serve the cheesecake topped with the raspberry sauce.

16 Servings

The official residence of the Governor of Illinois is the 16-room Executive Mansion near the Capitol and numerous Lincoln venues. The grand opening was on January 10, 1856. Lincoln visited often. A portrait of the Lincoln's, and Gilbert Stuart's portraits of Patrick Henry and Meriwether Lewis grace public areas. It is set in a beautifully landscaped square block.

## Swirled Fudge

| | |
|---|---|
| 18 ounces bittersweet chocolate, finely chopped | 2 tablespoons (1/4 stick) unsalted butter, softened |
| 6 ounces milk chocolate, finely chopped | 1/2 teaspoon salt |
| 1 3/4 cups marshmallow cream (fluff) | 1 tablespoon vanilla extract |
| 4 1/2 cups granulated sugar | 8 ounces white chocolate, cut into chunks |
| 1 (12 ounce) can evaporated milk | |

Line a 9 x 13 – inch metal baking pan with foil and then parchment paper. Combine bittersweet chocolate, milk chocolate and marshmallow cream in large mixer bowl. Set aside.

In a saucepan, combine sugar, evaporated milk, butter and salt. Bring to a boil over medium heat, stirring constantly, about 4 minutes. Reduce heat to medium low and cook stirring constantly and adjusting the heat as necessary to keep the mixture boiling for exactly 6 minutes. Remove from heat and gradually pour boiling syrup into the bittersweet chocolate mixture, mixing on low speed until chocolate is melted, about 2 minutes. Stir in vanilla. Pour into prepared pan and add white chocolate, stirring to create a swirl pattern. Smooth the top and cool completely at room temperature until firm before cutting, about 2 hours.

48 pieces

## Amaretto Truffles

*Note: Use pasteurized eggs in this recipe.*

| | |
|---|---|
| 1 cup whipping cream | 2 egg yolks |
| 1/4 cup sugar | 3 tablespoons cream cheese |
| 1 teaspoon vanilla extract | 1/3 cup amaretto liqueur |
| 2 cups semi-sweet chocolate chips | 1 cup finely chopped toasted almonds |
| 1/2 cup (1 stick) butter, softened | amaretto liqueur for serving |

Beat whipping cream, sugar and vanilla until stiff peaks form. Refrigerate until ready to serve. Melt chocolate chips in the top of a double boiler over low heat. Remove from heat and stir in butter one tablespoon at a time. Beat egg yolks into mixture (mixture will begin to thicken). Beat cream cheese and amaretto into chocolate mixture until smooth. Cover and chill until firm. Shape mixture into 1 1/2 – inch balls. Roll in almonds. Refrigerate until firm. To serve, pour 2 tablespoons amaretto into a wine glass. Place a truffle in glass and top with sweetened whipped cream.

36 truffles.

## Peanut Brittle

| | | | | |
|---|---|---|---|---|
| 1 | teaspoon baking soda | | 2 | tablespoons (1/4 stick) butter or margarine |
| 1 | teaspoon vanilla extract | | 1 | pound raw peanuts (about 3 1/2 cups) |
| 3 | cups sugar | | | |
| 1 1/2 | cups glucose | | | |
| 1 | cup water | | | |

Butter a large flat surface to use for spreading the hot peanut brittle. Measure the baking soda and vanilla into preparation containers so that they can be added quickly when needed. Combine sugar, glucose and water. Bring to a boil and cook until temperature on a candy thermometer reaches 275°. Stir to mix the ingredients; however, continuous stirring is unnecessary. When the temperature reaches 275° add the butter and peanuts. Stir very frequently until temperature reaches 310° to prevent the peanuts from burning.

Remove from heat and quickly add baking soda and vanilla. Stir well (it will foam up). Pour onto the middle of the prepared surface and begin to pull edges outward, working around the perimeter until mixture is pulled thin. You might want to use a small buttered spatula to pull the edges until you get a hardened cooled edge. You can also use the spatula to lift a bit and pull and use as a second hand. As the peanut brittle hardens, you can crack and or cut with scissors and move to another area until it is hardened. Cool before breaking into pieces and packing.

3 1/2 pounds

*Note: Glucose can be found at most specialty food shops and some larger grocery stores.*

*Tip: Use a buttered large piece of oilcloth on a table for access and ability to walk around and pull edges. You will want to do this fairly quickly as it cools and hardens quickly. Using a spatula helps to keep your fingertips from burning.*

## Peanut Butter Fudge

| | | | | |
|---|---|---|---|---|
| 1/2 | cup peanut butter | | 6 | ounces white chocolate chips (about 1 1/2 cups) |
| 1 | (14 ounce) can Eagle Brand Sweetened Condensed Milk | | 1 | teaspoon vanilla extract |

Butter an 8 – inch square pan. Combine peanut butter and sweetened condensed milk in a medium saucepan. Heat, stirring constantly, until mixture is smooth and peanut butter is dissolved. Remove from heat and add white chocolate chips and vanilla. The base must be hot enough to melt the white chocolate chips. Stir until chips are completely melted and mixture is smooth. Pour into the buttered pan. When cool, cut into squares.

36 servings

# Over the Top

*The crown indicates a celebrity's recipe.*

## Mike Aiello
# Marinara Sauce

Variation: For a
meat sauce, brown
1 pound of ground
pork, sausage or
ground chicken
or combination of
your choice prior
to beginning the
marinara. Add meat to
marinara mixture after
the tomatoes and mix
well.

Note: I prefer
using San Marzano
tomatoes, a variety of
plum tomatoes. They
are considered by
many chefs to be the
best sauce tomatoes
in the world.

- 1/4 **cup olive oil**
- 1/2 **medium onion, coarsely chopped**
- 5 **cloves garlic, minced**
- 1/4 **teaspoon crushed red pepper**
- 1/2 **cup Chianti wine**
- 1 **(28 ounce) can crushed tomatoes**
- 1 **(28 ounce) can tomato sauce**
- 1 **(6 ounce) can tomato paste**
- 2 **tablespoons dried oregano**
- 2 **tablespoons brown sugar**
- 2 **tablespoons fresh basil, chopped**

Warm the olive oil in a large saucepan over medium-low heat. Add onion, garlic and red pepper and cook for a few minutes, making sure not to brown the garlic. Add red wine and swirl to deglaze the pan. Add crushed tomatoes, tomato sauce, tomato paste, oregano and brown sugar. Cook over medium heat for 10 minutes. Reduce heat to low and simmer, stirring occasionally, for up to 1 hour. Add fresh basil during the last 10 minutes of cooking. Serve over pasta immediately or refrigerate for later use.

4 cups

# Stir Fry Sauce

Tip: Refrigerate for up
to a month. Save the
extra for the next stir
fry recipe or use as a
marinade.

- 4 **tablespoons brown sugar**
- 1 **tablespoon minced fresh ginger root**
- 1/4 **teaspoon red pepper sauce**
- 2 1/2 **cups chicken broth**
- 1/3 **cup cornstarch**
- 4 **garlic cloves, crushed or minced**
- 1/2 **cup soy sauce**
- 1/2 **cup dry sherry or dry white wine**
- 3 **tablespoons red or white wine vinegar**

Combine sugar, ginger root, pepper sauce, broth, cornstarch, garlic, soy sauce, sherry or wine and red or white wine vinegar. Stir the sauce well before pouring into the meat and vegetables. When meat and vegetables are almost done, pour approximately 1/2 of the sauce over them and bring to a boil until sauce thickens.

4 cups

## Béarnaise Sauce

| | |
|---|---|
| 2 1/2 tablespoons white wine | Pepper |
| 2 1/2 tablespoons white vinegar | 3/4 cup butter, softened |
| 1 tablespoon chopped shallot | 3 egg yolks |
| 1 tablespoon chopped chervil | A few tarragon leaves |
| 1 teaspoon chopped tarragon | Lemon juice |
| Salt | Pinch cayenne pepper |

Combine wine, vinegar, shallot, chervil, tarragon, salt and pepper. Boil until reduced by two thirds. Cool to lukewarm and strain. Gradually add softened butter to strained liquid. Using a double boiler, add eggs yolks slowly and stir until sauce thickens. Remove from heat. Add tarragon leaves and season with lemon juice and cayenne.

## Basil Sauce

| | |
|---|---|
| 8 ounces cream cheese, softened | 1 cup parsley, chopped |
| 1 cup pine nuts, toasted | 1/4 cup extra virgin olive oil |
| 1 cup basil | 1/4 cup yogurt |
| 1/2 cup Parmesan cheese | 1 teaspoon pepper sauce |
| 1/4 cup white wine basil vinegar | 1/2 teaspoon salt |

Combine cream cheese, pine nuts, basil, Parmesan cheese, vinegar, parsley, olive oil, yogurt, pepper sauce and salt. Serve at room temperature. Use on pasta or tomatoes.

## Ancho Chile Glaze

| | |
|---|---|
| 1/2 cup honey | Salt to taste |
| 2 tablespoons Dijon mustard | Freshly ground pepper to taste |
| 2 tablespoons ancho chile powder | |

Combine honey, mustard and chile powder in a bowl. Season mixture with salt and pepper to taste. Baste this on salmon, chicken or pork and cook for an extra minute on each side.

4 - 6 servings

## Carpenter Park Pork Marinade

Note: Margaret Garfield Orzo with Vegetables go well with meat cooked in this marinade. See page 82.

**Marinade:**

- 1/4 cup apple juice, concentrate
- 2 tablespoons Dijon mustard
- 2 tablespoons olive oil
- 2 tablespoons fresh rosemary, chopped
- 4 cloves garlic, minced
- 1 teaspoon black peppercorns, crushed

**Vinaigrette:**

- 1 1/2 tablespoons Dijon mustard
- 1 tablespoon minced shallots
- 3 tablespoons port wine
- 2 tablespoons balsamic vinegar
- 1 tablespoon olive oil
  Salt to taste
  Freshly ground pepper to taste
  Fresh rosemary

In a small bowl, whisk together apple juice, mustard, olive oil, rosemary, garlic and peppercorns. Marinade meat for at least two hours or overnight. Reserve about 1/3 of the marinade mixture for basting.

For the vinaigrette, combining the mustard, shallots, port, vinegar, olive oil, salt and pepper in a jar with a lid. Whisk or shake until blended. Serve over your choice of meat.

6 – 8 servings

## Franklin Flank Steak Marinade

- 2/3 cup vegetable oil
- 1/4 cup soy sauce
- 1/4 cup honey
- 1 garlic clove minced or 1 teaspoon chopped from a jar

- 2 tablespoons vinegar
- 4 chopped green scallions
- 1 1/2 teaspoon ground ginger

Place the oil, soy sauce, honey, garlic, vinegar, scallions and ginger in a bowl and mix well. Pour over flank steak and marinate overnight. Turn 3 – 4 times if possible. Meat is best if marinated for 24 hours and turned every 4 hours during the day.

Architect Elijah Myers built this Victorian Italianate home on North 5th Street for George and Isabella Brinkerhoff who then filled it with architectural objects; figures of humans, horses and other animals; relief sculpture and sculpture in the round. George transferred title to the Ursuline nuns nearby. It is now owned by Benedictine University, serving as office and meeting spaces.

## Koke Mill Chicken or Beef Marinade

| | | | |
|---|---|---|---|
| 1/4 | cup soy sauce | 1 | tablespoon oil |
| 1 | tablespoon honey | 1/4 | teaspoon ginger |
| 1/2 | teaspoon pepper | 2 | tablespoons water |
| 3 | garlic cloves, finely chopped | 3 | tablespoons brown sugar |

Combine the soy sauce, honey, pepper, garlic, oil, ginger, water and brown sugar. Put marinade into a plastic bag and add meat, making sure the meat is thoroughly coated. Seal the bag and refrigerate for about 2 hours, turning the package occasionally. When ready to cook the meat, remove it from the bag and throw away the marinade.

2/3 cup

*Note: If you wish to use marinade to baste the meat while cooking, make extra and put part of it aside while marinating the meat. NEVER use marinade that was used on the meat for basting.*

## Garlic and Oregano Marinade

| | | | |
|---|---|---|---|
| 1/4 | cup olive oil | 2 | tablespoons sherry vinegar |
| 1/2 | cup coarsely chopped garlic | 2 | tablespoons lime juice |
| 1/2 | cup coarsely chopped fresh oregano leaves | 1 | tablespoon honey |
| | | 2 | teaspoons ancho chile powder |

Combine the olive oil, garlic, oregano, sherry vinegar, lime juice, honey and chile powder in a large measuring cup. Mix well. Place marinade in a plastic container or plastic zip bag and add the meat. Refrigerate meat and marinate in mixture for at least 4 hours and up to 12 hours. This recipe works great when grilling.

1/2 cup

## South Fork Beef Rub

| | | | |
|---|---|---|---|
| 1 | teaspoon salt | 1 | teaspoon onion salt |
| 1 | teaspoon pepper | 1 | teaspoon celery salt |
| 1 | teaspoon garlic salt | 1 | cup beef bouillon |

Preheat oven to 425°. Rinse a 4 – 5 pound roast and pat dry with paper towels. Combine salt, pepper, garlic salt, onion salt and celery salt and rub the roast with the mixture. Place meat in a shallow roaster. Insert a meat thermometer in the middle of the roast. Bake for 30 minutes uncovered and pour 1 cup bouillon over the top. Reduce heat to 350°. Baste meat every 30 minutes. Remove from oven when thermometer reaches desired doneness. This may be used on all kinds of roasts, steaks, or as a stew seasoning.

## Island Bay Yacht Club
# Vanilla Vinaigrette Dressing

3/4   cup champagne vinegar
3/4   tablespoon lemon juice
3/4   tablespoon salt
3/4   tablespoon of pepper

2   tablespoons vanilla extract
2   tablespoons honey
2   cups of olive oil

Combine the vinegar, lemon juice, salt, pepper, vanilla, honey and olive oil and mix well. This dressing can be stored for several months in the refrigerator in a sealed bottle.

1 pint

# Apricot Balsamic Dressing

*Note: The dressing is sensational over garden greens, fruit salads or as a chicken marinade. It makes 1 cup. Refrigerate leftover dressing.*

**Dressing:**
1/2   cup pitted ripe apricots or canned apricots, drained
1/3   cup balsamic vinegar
1/4   cup honey
2   teaspoons Dijon mustard
1   clove garlic, minced

1/4   teaspoon dried tarragon
1/2   teaspoon dried parsley
1/2   teaspoon salt
1/4   teaspoon pepper
1   tablespoon virgin olive oil

Dressing: Puree apricots in a blender. Add vinegar, honey, mustard, garlic, tarragon, parsley, salt and pepper. Process ingredients until smooth. Pour oil slowly through the blender tube and blend until completely emulsified.

8 – 12 servings

# Walnut Oil Vinaigrette

*Note: Simple yet so delicious.*

2   tablespoons balsamic vinegar
1   tablespoon sherry (or red wine) vinegar
7   tablespoons walnut oil

3   tablespoons olive oil
Salt to taste
Pepper to taste

Combine balsamic vinegar and sherry. Gradually add the walnut oil and olive oil stirring constantly until they are emulsified. Add salt and pepper to taste.

3/4 cup

## KDO Kitchen Dressing

| | | | |
|---|---|---|---|
| 4 | tablespoons sugar | 8 | slices bacon |
| 4 | tablespoons red wine vinegar | | Milk to thin, if desired |
| 2 | cups sour cream | | Cherry tomatoes to garnish |

Combine sugar, vinegar and sour cream until smooth. Refrigerate. Fry the bacon until crispy, saving 1/4 cup of the bacon grease. Dry bacon on paper towels and chop into small pieces. To serve, heat the bacon grease and pour over chilled lettuce pieces. Toss to coat. Place individual servings on chilled plates and sprinkle with bacon pieces. Top with sour cream mixture and garnish with cherry tomatoes.

4 – 6 servings

## Nightingale Salad Dressing

| | | | |
|---|---|---|---|
| 3/4 | cup sugar | 1/4 | teaspoon white pepper |
| 1/2 | cup red wine vinegar | 2 | large cloves garlic, crushed |
| 1/2 | teaspoon salt | 1/2 | red onion, thinly sliced |
| 1/2 | teaspoon paprika | 1 | cup oil |
| 1/2 | teaspoon cayenne | | |

Combine sugar, vinegar, salt, paprika, cayenne, white pepper, garlic and onion. Slowly whisk in oil until it emulsifies.

1 1/2 cups

## Poppy Seed Dressing

| | | | |
|---|---|---|---|
| 1/2 | cup sugar | 1 | small onion, chopped |
| 1 | tablespoon dry mustard | 1/8 | teaspoon cayenne pepper |
| 1 | teaspoon salt | 1/2 | cup vinegar |
| 1/2 | teaspoon poppy seeds | 1 | cup salad oil |

Combine sugar, mustard, salt, poppy seeds, onion and cayenne in a blender. Add the vinegar and a small amount of oil. Blend well. Add remaining oil slowly until it is emulsified.

1 1/2 cups

*Note: Purchased poppy seeds should be immediately placed in a freezer for several months to a year. They will keep for 3 to 6 months refrigerated. Once they are ground their shelf life is shorter, about 2 months in the freezer. Without refrigeration the oils may go rancid quickly.*

## Mill Tavern Dressing

1 1/2　cups sugar
　1/2　cup prepared mustard
1 1/2　teaspoons salt
　　　　Water

Juice from lemon
　2　cups white vinegar
　1　cup oil
　1　clove garlic

Combine sugar, mustard and salt. Add scant cup of water, lemon juice, white vinegar and oil. Whisk until emulsified. Put in jar with a lid and add a clove of garlic. Remove garlic clove within 24 – 48 hours for food safety.

3 cups

## Italian Dressing Mix

1/4　teaspoon basil, crushed
1/8　teaspoon oregano
1/4　teaspoon sugar
　　　Pinch of garlic granules
1/4　tablespoon dry mustard

1/8　teaspoon pepper, cracked
2/3　cup oil
1/3　cup vinegar
　3　tablespoons lemon juice

In a glass jar add basil, oregano, sugar, garlic, mustard and pepper. Add oil, vinegar and lemon juice and shake well to incorporate.

1 cup

## Ranch Dressing Mix

Mix:
2/3　cup buttermilk powder
　3　tablespoons onion flakes
　2　teaspoons garlic powder or
　　　granules
　3　tablespoons parsley flakes

Dressing:
1/4　cup dressing mix
1/2　cup water
　1　cup mayonnaise

Combine the buttermilk powder, onion flakes, garlic powder, and parsley flakes and store covered in the refrigerator. When ready to make the dressing, combine 1/4 cup of mix with the water and mayonnaise. Chill for 2 hours before serving.

1 3/4 cups

## Buckhart Chili Sauce

12  pounds ripe tomatoes, skinned, drained and cut in halves

5  large white or yellow onions, chopped

5  small hot red peppers, stems and seeds removed, chopped

12  green peppers, seeds removed and chopped

1  whole large stalk of celery, stalks trimmed and chopped

4 1/2  cups brown sugar

6 1/2  cups cider vinegar

5  teaspoons mustard seed

5  teaspoons canning salt

3 1/2  teaspoons ground ginger

2 1/2  teaspoons ground cinnamon

3 1/2  teaspoons ground nutmeg

2 1/2  teaspoons curry powder

Combine the tomatoes, onions, red peppers, green peppers, celery, sugar, vinegar, mustard seed, salt, ginger, cinnamon, nutmeg, and curry powder in a large, heavy stockpot and bring to a boil. Reduce heat and simmer over low heat stirring frequently until this sauce reaches the desired thickness, 2 – 4 hours or so.

Makes approximately ten (10) quarts for canning.

## Horseradish Mustard

1/2  cup powdered mustard

1/8  teaspoon white pepper

1/4  cup water

1  tablespoon salt

1  teaspoon sugar or to taste

1  clove of garlic, peeled and minced

1 1/2  tablespoons horseradish, grated or prepared, divided

1/2  cup white wine or cider vinegar

Mix mustard and pepper with water. Combine salt, sugar, garlic and 1 tablespoon horseradish. Blend and then strain. Add salt mixture to mustard mixture. Cook covered over low heat, stirring constantly, until it thickens slightly. Cool. Stir in remaining horseradish for texture. Add additional horseradish if you prefer a stronger flavor.

3/4 cup

*Grace Lutheran Church is one of several churches in Springfield that have existed for at least 150 years. People drive from all over the city to attend this church that has remained downtown for generations. Established in 1841, the church building features a unique stone bell tower and steeple.*

## Tartar Sauce

| | | | |
|---|---|---|---|
| **4** | **tablespoons mayonnaise** | **1/2** | **teaspoon Worcestershire Sauce** |
| **1/2** | **teaspoon lemon juice** | **1** | **teaspoon sweet onion, minced** |
| | **Dash hot pepper sauce** | **1** | **teaspoon, minced dill pickles** |

Combine mayonnaise, lemon juice, pepper sauce and Worcestershire sauce and mix well. Fold in the onion and pickles. Refrigerate for 1 hour to chill and for flavors to meld before serving.

## Flavored Sugar

| | | | |
|---|---|---|---|
| **1/4** | **cup whole leaves of scented flowers or leaves** | **1/2** | **cup granulated sugar** |

Pick the herb or flower of choice immediately after dew has evaporated. Wash leaves and pat dry with a towel. Combine leaves and sugar and let mixture meld for 2 days. Sift to remove the herbs and store in a sealed jar.

Variation: Commonly used flowers and leaves include lavender buds, scented geranium leaves, lemon verbena leaves, dianthus pink leaves, nasturtium blossoms pistil's removed, flavored sages or any of the mints.

The Irish saying, "Céad Mile Fáilte," at D'Arcy's Pint is displayed prominently on a plaque in their entry way. With the meaning "100,000 welcomes," it is a invitation for many to feel welcomed. D'Arcy's Pint enjoys Irish Heritage by displaying this Traditional Irish Dance Uniform, and by naming their nachos "Irish Nachos."

# This & That

# Formal Table Setting

**KEY:**

1. Napkin
2. Salad Fork
3. Dinner Fork
4. Dessert Fork
5. Bread-and-Butter Plate, with Spreader
6. Dinner Plate
7. Dinner Knife
8. Teaspoon
9. Teaspoon
10. Soup Spoon
11. Cocktail Fork
12. Water Glass
13. Red-Wine Glass
14. White-Wine Glass
15. Coffee Cup and Saucer

*Wine*

| | Viognier | Sauvignon Blanc | Chardonnay | Reisling / Pinot Gris / Grigio | Pinot Noir | Syrah Shiraz | Merlot | Cabernet Sauvignon | Zinfandel |
|---|---|---|---|---|---|---|---|---|---|
| **Meat Poultry** | Thai or Spicy Chicken Dishes | Chicken Turkey Pork Chop | Veal Chicken Pork Loin | Smoky-Spicy Sausage/Ham Duck | Lamb/Veal Sausage Filet Mignon | Game/Ribs Beef Brisket Spicy Sausage | Grilled Meat Steak/Bacon Charred Meat | Grill Steaks Beef Stew Venison | Pork/Beef Spicy Meats Duck |
| **Seafood** | Lobster/Crab Shrimp Scallops | Lobster/Sole Oysters Scallops | Lobster/Crab Halibut Shrimp | Sea Bass Trout Swordfish | Salmon Orange Roughy Swordfish | BBQ Salmon | Trout | Trout | Cioppino Blackened Fish |
| **Nuts Cheese** | Goat Cheese Gouda | Goat Cheese Feta Pine Nuts | Asiago Havarti Almonds | Havarti/Swiss Gouda Candied Walnuts | Goat Cheese Brie Walnut | Sharp Cheddar Roquefort Hazelnuts | Parmesan Romano Chestnuts | Cheddar Gorgonzola Walnuts | Ripe Brie Aged Cheese |
| **Appetizers** | Wontons Sushi Rolls Hot Wings | White Pizza Spinach Dip Ceviche/Sushi | White Pizza Fried Zucchini Ceviche/Sushi | Tuna Tartare Ceviche | Tuna Tartare Baked Brie Simple Sliders | Pizza/Ribs BBQ Chicken Pulled Pork | Pizza Prosciutto Burgers | Pizza w/Veg's/ Meats Burgers | Pizza w/Spicy Meats Burgers |
| **Sauces** | Indian Curries Asian Sauces | Citrus/Pesto Asian Light Sauces | Cream and Pesto Sauces | Sweet BBQ Spicy Chutney | Mushroom Light-Med. Red Sauces | Heavy Red BBQ | Bolognese Bearnaise | Brown Tomato Rich | Spicy Cajun Salsa |
| **Herbs Spices** | Chili and Ginger | Tarragon Chives Cilantro | Tarragon Sesame Basil | Rosemary Ginger | Nutmeg Cinnamon Clove | Oregano and Sage | Mint Rosemary Juniper | Vanilla Rosemary Juniper | Pepper and Nutmeg |
| **Vegetables Fruit** | Artichoke Asparagus Citrus | Asparagus Green Apple Citrus | Potato/Apple Squash Mango | Chili Peppers Apricots Pears | Mushrooms Dried Fruit Figs Strawberries | Tomatoes Beets Currants | Caramelized Onions Tomatoes Plums | Broccoli Tomatoes Black Cherry | Peppers Eggplant Cranberries |
| **Desserts** | Vanilla Ice Cream | Sorbet Key Lime Pie | Banana Bread Vanilla Pudding | Apple Pie Caramel | Crème Brûlée White Chocolate | Black Forest Cake Rhubarb | Dark Chocolate Berries Fondue | Bittersweet Chocolate Espresso | Spice Cake Gingerbread Carrot Cake |

# Roasting Vegetables

Roasting is an excellent way to prepare vegetables. The high, dry heat of the oven concentrates their flavors and the natural sugars caramelize, transforming them into richly satisfying sides. For every 2 pounds of vegetables, toss with 1 tablespoon olive oil prior to roasting and roast at 450°.

Spread in a single layer on a lightly oiled shallow roasting pan or jelly roll pan with space in between pieces, if possible, or they will steam instead. Roast different veggies together if their cooking times are similar and top with a sprinkling of coarse or kosher salt. Vinaigrettes, a drizzle of balsamic vinegar or a squeeze of fresh lemon also make fine toppings.

| | | |
|---|---|---|
| **Asparagus** | Trim woody bottoms and peel first 3 – inches, if desired | 10 – 15 minutes |
| **Broccoli** | Trim and peel stem: split florets into 1 1/2 to 2 – inch pieces | 10 – 15 minutes |
| **Brussels Sprouts** | Trim and cut an X through stem end | 15 – 20 minutes |
| **Butternut Squash** | Peel and cut in 2 – inch pieces | 40 minutes |
| **Carrots / Parsnips** | 1 – inch pieces | 30 – 40 minutes |
| **Cauliflower** | 1 1/2 – inch florets | 20 – 30 minutes |
| **Eggplant** | 1/2 – inch slices | 20 – 25 minutes |
| **Fennel** | Trim and cut into wedges | 35 – 40 minutes |
| **Green Beans** | Trimmed | 20 – 30 minutes |
| **Onions** | Peel and cut in 8 or more wedges depending on size | 20 – 30 minutes |
| **Potatoes** | 2 – inch pieces | 30 – 40 minutes |
| **Sweet Peppers** | 1 – inch strips | 30 minutes |
| **Sweet Potatoes** | Cut crosswise in half then lengthwise in 1 – inch wedges | 30 minutes |
| **Turnips** | Peel and cut into wedges | 45 minutes |
| **Zucchini** | Trim and cut in half crosswise, then quarter each half | 15 – 20 minutes |

# Cooking with Herbs

**Description:** Fresh herbs, which naturally enhance fresh produce are varied: annuals, biennials, and perennials; strong or mild, sweet or sour. They can be grown year-round in mild climates or in a sunny window sill.

**Selection:** Choose herbs that are fresh and green. Avoid those that are shriveled or have dark spots.

**Storage and Handling:** Once picked, herbs do not keep long. First removing any damaged leaves and trim the stalks. Store them upright in a glass of water in the refrigerator. They also keep well wrapped in a damp paper towel in a zippered plastic bag in the refrigerator.

**Preparation:** When ready to use, swish in a bowl of cold water, wrap in paper towels (or a clean dish towel), and shake dry. Chop and use in recipes; or tear or snip fresh herbs for better flavor.

**To Dry Herbs:** Tie bunches and hang upside down in a cool, dark place. When dry, crumble dried leaves and store in small airtight jars. *Note:* When dried, herbs have stronger flavor than fresh: use 1 teaspoon of the dried herb where you would use 2 – 3 teaspoons of the fresh.

---

**BASIL:** Found in most Italian cooking. Tear leaves to sprinkle over salads and sliced tomatoes or add to pasta sauces and Mediterranean cooked dishes at the last minute.

**BAY LEAF:** Use whole in stews, soups and sauces. Add to marinades and stock; always remove leaves before serving.

**CHIVES:** Finely snipped chives add flavor and garnish. They are excellent with eggs, salads, soft cheeses, potatoes and fish. Add at the last minute to retain their delicate flavor.

**CILANTRO:** Its distinctive flavor and fragrance are frequently found in Mexican, Middle Eastern, Asian cuisines. Use fresh in salad, salsa, dip, curry and chili; it is best included at the end of cooking time.

**DILL:** Dill leaves also known as dill weed, combines well with potato dishes, yogurt dips, cucumber salads, dressings, fall and winter stews, green beans and fish dishes. Use the flowering tops or seed in egg, seafood and potato dishes, or for pickling.

**MARJORAM:** A taste reminiscent of oregano, but with a sweeter flavor. Can be used in soups, stews, bean dishes, dressings and sauces, and in marinades for vegetables, fish or lamb.

**MINT:** Mints can refresh, cool and invigorate. Add mint to new potatoes, peas, fruit salads and drinks.

**OREGANO:** Found extensively in Mediterranean cooking. It is particularly well-suited to tomato-based sauces. Try rubbing on roasting meat or using in meatballs.

**PARSLEY:** Flat-leaf parsley has the most flavor and is best for cooking. Sauté finely chopped leaves with garlic and add at the last minute to steak, fried fish or vegetables. Sprinkle finely chopped curly parsley over boiled potatoes.

**ROSEMARY:** Add sparingly to meat dishes, particularly lamb and pork. Sprinkle over focaccia. Makes a delicious herb butter for vegetables.

**SAGE:** This strong-flavored herb combines well with other strong flavors. Mix leaves with onion for poultry stuffing. Cook with rich, fatty meats such as pork and duck or with vegetables. Blend into cheeses or butter.

**SAVORY:** Its peppery spiciness improves the flavor of legumes and all kinds of beans, even frozen or canned. Use in sauces.

**THYME:** Fresh thyme is very pungent – use sparingly. Add to stocks, marinades, stuffings, sauces and soups. Sprinkle over roasted vegetables. Also suits shellfish, and game Lemon thyme is a wild variety with a more pronounced lemon aroma. Great in bread.

# Appropriate Equivalents

| | |
|---|---|
| A pinch | 1/8 teaspoon or less |
| 3 teaspoons | 1 tablespoon |
| 4 tablespoons | 1/4 cup |
| 8 tablespoons | 1/2 cup |
| 12 tablespoons | 3/4 cup |
| 16 tablespoons | 1 cup |
| 1 ounce | 2 tablespoons |
| 8 ounces | 1 cup |
| 2 cups | 1 pint |
| 4 cups | 1 quart |
| 4 quarts | 1 gallon |
| 16 ounces | 1 pound |

Use standard measuring spoons and cups.
All measurements are level.

# Acknowledgements

**Dining with the Daughters** began as a vague vision. Today, through the selfless efforts of many individuals participating in our project and thousands of volunteer hours, it is a glowing reality!

We extend a heartfelt THANK YOU to our members, family, friends and businesses who provided assistance with our cookbook **Dining with the Daughters, Recipes Galore from King's Daughters and More**. We sincerely hope that we did not overlook anyone that has participated. We believe it to be a means of serving the entire community with a beautiful memento of our fundraising efforts towards our mission, to serve the elderly.

## Contributors

Jill Aiello
Ingrid Alexander
Karen Alexander
Norma Altman
Patricia Altorfer
Joan Anderson
Barbara Archer
David Archer
Iris Archer
Elise Arnold
Kathy Badger
Karen Barber
Jode Barrows
Sheri Barry
Jo Ann Bartolomucci
Manjula Batmanathan-Rigg
Susan Beard
Nancy Beatty
Frances Beaver
Vickie Beaver
Linda Bee
Francie Black
Betty Boardman
Mary Lou Booker
Connie Bostick
Sylvia Brewer
Evie Brodland
Katie Brown
Shirley Bruner
John Bryden
Jeanette Buie
Jeanne Buie
Florence Bunn
Nancy Bunn
Sarah Bunn
Cindy Burke
Janice Butler
Sally Cadagin
Laura Carmody
Mary Carmody
Sue Carroll
Grace Carvahlo
Joan Casper
Susan Cassiday
Linda Chronister
Gloria Cisna
Lisa Coakley
Beverly Collins
Kim Collins
Diana Copper
Shirley Crawford
Pat Cross
Caroline Cunningham
Lori Curry
Deloris Dedrick

Diana Dedrick
Irene Dedrick
Nancy DeMarco
Cindy Denby
Anne Dondanville
Carolee Drennan
Helen Everson
Lynne Ewan
Virgene Fair
Constance Feldhausen
Emilee Feldhausen
Dorothy Fitzgerald
Rozanne Flatt (Posy)
Linda Flowtow
Naomi Fowler
Donna Freeman
Susan Fulks
Dee Dee Gain
Bonnie Gates
Donna Jean Gibney
Mary M Gill
Becky Glazier
Cressie Gorgerson
Kandy Grafton
Terri Greenwald
Shirley Greenwalt
Ellen Griesemer
Donna Grove
Kay Gulley
Nancy Hahn
Pat Hanken
Helen Harmony
Becky Harting
Jannette Hassebrock
Sharon Heflin
Brynn Henderson
Ferol Henry
Mary Kay Hinkle
Elaine Hoff
Dana Homann
Sue Howell
Judy Inslee
Sally Jones
Sarah Jones
Willa Jean Jones
Jayme Joyner
Wanda Keil
Barbara Kenney
Tammy Klein
Susan Kock
Joy Kroeninburg
Amanda Kurman
Gloria Lamb
Cleo Lee
Rosemary Leistner
Donna Ley

Wilda Lunt
Jeanne Madden
Laurie Maddox
Susan Madison
Bonnie Malcor
Katie Marinelli
Lisa Marinelli
Maureen Marker
Bobbie Maupin
Helen McDonald
Teresa McElwee
Barbara McKean
Tara McVary
Lisa Metzger
Paula Milling
Karen Moffat
Maritza Monk
Bev Neisler
Alice Nelle
Donna Nelson
Trudy Nelson
Nadine Neumister
Judy Oxtoby
Jan Parr
Clemilee Patterson
Mary Beth Patterson
June Paul
Shirley Penewitt
Gaile Phillips
Hiram Phillips
Janet Plohr
Judy Rader
Pearl Rank
Bitsy Reisch
Elizabeth Reyhan
Sue Reynolds
Jo Ridley
John Rigg
Doug Ringer
Sandy Robinson
Joanne Roderick
Polly Roesch
Joan Rothfuss
Kim Rusciolelli
Myrtle Rusciolelli
Martha Rushton
Norrie Russell
Paula Ryan
Jan Sables
Suzie Sables Fessler
Nancy Salefski
Karen Sanders
Cathy Schwartz
Fran Schwartz
Margaret Schwartz
Marie Secker

Kathy Sees
Pat Shafer
Sue Shevlin
Bertha Siddens
Rhondda Siddens
Nancy Simpson
Suzy Smiley
Kay Smith
Mary Smith
Ben Sowle
Todd Sowle
Donna Spencer
Polly Spengler
Connie Sprague
Brenda Staab
Jean Staab
Ruth Anne Staab
Mary Staudt
Paula Stewart
Carolyn Stone
Candy Stout
Margie Stuart
Jan Sullivan
Phyllis Sweeney
Mona Taylor
Leda Thorp
Dee Tozer
Mary Trask
Sharon Turner
Kay Usher
Jone Van Winkle
Lin Vautrain
Maryann Walker
Carol Walton
Deb Wargo
Glenda Warren
Dave Watson
Samantha Watson
Nancy Watson
Jean Weiss
Ayten Welch
Laverda Wenzel
Judy Wheaton
Sue White
Maxine Whitlock
Janet Wilson
Mary Ann Wood
Jackie Woodruff
Kathie Wozniak
Linda Younkin
Evelyn Yurdin
Sarah Zerfas
Chris Zuck
Fern Zuckworth

# CELEBRITY CHEFS

5flavors .................................. Chip Kennedy and Fallon Achas
American Harvest ................................ Jordan and Aurora Coffey
Apple Barn ............................................ Gayle Johnson
Augie's Front Burner .............................. August Mrozowski
Cafe' Moxo ............................................ Mark Forinash
Caitie Girl's .......................................... In Memory of Caitie Barker
Carol Jean's Fine Cuisine ..................... Carol Jean Fraase
D'Arcy's Pint ......................................... Hallie Pierceall
Gloria Schwartz
HG's Steakhouse .................................. Jeff Griswold
Illini Country Club ................................. Robb Wyss
Incredibly Delicious .............................. Patrick Groth
Island Bay Yacht Club ........................... Robert Tregoning
Julianne Glatz
LLCC Culinary Arts Center ..................... Denise Perry
LLCC Culinary Arts Center ..................... Jay Kitterman
Maldaner's Restaurant .......................... Michael Higgins
Maldaner's Restaurant .......................... Steve Sowers
Mike Aiello
Sangamo Club ....................................... Larry Langley
Sangamo Club ....................................... David Radwine
Sebastian's Hideout Restaurant ............. Chris Hanken & Vic Lanzotti
State Journal-Register ........................... Cookie Contest (with permission)
The Feed Store ...................................... Ann Laurence, Ross Richardson

# WINE SELECTIONS

King's Daughters Organization would like to thank Dr. Geoffrey Bland and The Corkscrew Wine Emporium for sharing their expertise in recommending wines to compliment many of the recipes in our Main Events chapter.

# CIRCLES OF KING'S DAUGHTERS

In the long history of the King's Daughters Organization, there have been over 100 circles. All of our former circles have played a significant role in our history. Some have stayed the course and others have disbanded while new ones formed or joined forces. We have used some of these names in recipe titles. The names in bold represent the eight current circles.

Ann Clark Circle     **Mary H. Blackstock Circle**
**Friendship Circle**     Mary Vienna Circle
Golden Hour Circle     Nightingale Circle*
**Grateful Daughters Circle**     **Progress Circle**
**Margaret Garfield Circle**     Sunny Circle
Marjorie Post Circle*     **Willing Circle**
**Mary A. Lawrence Circle**

*Marjorie Post and Nightingale merged to become **Marjorie Post/Nightingale** Circle.

# COMMITTEES

## Cookbook

Barbara Archer
Diana Dedrick
Suzie Sables Fessler
Rozanne (Posy) Flatt
Donna Freeman
Katie Marinelli
Cathy Schwartz
Brenda Staab

## Editors

Barbara Archer
Rozanne (Posy) Flatt
Donna Freeman
David Grimm
Barbara McKean
Brenda Staab
Candy Stout
Jan Sullivan
Jone VanWinkle
Maryann Walker
Jean Weiss

## Photography

Lisa Coakley
Polly Danforth
Robert W. Fox
Shelley Lamantia
Katie Marinelli
Paula Ryan
Suzie Sables Fessler
Kyle Schultz Photography
Erin Weller

## Marketing

Cindy Denby
Rozanne (Posy) Flatt
Sarah Jones
Bev Neisler
Karen Sanders
Cathy Schwartz

# Index

— continued on next page

— continued on next page